D0875051

TO

MY BROTHERS

OF

BLUE CLOUD ABBEY

They ate and were satisfied.

They gathered up the fragments.

ACKNOWLEDGEMENTS

The author expresses his appreciation to the following publishers and editors for permission to use material that previously appeared under their imprint:

American Benedictine Review	Richardton, ND
Chicago Studies	Mundelein, IL
Grail Press	St. Meinrad, IN
Liturgical Press	Collegeville, MN
Living Light	Washington, DC
National Catholic Reporter	Kansas City, MO
New York Times	New York, NY
North Central Publishing Co.	St. Paul, MN
Our Sunday Visitor	Huntington, IN
Pastoral Life	Canfield, OH
People of God	Albuquerque, NM

All quotations from Sacred Scripture are from *New American Bible*, with the exception of the essay, *Great and Holy Week*, with the permission of the Confraternity of Christian Doctrine, Washington, DC. Scriptural quotations from *Great and Holy Week* are from *Revised Standard Version of the New Testament* with the express permission of the Division of Christian Education of the National Council of Churches of Christ in the United States of America.

Cover: Brother Placid Stukenschneider, O.S.B.
Typesetter: Robert Briggs

Printer: Park Press, Inc.
           P.O. Box 475
           Waite Park, MN 56387

Gatherings

Vincent A. Yzermans

Park Press, Inc. • P.O. Box 475 • Waite Park, Minnesota 56387

INTRODUCTION

For three years my health has been in a precarious state. As I enter this period of my life, which some call the twilight years, I joyfully feel the Angel of the Resurrection approaching me more closely. I frequently repeat in my heart and soul the words of Francis Thompson:

> Halts by me that footfall:
> Is my gloom, after all,
> Shade of His hand, outstretched caressingly!
> "Ah, fondest, blindest, weakest,
> I am He Whom thou seekest!"

With a confident hope I say with good Pope John: "I have my bags packed and I am ready to go." My Christian faith endows me with a daily increasing awareness of God's great love. His everlasting love sustains me with the firm conviction that I shall soon hear my Brother and Friend say to me: "Come, blessed of my father...."

A good father tries as best he can to leave a legacy to his children. I have been blessed with God's gift of the priesthood for forty-two years and a writer for more than those years. All of the People of God are my children – my brothers and sisters in Christ. With St. Peter I must say, "Gold or silver I have not." My legacy is the gifts God gave me: to be His priest and writer. In these pages I bequeath my brothers and sisters – the readers – some of these gifts God gave me.

For twenty-two months I worked night and day on my personal memoirs. In God's good time – for all of time is God's good time – they may someday be published either while I am still in the land of the living or sharing more fully in the glory of God. That will be His holy will.

However, I have reflected for some time upon what I consider to be my best writings both in the world of grace and nature. These I give with a wounded, loving heart as my gift to you. One day the great St. Augustine of Hippo heard a child's voice singing, "Take and read." With joy in my heart I sing to you, my brothers and sisters, "Take and read."

VINCENT A. YZERMANS
Oblate of Saint Benedict
Priest of the Church of St. Cloud

All Saints
November 1, 1993

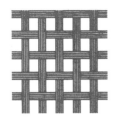

ABLE OF CONTENTS

1958

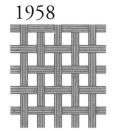

HE DIOCESAN PRESS

In November, 1958, almost a year after I became editor of the St. Cloud Visitor *I wrote this essay. It was not only my attempt to express my philosophy at that time but also to state it as my platform as an editor for others. It was printed in pamphlet form by North Central Publishing Company, St. Paul, Minnesota, and distributed to the priests and religious of the Church of St. Cloud and some of my colleagues in the Catholic Press Association. The Postscript was written in April, 1993.*

The diocesan paper is like a parish church. The relationship between the two is so intimate that the conduct of a successful diocesan paper is most similar to the manner that a good pastor conducts his parish.

The parish church is the meeting place of the people of God where the Sacraments are administered and Word of God is preached. The diocesan paper is the extension of the parish pulpit. It continues the work of the good pastor who is commissioned by his Bishop to preach the truths of God and His Church.

In the parish pulpit the good pastor explains, urges and appeals to his people to be frequent and fervent in the reception of the Sacraments of God. The diocesan paper continues this work throughout the year by showing forth in pictures, articles, features and art work the beauty, excellence and benefits of the Christian sacramental order.

In the pulpit, too, the good pastor explains the teaching of the Church, her dogma and moral law. This, too, the diocesan paper does. Because it is a different medium of communication, however, its tone will be factual and informative rather than pastoral and homiletic.

A good pastor is "all things to all men." In the pulpit, therefore, he will always be conscious of the intelligence, interests and needs of his people. The diocesan paper, too, must keep its readers in mind. If its language is "highbrow" it may win all the Catholic Press awards in the book, but it will fail in its mission of being "all things to all men."

The diocesan paper, like a good pastor, must know its readers. A pastor finds this out by taking census, mixing with his people, and literally going out into the homes and institutions of his parish to come to know his people better. The diocesan paper must imitate his aspect of the pastor's duty. It must attend meetings, be present at every event that is of significance or importance to the people of the diocese. It must represent its readers at any state or national function that has a bearing on their lives. In this respect it must take on the role of being a "witness" to the people of Christ, just as an apostle is a witness to the truth of Christ.

This does not mean to say that the diocesan paper, any more than the good pastor, is satisfied with the lowest common denominator. A good pastor does not water down his teaching merely because there are some who are simply incapable of understanding it or too indifferent to accept it. So too, the diocesan paper will not stoop to the level of its lowliest subscriber. Rather, it will embark on a mission of elevating minds through patient, studied use of literary and typographical aids that modern science and research have introduced to the field of journalism. The diocesan paper will strive gradually, over a period of time, to raise the intellectual level of its readers. Like any true Christian, the diocesan paper will be restless with the zeal of Christ to elevate human nature. But the restlessness, like Christ's, will always be tempered with patience, prudence, and charity.

Need of Policy

No institution can long endure that does not have a policy. Mother Church's policy is set forth in Canon Law: The Salvation of Souls is the Supreme Law of the Church. Fraternal, political, social organizations all have a policy that sets forth their aims and the means they choose to arrive at their goals. A parish, too, must have a policy. To a large extent, that policy will be directed by the Bishop and the pastor. A diocesan paper is no exception. Unfortunately, history shows too many examples in our country of diocesan newspapers that were left to shift for themselves. The net result was they either collapsed or withered away in an enfeebled condition for lack of a strong, vital policy.

The editorial policy of the diocesan newspaper is one that is necessarily set up in its very purpose; namely, to inform and form the Catholic people. But in itself, that is too general. It must be delineated down to the smallest incident that can arise in its existence. Thus it will include the position types of news stories have, the extent of subject matter that will fill its editorial columns, the kind of advertising that will be accepted. Since, however, the diocesan newspaper is diocesan in scope, its policy cannot be established either by a touch-and-go manner or the desires and preferences of any one man or group of men that form its editorial board. Ultimately, its policy will be established by the Bishop of the diocese. The paper is, in a very real way, an extension of the Bishop's thinking in the homes of his diocese. Therefore, the excellence or altogether lack of an editorial policy will reflect to a large extent the thinking of the Bishop of the Diocese.

A Paper's Personality

To speak of the nature of a diocesan newspaper presupposes that it is something that lives. Too many diocesan papers are dead, lifeless. If they have a nature at all it is so twisted and disfigured by a lack of clearcut policy that it cannot easily be recognized. The nature of the parish church is to be the Gate of Heaven through which the children of men pass from death to life. How that nature is manifested in the everyday lives of the men in a community largely depends upon the personality of the pastor of the parish. His personality will be stamped on the activities – even on the people – of his parish. They will be as alive and receptive to God's grace as he, the pastor, is himself.

A diocesan paper, too, must have a personality. Normally, the personality it receives is that of the editor himself. In a very real way, the personality of the editor finds a vicarious existence in the pages of the diocesan paper. It will be as alive, vibrant and appealing as the personality of the editor. His love for God, devotion to the Church, interest in the diocese and zeal for souls will be combined with his own native and acquired journalistic gifts and ability that will make the diocesan paper a living reality in the life of the diocese.

We should add here that unless the diocesan paper lives it will not be able to fulfill its mission. It must have a personality before its readers will come to know it through reading its columns. This life that comes for the diocesan paper comes, too, from the editor's own personal contact with his readers. He can delegate paper work to a secretary. He can hire a janitor to sweep the floor. But his public relations must be a work that rests squarely on his own shoulders.

The late Cardinal O'Connell succinctly stated the purpose of the diocesan paper when he said: "A Catholic paper is as much a necessity as a church. It as much the duty of every priest in the diocese to stand for it, aid it, and work for its widest diffusion among the people as it is to build and support a school. It is for the self-same purpose, object and aim – the propaganda and defense of Christian principles."

The diocesan paper will do this by fulfilling its mission of being an educational institution that embraces the whole diocese. As a teacher it has the twofold purpose of information and formation. If it is mindful of this twofold role of teaching, it will, in turn, be both interesting and entertaining. By doing this, week in and week out, the diocesan paper performs two invaluable services to the diocese that no other agency or institution can render. These two services are the formation of a healthy, Catholic public opinion and the unification of the diocese as a whole.

The information the diocesan paper gives its readers will be of three kinds: namely, temporal, social and spiritual. Temporal information will deal with the international, national and local affairs that are secular in themselves, though they have religious implications. When this information is purely secular (if that phrase can possibly be used), the editor will be certain that an opinion expressed in no way reflects the attitude of official Church authority. This he can do by means of a byline or by placing such items on a page that is given over to temporal affairs.

The social information that the diocesan paper will supply its readers is what some may call trivial in importance. It will be the announcements or recording of parish meetings, first Communions, local events in various schools, and such like. Though some may think these events are of little importance, the diocesan paper cannot overlook the fact that these are the warp and woof of the daily lives of its readers.

It remains as true today as a century ago that "names make news" and "a dog-fight on Main street is of greater importance than a war in Europe." The diocesan newspaper will, therefore, be interested in these local, social activities, if for no other reason than their importance as the bond that draws its readers into more intimate converse with its pages.

Spiritual formation will flow from information. This will not be "preachy" coverage nor pious platitudes. At times it will be factual series on the Creed or Commandments. At other times it will be photo stories on liturgical celebrations or sacramental ministrations.

Here especially the diocesan paper must employ every trick of the trade both in typography and design so that the most appealing and interesting items in its pages will be those which deal with the spiritual. Its object will be to instill a love, devotion and reverence for spiritual things in the minds and hearts of its readers. Here, above all else, the editor must bear in mind the saying: If you can't do it well, don't do it at all.

A Proper Balance

The diocesan paper that strives to give its readers a proper balance of temporal, social and spiritual coverage and does this with intelligence, spirit and craftsmanship, will automatically have readers who are both interested and entertained. Their entertainment will not be the raucous type, to be sure. It will be the calm, silent appreciation of knowing they and their lives are important, that their Church's liturgy is compelling and moving, that they have a sound opinion concerning the temporal affairs that form so much the topic of their daily conversation.

The formation of Catholic public opinion will necessarily be a much more difficult effect to gauge. It will take hold only over a long period of time. It will be instilled unconsciously, so much so that the reader himself will be unaware of its origin. But the diocesan paper, sometimes in spite of seeming failure, must continue to develop Catholic public opinion. This will be achieved by setting up several general goals that will color the editor's choice of articles and position of news items in the columns of the diocesan paper.

Thus, for example, the diocesan paper will strive to cultivate a respect for authority, a love for learning, an appreciation of Christian culture. In its coverage, its layout, its editorial comments it will strive to bring these attitudes to the attention of its readers. Only God and the recording angel will be able to measure the success. Yet, a diocesan paper that has no over-all general objectives, clearly enunciated and maturely developed in the editor's mind, will lack the color and vitality that keeps the diocesan paper alive from one week to the next.

Looked at from another point of view, one might call this two-fold role of formation and information the educational mission of the diocesan paper. When we come to examine this role more closely – even if it means here that we do it by way of digression – there is one papal document that forms sort of a *Magna Carta* on the subject. This is the address of Pope Pius XII delivered to the forty-seventh annual convention of the Catholic Press Association which met in St. Louis in 1957.

MAKING OF A CATHOLIC MIND

Editors throughout the country have a conviction that there will never be a strong, virile diocesan press until the day dawns when this common desire becomes a reality in every classroom of every Catholic school in our country. This conviction is born out of the opinion that a strong, virile diocesan press demands active, intelligent readers – not just an imposing subscription list. They can even help in making the kind of readers they would like. But when all is said and done, active, intelligent readers are made, not born.

This making is a task that no one can do better than a teacher in a classroom. By beginning in the grades and working through the high school and college years, a teacher can build up patterns of reading in students. By using the diocesan press not only as reference works gathering dust in the library, but also by using the diocesan newspapers when they come rolling off the press – students will develop the habit of making the diocesan press their weekly guide in search for that information and formation so necessary for the making of a Catholic mind.

CATHOLIC PRESS AND CATHOLIC SCHOOLS

This very point was made by Pope Pius XII in his address. Said the late Pontiff: "Obviously the influence of the diocesan press will be in proportion to the influence and number of its readers....Is it not right to expect the students and graduates of the (Catholic) schools should be a chief support of the diocesan press and literature? Are they?"

In response to this question, Catholic educators themselves must realize the need of using the diocesan press as a teaching aid. If they have such a conviction, the diocesan press will grow – not only in numbers but more importantly, in influence throughout the coming years.

Pope Pius XII did not rest at merely pointing out the importance of building a bridge between the diocesan press and the Catholic school. He went further, explaining why this bridge must be built. He listed three reasons why the diocesan press must penetrate – infiltrate, if you will – the Catholic school. These are:

1. "To guide the students' taste in reading;

2. "To bring them to realize the responsibilities which await the Catholic laity today and their consequent need to deepen by continued study their understanding of the Faith;

3. "To help them grasp the nature and magnitude of the issues at stake in the personal struggle that the Church has to wage in the face of those who through ignorance or evil-minded enmity revile and misrepresent her and her teachings."

These objectives are a big order. At the same time, neither the enormity of the task nor the feelings of futility are valid reasons for neglecting the need of at least continually striving to bring these three attitudes week after week and month after month to the attention of readers – and in this case, especially younger readers.

From time to time the diocesan paper must reset its goals and remind itself of its part in that total Christian revolution Pope Pius XII talked about when he said in February, 1952: "It is an entire world which must be rebuilt from its foundations, transformed from savage to human, from human to divine, that is to say, according to the Heart of God."

"Good Enough" Not Good Enough

To achieve these goals, we must strive daily for professional competence. This thought Pope Pius XII expressed to a group of book publishers in 1954. Said the Holy Father: "Though commercial interests might induce him (the publisher) to bargain with morals, he refuses to make any concessions to anything his conscience would condemn. Furthermore, he takes the greatest care in respect to quality. He accepts for publication only a book which is accurate and correct; he strives to give a worthy form to such solid foundation. He does not fail to recognize the sum-total of knowledge and work which this requires, and he does not spare efforts to attain that perfection which his means allow." What the Pope said here to book publishers applies with equal – if not greater – value to the diocesan newspaper.

Secondly, these goals demand unity. Pope Pius XII expressed this thought in this way: "This desired bond of union, assured and sealed by justice and charity, will be unbreakable if all are ever conscious of the one, sublime goal each and everyone of you is striving to gain: the spread of Christ's Kingdom of Truth and Salvation among men."

SOURCE OF UNITY

The Bishop is both the symbol and person of unity in a diocese. In his person he unites the activities and parishes, people and clergy, of his diocese. The diocesan paper is his adjunct in his role as unifier. Through use of local items in its columns, through proper publicity of diocesan news items in its headlines, through episcopal letters and comments in its pages, the diocesan paper assists in forming the diocese into a unified whole.

Significantly, the people look for this diocesan news in a diocesan paper. If they do not find it (or if they find it cut down to a one inch item on the bottom of page thirteen sandwiched between two overwhelming advertisements) they complain that there is "nothing" in the paper. A diocesan paper that consciously uses its ability to aid in the unification of the diocese is chartering a wise editorial policy. It thereby assures itself of greater reader-interest among its subscribers.

We should briefly recount here some motives that are ignoble and consequently unworthy of a diocesan newspaper. It goes without saying that a diocesan paper does not engage in sensationalism. It does not embark on break-neck, cut-throat competitive war with local daily or weekly secular newspapers. It does not seek to arouse factions in the diocese and sedulously, but prudently, strives to avoid anything that would be offensive. Thus it will be completely impartial to persons and institutions and strive at all times for that severe objectivity in reporting that is the goal of every worthy journalist. Too, it does not court the favor of individuals or parties, and never stoops to pampering the vanity of individuals or groups. Like a Catholic school, its principal concern is to teach the truths of Christ in the manner of Christ.

We know the value of Catholic education and are willing to sacrifice for it. We maintain and operate Catholic schools to form Christ in the souls of those regenerated by Baptism.

On the same count, we maintain and operate diocesan newspapers. We are primarily concerned with educating Catholic people. Hence, money is not the primary purpose of the diocesan paper. In many cases, money must be expended to build up a top-notch diocesan paper, the same as money must be invested in the building of a Catholic school. We can only boast of our splendid parochial school system in this country because American Catholics have been willing to make almost heroic sacrifices on behalf of this aspect of Catholic education. Unfortunately, we cannot boast of too many excellent Catholic diocesan newspapers because American Catholics have not been willing to spend money in building up papers of superior craftsmanship.

Mr. Gardner Cowles, Sr., of the *Des Moines Tribune* once said in a talk to his staff, "We must have more circulation to get more advertising to make a better paper..." and so on, like a broken phonograph record. On such a vicious circle Cowles built a newspaper empire. In many ways, the operation of any newspaper, religious or secular, is based on that same simple, obvious, vicious circle.

Advertising is the life-blood of a newspaper. But advertising demands over and above circulation, reader-response. Circulation and reader-response will only be gained by a "good" newspaper. A diocesan newspaper is not good merely because it has a religious purpose. It must be able to stand on its own two feet from a professional point of view. A good diocesan paper will be journalistically a good paper.

The closest a diocesan newspaper can come to breaking into the vicious circle is to start with a "good" paper. To make a poor diocesan paper a good one will demand an outlay in money. The old saying, "It takes money to make money," applies with equal certainty to a diocesan newspaper. Once capital is put into making the diocesan paper acceptable according to the canons of sound journalism, it is assured of financial success. The report of the Commission on the Freedom of the Press reported back in 1947 that "Good morals are good business." From a diocesan paper's purpose we are assured of a paper with good morals. Yet too many diocesan papers fail because they ask their readers to accept second-rate journalism in reporting first-rate information. Beginning with a "good" newspaper, it will not be long before reader-interest and reader-response come forth.

NEW APPROACH

What, then, makes a "good" diocesan paper? Obviously, it cannot compete with the secular dailies in that most precious commodity of "timeliness." It must seek other channels of interest.

Fortunately, the diocesan newspaper can learn much from its big city cousin, the secular daily. Radio and television, by their very nature, can always "scoop" the newspaper. Their advent was the death warrant of the "extra." The secular dailies did not fight back. They recognized that they had lost the battle of "timeliness." Instead, they changed their tactics. They leaned more toward the feature and interpretative type of reporting. They dug up the little details, the hidden facts in the current news stories, and exploited these in their columns. They went back to history and geography books to learn the background of modern events and entered upon a new phase of American journalism that lay midway between the news story and the editorial, namely, interpretative reporting. They resurrected the truism, "Names make news" and behind the great events of the day they hung a backdrop of biography and personal interviews. In such a way they learned how to complement the more rapid media of television and radio. The success of their adjustment can be seen in the fifty-seven million copies of daily newspapers sold in America – the largest figure ever attained in the history of the American press.

So, too, the diocesan paper must look for different ways and means of making itself journalistically "good." It will seek out the human touch behind the news stories. It will interpret current events in the light of Christian principles. It will rely on history and geography to supply details the secular press overlooks. It will track down biographical sketches of personalities within the diocese and come out with gaily-decked feature stories. By such means and ingenuity the diocesan paper will be able to hold its own against the secular daily.

News isn't something that just happens. News is made by hard work, and the harder the work, generally speaking, the more appealing the news.

In summary we might say simply that circulation is not the main problem of the diocesan newspaper. Nor is reader-response on which advertising is based. The basic, fundamental problem is a problem of news. Get it, and the rest will follow. Perhaps not at once, but suddenly it will develop as light follows darkness.

COMPETENT STAFF

The second aspect of the operation of a diocesan newspaper involves the personnel. Wisely the state makes laws that school superintendents be qualified, mental hospital chaplains have on-the-job training, and definite standards must be met in our schools, hospitals and public buildings.

The Church, too, makes wise laws concerning the qualifications of Bishops, chancellors, seminary professors and other officials. For the very same reason that the Church and State make these standards, the diocesan newspaper should have standards that its personnel should be expected to meet.

In the secular field editors don't just happen. They are educated and trained for their job. Any "shutter-bug" does not get his pictures in print. Reputable photographers are hired. Secretaries and file clerks are not just employed because they are supporting an invalid aunt. They are carefully screened (and adequately paid) so that they will fill the demand of stenographer, typist, receptionist and public relations expert.

The diocesan paper cannot expect to operate efficiently if it does not observe the same minimum expectations that the secular press demands. Journalism is a profession, like medicine or law. A good newspaper is the result of highly professional, skilled, diligent journalists. A diocesan paper will be, from a natural point of view, as good a newspaper as its personnel are trained and prepared for this function in the life of the diocese.

A Truly Diocesan Paper

A final observation. A diocesan newspaper will best be able to fulfill its function if it be truly a diocesan newspaper. By that we understand a diocesan paper that is published and printed within the diocese itself.

Recently, a distinguished Catholic editor expressed this thought when he said: "One of the most vital aspects of the Catholic Press is to have a diocesan paper to make the people aware of their obligations to and their unity with the Holy See. It is through the diocese to the Holy See. This basic unity of jurisdiction needs to be developed today....What is needed primarily in our country today to bring the Church to full maturity is to have a strong publication within every diocese."

There, briefly, is a course for the diocesan newspaper to follow. It demands the support and assistance of every individual in the diocese. Given this, it cannot help but be successful, for it has as its powerful patron, St. Francis de Sales.

It has, too, a challenge. This was given it by Pope Pius XI, who once said to a group of Catholic writers, "You are my voice. I do not say that you make my voice heard, but that you are really my voice itself." Wrote Pope Pius XI in the same encyclical letter that names St. Francis de Sales as patron of the Catholic Press:

"It is necessary that they (Catholic journalists), in their writings, imitate and exhibit at all times that strength joined always to moderation and charity, which was the special characteristic of St. Francis. He, by his example, teaches them in no uncertain manner precisely how they should write. In the first place, and this the most important of all, each writer should endeavor in every way and as far as this may be possible to obtain a complete comprehension of the teachings of the Church. They should never compromise where the truth is involved, nor, because of fear of possibly offending an opponent, minimize or dissimulate it. They should pay particular attention to literary style and should try to express their thoughts clearly and in beautiful language so that their readers will the more readily come to love the truth. When it is necessary to enter into controversy, they should be prepared to refute error and to overcome the wiles of the wicked, but always in a way that will demonstrate clearly that they are animated by the highest principles and moved only by Christian charity."

An Importrant Postscript

I was, indeed, a novice editor when I wrote those words. I believe they reflected the thinking of the Catholic press in the United States in 1958. I recall attending annual conventions of the Catholic Press Association during the decade of the 1950's and early years of the 1960's when the delegates were about 90 percent priests and a mere ten percent lay people. Such editors as Donald Quinn of the *St. Louis Review* and Donald McDonald of Davenport's *Catholic Messenger* were conspicuous because as lay people they were so few.

Catholics generally considered the diocesan newspaper as a teaching aid used by the bishop of the diocese and did not even give the fact that he was its publisher a second thought. As a matter of fact, the diocesan newspaper of the Church of Sioux Falls was initiated during this period called *The Bishop's Bulletin*.

Looking back at this essay now, years later, some of its contents still have merit. The fact remains that the Catholic press exists to form and inform the Catholic body. It remains a powerful educational and pastoral instrument of the Catholic Church in the United States. But today I would make major changes in that philosophy because both the world, the printing industry and the Church have undergone major changes. Without attempting to write another lengthy essay, I will state my present thinking concerning the diocesan newspaper in three brief points.

1. I do not think the bishop of the diocese should be the publisher of the diocesan press. Fortunately, in many cases a lay person is the actual publisher. The diocesan newspaper belongs to the People of God in a given area. I believe it should be governed by a board of directors, one being chosen as the publisher.

2. As early as 1962 I began promoting the idea that the Catholic

newspaper should be one and the same for all the dioceses in a state. The existence of a diocesan newspaper is a luxury that a Church dedicated to "a preferential option for the poor" cannot and should not enjoy. The repetition of the same international and national news and commentary in five or six or more diocesan newspapers is a terrible duplication of expenses. The rising costs of mailing the paper to subscribers further makes individual diocesan newspapers a luxury. The principle of collegiality, as co-responsibility, should apply to the diocesan newspaper.

The Church after the Second Vatican Council has changed in many of its institutional aspects. Most states now have their own state-wide Catholic Conference with related areas of the Church's concerns working within that framework. The diocesan newspaper continues to operate as it did in 1910 or 1950 – independently. The major concerns of Catholic people are the same whether they are members of the local churches of St. Paul-Minneapolis, St. Cloud, Winona, Duluth, Crookston or New Ulm.

The printing industry has advanced so rapidly in the past 20 years that it is possible to deliver one state-wide paper the same day in every Catholic home and institution. By sharing the same international and national news costs are drastically reduced. This can readily be seen by the cooperation new existing between the *Catholic Bulletin* of St. Paul-Minneapolis and *The New Earth* of Fargo.

3. The sole objection, as I see it, is that coverage of diocesan events would suffer. Not so! I believe that each diocesan newspaper in the state should have as many pages as needed from week to week. The office of a diocesan editor would not be eliminated. The editors of each diocese would also be members of the board of directors of the state-wide Catholic paper.

As every parish struggles with mounting costs, as does every diocese, a state-wide Catholic newspaper would decrease the costs considerably. Such a newspaper would also attract more advertising revenues and a professional staff of high calibre. What I fear most is that the time will come when parish councils will eliminate any subsidy for the diocesan newspaper because of budgetary demands in other areas. A state-wide Catholic newspaper, in my mind, is the only route to go for the good of the People of God. ↞

1961

HRISTMAS MEDITATION

This meditation was written following a request by Rev. Colman J. Barry, O.S.B., a monk at St. John's Abbey, Collegeville, Minnesota, and at that time director of the American Benedictine Academy. It appeared in the December, 1961 issue of the American Benedictine Review.

Christmas is a time for meditation. It is our time to grasp the love of a God-made-man, to learn to become like God. This is the time of meditation because Christmas is a time shot through with mystery. Christmas is the world mystery that has seized the minds of millions for almost two thousand years. All the mysteries of man and nature are as child's play when compared with God's great mystery of the incarnation. The mystery of Christmas makes this a time of joyful meditation.

Who can ever comprehend the Christmas mystery? Who can exhaust it? It is full of paradoxes, complicated by the fact that they are both real and symbolic. Saint Ambrose asks: "Can anyone say that the Lord is made known to us by signs of little significance when the Magi come and adore him, the angels serve him and the martyrs confess him? He comes forth from a womb, but he shines like lightning from above. He lies in an earthly resting place, but round about him is the brightness of heaven. The espoused has brought forth, but a virgin has conceived. A wife has conceived, but a virgin has given birth." Such are the paradoxes of the Christian mystery; but paradoxes only until they are solved by Christian faith.

We are not alone in exploring the Christmas mystery. If it seems too noble or inexplicable for the weakness of our minds, God in his goodness has given us guides, the Fathers of the Church. Although they followed the apostolic Fathers by several centuries, they deserve to be called, in the words of Charles Peguy: "the first Christians of Christianity, the inaugurators, the authors of it under God, the creators of it all along with him…. They build the house for others, for all others, therefore for ourselves…these old saints, the first of all old saints, those of the earliest days…. Now that it is made, it is not so bad after all…and they made it for us. We work on what exists. But when they worked, it was not so…. They began Christian living. We have only followed them, and that is quite different. They inaugurated the Kingdom of God upon earth, the initiators of it all." These Fathers will help us make our Christmas meditation.

Our limited knowledge of the Christmas mystery in no way should diminish our joy in meditating on this singular manifestation or divine love. From the mystery of the Incarnation, many mysteries shoot out in every direction, like rays from a flaming sun. So Leo the Great told the Romans fourteen hundred years ago:

"The truths that belong to this day's solemnity are truly well known to you, dearly beloved, and you have frequently been instructed in them; but just as the visible light delights the healthy eyes, so unceasing joy comes to the heart that is healed from the birth of the savior. We must not pass over this in silence, though it can never be spoken of in a worthy manner. For the words of the prophet, 'Who shall declare this generation?', refer not only to that mystery in which the Son of God is coeternal with the Father, but also to this birth in which 'the Word was made flesh.'"

Above all else, Christmas is the feast of faith. With faith burning in our souls we approach the crib of Christ. Saint Leo the Great again admonishes us: "When we try to understand the mystery of Christ's nativity, by which he was born of a virgin mother, let the darkness of our human minds be driven far away and let the fog of worldly wisdom depart from the eye of illumined faith.' This faith must be our guide, our constant companion in contemplating the Christmas mystery. Faith, and only faith, prompted the Magi to fall down and worship the Christ Child. The same faith will help us penetrate the brilliance of the mystery, see divinity clothed in humanity.

Faith will unfold the paradox of Christmas. Saint John Chrysostom explained this when he said:

"The Son of God, who is the God of all things, is born a man in body. He who holds the heavens in his hand permits himself to be placed in a crib. He whom the world cannot contain is confined in a manger. He whose voice in the hour of his passion caused the whole earth to tremble is heard in the voice of a wailing infant. The Magi, beholding a child, profess that this is the lord of glory, the lord of majesty, whom Isaias has shown was both child and God and king eternal, saying: 'For a child is born to us, and a son is given to us, and the government is upon his shoulder: and his name shall be called wonderful, counsellor, God the mighty, the father of the world to come, the prince of peace.'"

Christmas is also the feast of hope. It is more than an historical event, albeit the greatest event of history. It looks to the future as well as the past. It began in paradise and will end only in heaven. The Christ who came as the child in Bethlehem is the same mighty savior promised at Eden's gates and the same eternal judge who will appear in majesty when time will be no more. This earthly Bethlehem, a small, out-of-the-way, dusty village in a despised country was both a rebuke and an image. Bethlehem rebuked the haughty messianic hopes of a downtrodden people. Bethlehem pointed, as wretchedly as all earthly symbols, to the glorious heavenly Bethlehem.

The Venerable Bede saw this amalgamation of time and eternity centuries ago:

"Let us go over in thought to Bethlehem, and in love recall to our minds that there the Word was made flesh. Let us celebrate his incarnation with honors worthy of him. Throw off worldly desires. With all the desire of our minds let us go over to the heavenly Bethlehem, that is, the house of bread, not made by hands, but eternal in heaven, and in love recall that the Word was made flesh. There in heaven he has ascended in the flesh. There he sits at the right hand of God the Father. There let us follow him with a firm will and by steadfast mortification of heart and body, merit to see reigning on the throne of his Father him whom the shepherds saw crying in the manger."

Bethlehem pierces time and points to eternity. Bethlehem is dear to Christians more for what it means than for what it is. "Rightly," said

Saint Gregory the Great, "is Christ born in Bethlehem. For Bethlehem means *the house of bread*. And he who was born there said: 'I am the living bread which came down from heaven.' The place, therefore, where the Lord is born was called *the house of bread* because he was to appear there in the flesh who was to fill the souls of the faithful with an eternal abundance."

There are many mysteries about Christmas. Why was there no room in the inn? It would surely be injurious to say that Joseph whom we know was so good a provider was improvident on this holy night. But there was a providence far greater than Joseph's. In this divine providence the Venerable Bede sees a lesson that the Christ Child himself wished to teach us.

"He who sits at the right hand of the Father goes without shelter from the inn in order to prepare for us many mansions in the house of his heavenly Father.... He was born, not in the house of his parents, not in the inn, but by the wayside, because through the mystery of the incarnation he is to become the way who guides us to our home where we shall also enjoy the truth and the life."

Some may think the census of Caesar Augustus was merely coincidental. But faith tells the believer that there are no accidents in the providence of a loving Father. The decree of Augustus "that the whole world should be enrolled" was more than an act of officialdom. Augustus' census, according to Gregory the Great, revealed that "he who then appeared in the flesh, wanted to enroll his elect for eternity." Origen perceived another meaning behind the census. "Anyone who considers this closely," he wrote, "can see a certain mystery prefigured. Christ was enrolled in the census of the whole world so that he might sanctify all men. He was recorded with the whole world in order that he might unite all men in himself."

With the same eyes of faith, Saint Ambrose perceived another meaning:

"While the secular census is referred to, the spiritual is implied. The latter is to be made known, not to the king of the earth, but to the king of heaven. It is a profession of faith, an enrollment of souls. The ancient enrollment of the synagogue is ended, while the new one of the Church has begun. Finally, in order that you may know that this is

Christ's census, not Augustus', the whole world is ordered to be enrolled. He alone could decree the enrollment of the whole world who has dominion over the whole world. It is written not of Augustus, but of the Lord: 'The earth is the Lord's and the fullness thereof.'"

The inn, the census, were providential designs. So too was the night. Christ would teach his first lesson the moment of his birth. Although he was a child, he revealed his power through the virgin who is his mother. Although the world slumbered in darkness, he would penetrate the shadows by the bright rays of his light. So Gregory of Nyssa analyzes the night of the virgin birth:

"Although he appeared as man, he was, nevertheless, not subject in all things to the laws of humanity. That he was born of a woman savored of lowliness; but the virginity that attended his birth revealed his transcendence of mankind. His carrying in the womb was joyful. His birth was immaculate. His coming forth was without pain. His nativity was free of blemish, neither taking rise from the will of the flesh, nor brought forth in sorrow. Since she who brought death by sin to our nature was condemned to bring forth in sorrow, it was fitting that the mother of life should bring forth in joy. In that hour when the shadows began to retire and the immense gloom of night was forced back by the splendor of this light, through this virginal incorruption, Christ comes to share the life of mortal men. At that moment death reached the boundary of sin's dominion and moved towards nothingness, because the true light arrived and his evangelical rays had given light to the whole world."

Although he was more brilliant than the sun, Mary "wrapped him up in swaddling clothes" so that the Christ Child may show the world his humility. He who clothed the world with a myriad of ornaments is folded in poor swaddling clothes that we may receive his gift. He through whom all things were made is bound both hand and foot, that our hands may be employed in every good work, and our feet directed in the way of peace.

The way of peace: there is no safer way to peace than the road that leads through Bethlehem. With faith we must approach the Christmas mystery. If we do, we will return with peace. "This peace," says Saint Cyril, "was made through Christ. By himself he reconciled us to God the Father, taking from our midst the inimical guilt, reconciling two peoples through one man, and joining together into one flock both those in heaven and those on earth.' The condition of peace was contained in the angels' hymn: Only to men of good will would God grant peace. These, says the Venerable Bede, are "those who shall receive the newborn Christ."

The message of peace was proclaimed to shepherds. Humility is the foundation of peace, just as faith is the condition of peace. "Let not the shepherds' example of faith," said Saint Ambrose to his people in Milan, "seem of little worth to you because the person of the shepherd is lowly. Surely, the poorer a person is in regard to worldly wisdom so much more precious is he in his faith. Our Lord did not seek out the schools packed with assemblies of wise men, but rather the simple people who did not know how to elaborate and exaggerate the things they had heard. Simplicity is sought: ambition is not desired." Echoing the same sentiments, Saint John Chrysostom told his people in Constantinople: "An angel neither went to Jerusalem nor sought out the Scribes and Pharisees because they were corrupted and tormented with envy. But the shepherds were sincere of heart, observing the ancient teaching of the patriarchs and Moses. Blamelessness is one of the paths that leads to wisdom."

Humility is the example the shepherds give both clergy and laity. The Venerable Bede sees them as a type of all ministers of the new law. He writes:

"These shepherds of the flocks mystically signify the teachers and rulers of the faithful. The night, in which they keep watch over their flocks, stands for the danger of the temptations against which they must unceasingly defend both themselves and the flocks committed to them. Fittingly, since the Lord is born, the shepherds keep watch over their flocks, since he is born who has said: *I am the good shepherd.* The time was now approaching when this shepherd would recall to his own living pastures those of his sheep who had strayed. Each one, though he seems to live simply as a private person, holds the office of shepherd if, gathering together a flock of good deeds and chaste thoughts, he endeavors to guide it with a suitable rule, nourishing it on the pastures of the scripture, and defending it against the snares of the demons."

No sooner was the Christ Child born than he began to radiate that grace of which he alone was the source and plenitude for all mankind. The ancient law of fear was dead; the new law of loving grace began. Saint John Chrysostom draws the parallel: "Where before angels were sent to punish, as to the Israelites, to David, to the Sodomites, and to the valley of tears, now they sing on earth, giving thanks to God because he had revealed to them his coming down among men."

To share the grace of Christmas God sent an angel to the Jews and a star to the Gentiles. If we ask why the messengers of the good news were so different, Saint Gregory the Great gives the answer: "It was fitting that to the Jews, as rational creatures, a rational creature (that is, an angel) should preach, while the Gentiles who knew not how to use their spiritual reason, came to know their Lord not by the rational word, but by signs. For this reason, to the Jews, as believers, were given the prophecies of old and the message of the angels; while the Gentiles, who were unbelievers, were given signs, such as the star."

The Magi came to Bethlehem in our name, mysterious visitors at the time of their coming, mysterious throughout history. The strangest fact about the Magi is that they were not kings at all and yet, Christian tradition delights in making them kings. At most, they were learned men, scholars from strange lands of the East. They are called astronomers, but no greater insult could be offered them than to call them astrologers. We do not even know their names. The Roman Church calls them in her liturgy Caspar, Melchior, and Balthazar. But this is only a seventh century tradition. Earlier they had almost as many names as nations. The Syrians, for example, called them Larvandad, Hormisdas, and Gushnasaph. The Armenians knew them by such names as Kagba and Badadilma.

Nor do we know how many Magi suddenly appeared in Bethlehem and just as suddenly disappeared. Many of the eastern churches commemorate twelve wise men. The Latin Church number three. A painting in the cemetery of Saint Peter and Saint Marcellinus shows two; another painting in the cemetery of Domitilla shows four.

Confusion about the Magi was prevalent even on the rim of the empire in the fifth century. Summarizing current opinion, Saint Remigius, apostle of the Franks, wrote:

"We must keep in mind that there is a variety of opinions regarding the Magi. Some say they were Chaldeans. The Chaldeans worshipped a star for god, and accordingly they said that their so-called god had declared that the true God was born. Others say there were Persians. Some say that they came from the farthest parts of the earth. Others say they were descendants of Balaam, which is more credible. For among the things which he prophesied, Balaam said: A star shall rise out of Jacob. They knew this prophecy; as soon as they had seen the star they understood that the king was born and they set out on the journey."

Regardless of who they were or where they came from, the Magi like the shepherds were instruments God used to enlighten us further about the Christmas mystery. "These wise men," asks Saint Augustine, "what were they but the first fruits of the Gentiles? The shepherds were Israelites, the Magi Gentiles. The former from close by, the latter from far away; both hastened to the cornerstone. Jesus revealed himself neither to the learned nor the self-righteous. Ignorance dominated the rusticity of the shepherds and impiety the practices of the Magi, but that cornerstone joined both to himself. In such a way he chose the foolish to confound the wise and called the sinners, not the self-righteous, to repentance. Accordingly, no great one should take pride in himself and no lowly one should despair."

To be sure, the Magi had a star to lead them. But that Christmas star, like so many material things, might well have been hung in the heavens more to glorify God than to be of service to man. Saint Augustine makes this point: "The angels show Christ to the shepherds; the star reveals him to the Magi. To both the voice of heaven speaks, since now the prophet's voice is silenced. The angels dwell in the heavens; the star adorns them. Through both, the heavens *proclaim the glory of God.*"

The star is another facet of the jewel of the Christmas mystery. First and foremost, it glorified God. It was God's own special creation, his ornament in the heavens, joyfully announcing the birth of his Son. The star was nature's way of recognizing her creator. The universe could not contain its joy because of its creator's willingness to be clothed in the garments of nature. If men would not recognize their creator's birth, nature itself would shout out its joyful and grateful acceptance of this child as the lord of the world. Thus Saint Gregory the Great remarked: "The heavens recognized him as their God and sent a star to shine over where he lay. The sea knew him and offered itself as a solid basis for his feet. The earth knew him and when he died it quaked. The sun knew him and it hid the rays of its light. The rocks and walls knew him and at the time of his death they were rent asunder."

Some have tried to prove that this star was just another comet; others that it was the conjunction of two planets, Jupiter and Saturn. But it was a special creation, as Saint John Chrysostom took pains to prove to his people:

"That this was not one of the heavenly bodies seems manifest. No other star moved in this way. This moved from the east to the south, for so Palestine lies in relation to Persia. In the second place, this is evident also from the time of its appearance, for it seems to have been visible not only in the night but in the full light of day, which is not within the nature of any star, or even of the moon. Thirdly, this star at first appears and then hides itself. After they had entered Jerusalem it hid itself; when they had left Herod it showed itself again. Neither had it any course of its own; but when the Magi travelled, it travelled with them. When they halted, it likewise halted as the pillar of cloud in the desert. Fourthly, it pointed out the offspring of the virgin, doing this not by remaining on high, but coming low, which indicates not the action of a star but of some rational power. So this star was but the sign of invisible power, revealing itself in this form."

Saint Ambrose sees an even more noble symbol in the star. He does not hesitate to call the star Christ. "Do you desire to know how precious was their reward?" he asks. "The star is seen by them, but where Herod is it is not seen. It is seen again where Christ is and shows them the way. Therefore this star is the way, and the way is Christ: for in the mystery of the incarnation Christ is a star…. Where, then Christ is, the star is. For he himself is *the bright and morning star*. He shows us himself, therefore, by his own light."

More than the star, however, guided the Magi. They were coming to the Christ Child who, by his birth, opened a world of faith. From the shadows of paganism they were entering into the brilliance of faith. This was the Magi's constant companion; this same faith is the lesson they teach us. Saint Leo the Great delighted in telling his people about it.

"Besides the image of the star, which strikes upon the bodily eye, more brilliantly had the light of truth illuminated their hearts, leading them, even before they had set out, to prepare gifts that were worthy of his dignity…. They needed not, with the eye of the body, to look upon that which they already beheld with the fullest vision of the mind. Persevering in the ardor of their discerning allegiance until they beheld the child, they did a service to the peoples of future times, to the men of our own day. Just as we all gained when after the resurrection of the Lord the hand of the apostle Thomas explored the places of his wounds, so also we profited when the eyes of the Magi looked upon his infancy."

The Magi knew well that the object of their quest was no ordinary king. If the star did not tell them, their faith shouted out the deafening noises of paganism. They knew the prophecy of Balaam which foretold the coming of the king of the Jews. They knew, too, that, more than a king, he was to be the king of all kings. They watched the heavens, hoping this would be the way the true God would inform them. With the same expectancy, they prepared gifts for the new-born king. Again, faith dictated the nature of their gifts – gold, frankincense, and myrrh.

"Gold," said Saint Augustine, "is offered to a great king; incense is immolated before God: myrrh is given to him who is to die for all men." The choice was not mere chance. That same providence who directs all men of faith directed the selection of gifts, just as he directed the decree of the census. In explanation Chrysostom offers: "Although the Magi at the time understood neither the mystical meaning when they offered the gifts nor what each single gift might signify, there is nothing out of place in their offerings. The grace that had stirred them to do all these things is the same which orders the universe."

The Magi's gifts, like everything about the Christmas mystery, offer us more oil for the lamp of meditation. The gifts are symbols. "Gold," says Saint Gregory the Great, "symbolizes wisdom, as Solomon testifies saying: *There is desirable treasure in the mouth of the just.* Frankincense, which is burnt before God, symbolizes the power of prayer, according to the psalm: *Let my prayer be dircted as incense in thy sight.* Myrrh typifies the mortification of the flesh. We offer incense when by the fervor of our prayers we offer up that which is agreeable to him. We offer myrrh when by abstinence we mortify the vices of the flesh."

Saint Gregory was not content with one mystical significance of the gifts. In another sermon he admonished his flock:

"The wise men proclaimed by their mystic gifts him whom they adored. By the gold they proclaim him king; by frankincense, God; by myrrh, a mortal man.... Let us, therefore, offer gold to our new-born Lord that we may acknowledge his universal dominion over us. Let us offer frankincense, that we may believe him who appeared in time and existed as God before all time. Let us offer myrrh in order that we may believe him whom we know to be immortal in his divinity and mortal in our humanity."

Again, the theme is faith. The same faith in the Christ Child that moved the magi to offer material gifts will prompt us to offer the spiritual gifts their offerings prefigured. No wonder, then, that Chrysostom exclaims: "Behold the faith of the Magi! See how they are not scandalized, saying to themselves: 'If this child is mighty, where is the need of flight and remaining hidden?' It is ever the way of true faith that it seeks not to know the reasons of the things that are commanded, but is persuaded to obey simply by the command."

That same faith also directed their actions after they had adored the Christ Child. The same patriarch of Constantinople tells us: "Had the Magi been seeking Christ as an earthly king, having found him they would have remained with him. Instead, they adored him and then returned to their own home. When they had returned, they continued to worship him, more than before, and they preached him and instructed many. Finally, when Thomas came to that region they joined him and were baptised, and they became his helpers in the work of preaching the Gospel."

In a most special way we are indebted to the Magi, our representatives. They give us cause to rejoice, for in them each of us finds his place around the crib of the Christ Child. This, too, was a part of God's plan. Saint John Chrysostom maintains:

"The Magi, teachers of a false faith, could never have come to know Christ our Lord had they not been illumined by the grace of this divine condescension. Indeed, the grace of God overflowed at the birth of Christ, enabling every soul to be enlightened by his truth. The Magi are enlightened, making the goodness of God manifest. Seeing that he bestowed salvation through faith on the Magi, no one need despairingly lose hope. The Magi who were think he will not receive it. Therefore, the Magi were the first from the Gentiles were chosen for salvation so that through them a door might be opened to all the Gentiles." Their presence at the crib demands our gratitude. Following the admonition of Saint Gregory the Great, "Let us acknowledge the Magi, the adorers of Christ, the first fruits of our calling and our faith. Let us, with souls rejoicing, celebrate the beginnings of a blessed hope. Through the Magi we began to enter an eternal inheritance when the secrets of the scriptures – speaking to us of Christ – were laid open and the truth…gave forth his light to all nations."

How fruitless our meditation would be if we made it no more than an intellectual gymnastics. Christ came for a greater reason than to give us the joy of intellectual contemplation. The lessons he teaches by his birth have a greater purpose. The census, the inn, the shepherds, the star, the Magi – these are types and symbols for us to follow. Christmas is to be lived. More than a day or a month or a year, Christmas is a way of life.

The Church Fathers understood this meaning of Christmas. Their sermons and writings are more than scriptural exegesis or historical research. Above all else, they spoke and wrote to help us understand how we can make Christmas a part of our lives. Saint Gregory the Great, for example, draws this lesson from the Magi:

"In returning to their own land by another way the Magi suggest something of great significance for us. Our true country is paradise. Having now come to the knowledge of Jesus, we are forbidden to return to it on the path by which we left it. For we left our land by the path of pride, of disobedience, by following after wealth, by eating forbidden food. So we must now return another way: by way of tears, by way of obedience, by contempt of the world, by restraining the desires of the flesh."

In the same tones, Saint Leo the Great exhorted his people to seize the grace of Christmas for a change of life.

"Dearly beloved, lift up your hearts to the shining grace of the sempiternal light and, adoring the precious mysteries of man's redemption, give earnest thought to what has been done for you. Love the purity of chastity, because Christ is the son of virginity. Refrain from carnal desires which war against the soul…. In malice be like children, because the Lord of glory has subjected himself to the childhood of mortal man. Follow in the way of humility, which the Son of God deigned to show his disciples. Clothe yourselves with the strength of patience, in which you shall have the power to possess your souls, because he who is the redeemer of all men is also the strength of all men. Mind the things that are above, not the things on earth. Walk in steadfastness along the way of truth and life. Do not let the things of earth ensnare you, for whom the things of heaven are prepared."

Moral transformation is the result of Christmas meditation. When we gaze into the crib and know who he is who cries as a babe yet rules as the Lord, we realize more deeply the need of moral reform. In this Christ, "set for the fall and the rise of many," we discover who we are. In his life we find our life; that is another reason why Christmas will continue to be celebrated until the end of time. Christmas is Christ's birthday, and ours too. As long as men continue to long for life there will be a Christmas.

Saint Leo the Great urged his people to give thanks on this most holy night:

"Thanks to God the Father through his Son, in the Holy Spirit, who has had mercy on us because he has loved us so much. Even when we were dead by sin, he has restored us to life in Christ so that we might be in him new creatures and new images. Therefore, through this new participation in the life of Christ, now let us put off the old man with his works and renounce the works of the lustful flesh. Recognize, O Christian, your dignity! Now that you are a partaker of the divine nature, do not return to the old misery by an evil way of life. Be mindful of whose head and body you are a member! Now that you have turned from the power of darkness, remember that you have been born with Christ into the light and kingdom of God."

Here is the Christmas mystery, unfolded by the Fathers of the Church, but never completely revealed. It will ever be a mystery because it was and is and always shall be the unfolding of God's love, the story of God's falling in love with man and, out of love for man, becoming man for man's sake. It is God's eternal love song, God's always recurring love story. It is a story ever-ancient, ever-new. No one will ever comprehend the love of God. ❧

1963

REAT AND HOLY WEEK

The Liturgical Press, Collegeville, Minnesota, published this meditation as part of the book, Death and Resurrection, *in 1963. The book was significant inasmuch as it was the first work printed by a Catholic publishing house with an Imprimatur of the Most Rev. Peter W. Bartholome, Bishop of the Church of St. Cloud, containing passages from the Revised Standard Version of the Holy Bible. This was an historic ecumenical breakthrough in the United States. I wrote these meditations in Puerto Rico in early 1962.*

The sacred drama of Holy Week begins with a shout of praise: "Blessed is He who comes in the name of the Lord!" Today, too, children raise the cry: "Hosanna in the highest!" This is the day of triumph. Christ rides into the holy city Jerusalem and is hailed as King.

This is the week of triumph. Christ lives in the holy city which is His Church, and His people joyfully acclaim Him King. The holy bishop Methodius cries out for all of us:

"Blessed is He who comes in the name of the Lord, for He is the Lord who will have mercy upon the creatures of His hands.... Blessed is He who comes in the name of the Lord, for He is the Lord who will save all men who have been lost in error by putting away all error and sending light to those who are lost in darkness.... Blessed is He who comes in the name of the Lord, for He is the one who will give Himself for all of us. He will deliver the poor from the hands of their oppressors. He will pour wine and oil upon him who had fallen among thieves and had been overlooked by so many.... Blessed is He who comes in the name of the Lord for He is the Lord who will save us by Himself. No ambassador, no angel, but the Lord Himself will save us."

The triumphal entry of the Holy One sets the theme for our hymn of praise and adoration this week. We become a part of the throng who welcome the Savior every Palm Sunday; we go forth with joy to meet Him, inviting Him to come into the holy city of our souls. We take to heart the advice of Methodius:

"Let us, with the children, raise our branches on high and with them make a joyous applause so that the Holy Spirit will breathe also upon us and enable us in our own way to cry out the hymn taught by God Himself, "Blessed is He who comes in the name of the Lord"…. Today the King of glory is praised throughout the world and invites us to be partakers of His heavenly banquet. In this way He shows that He is the Lord of both heaven and earth, just as both those in heaven and upon earth now glorify Him with the same hymn of praise."

With this spirit, Holy Week will have a deeper meaning for all of us. It will be infinitely more than a rigorous spiritual marathon. Rather, it will be the time of our renewal, the time of joyous praise, the time of loving and grateful union with Christ who is our love and joy. This was the week for which the Son of God was born; this is the week for which each Christian is born.

We were created to share in the suffering and death and, at the very same time, in the glory and resurrection of our Savior. The response we give the Savior in His agony is the measure of our sharing in His glory. Thus Saint Augustine admonishes us today with the words he addressed to his flock in northern Africa centuries ago:

"Although Christians should be conspicuous in every season of the year by their prayers, fasts, and alms-deeds, this season especially should arouse even those who are indifferent at other times. Even those who are conscientious in performing these works at other times should now perform them with even greater diligence. These days, when the sufferings of the Lord Christ are renewed, should remind us that our life in this world is a time for continually practicing humility."

That humility which is the cornerstone of the Christian life is the necessary condition for fruitful participation in the events of this great week. Setting before us the example of Christ's humility, the Bishop of Hippo continues:

"What mercy could be greater, so far as we poor sinners are concerned, than that which drew the Creator of the heavens down from heaven, clothed the maker of the earth with earthly garments, made

Him, who in eternity remains equal to His Father, equal to us in mortality, and imposed on the Lord of the universe the form of a servant? He who is our food hungers; He who is our fulfillment thirsts; he who is our strength becomes weak; He who is our health suffers; He who is our life dies."

We shall not be able to enter into the spirit of these sacred days unless we have a humble and contrite heart. Without humility, we cannot begin to comprehend the meaning that pierces every moment of these days. Saint John Chrysostom gives us this counsel:

"Think of who He is who is so close to you in this tremendous sacrifice and with whom you are invited to call upon God…. This will help you to be recollected in spirit when you reflect that, in spite of being enclosed in a body and clothed with flesh, you have been deemed worthy to praise the Lord of all with the citizens of heaven. Do not, then, take part in this holy praise, in these sacred mysteries, with a dissipated soul. Let not your thoughts during these days be occupied with worldly matters. Rather, casting all earthly things from your mind…offer your holy praise to God for all that He has done for you."

Without humility we cannot worthily offer God that praise which is His due. Each of us must be so thoroughly convinced of our need for humility that we are constantly conscious of it. This conviction is born only after serious reflection and meditation. Holy Week is the time for us to begin or to continue this serious meditation. During these days we should abstain from worldly interests just as rigorously as we abstain from worldly pleasures. This is the type of fasting Saint John Chrysostom enjoins when he says:

"When you were fasting I used to say to you that there could be one of you who, while fasting, was not fasting. So now I say that it is possible that a person can fast by not fasting. Perhaps you think I am speaking in riddles, so I shall explain. How can it be that a person who is fasting does not fast? When a person abstains from food but not from sin. How can it be that a person who is not fasting still fasts? When he partakes of food but abstains from sin. This latter fast is better than the former – not only better but also easier."

Through such fasting, both from sin and from the enticements of the world's distractions, we shall find time for quiet meditation.

Foregoing unnecessary involvement in daily living will give us leisure – leisure, as Saint Augustine says, "not for indulging in pleasure but for searching after wisdom." Quoting Holy Scripture, he continues: "The wisdom of the scribe comes in leisure time and he who abstains from unnecessary business shall receive wisdom. In this way the mind has time for thoughts of God."

The Christian should strive after this quiet meditation every possible moment during this great week. The subject of his meditation is given by holy mother Church, thoughts that recur day after day, beginning as an imperceptible cloud during the triumphal entry into Jerusalem until it rumbles in the heavy overcast on Good Friday and is finally dissipated by the glorious rays of the rising Son on Easter morning. The theme is the text of Saint Paul: "And being found in human form He humbled Himself and became obedient unto death, even death on a cross. Therefore God also has exalted Him and has bestowed upon Him the name that is above every name, so that at the name of Jesus every knee should bend of those in heaven, on earth and under the earth, and every tongue should confess that the Lord Jesus Christ is in the glory of God the Father" (Phil. 2:8-11).

Our reflection on this central idea of Christianity will form the solid foundation for our humility. From the shame of the cross to the glory of the resurrection, we learn the path that each of us must follow in our journey to everlasting glory. In His footsteps we shall find our sure footing. His actions become our examples, as Saint Hilary of Poitiers saw so clearly:

"Christ prayed for His persecutors because they knew not what they did. He promised paradise from the cross, because He is God the King. He rejoiced upon the cross, that all was finished when He drank the vinegar, because He had fulfilled all the prophecies before He died. He was born for us, suffered for us, died for us, rose again for us."

Christ is our model. We must follow Him. His purpose must be our purpose. The Venerable Bede explains that divine purpose in these words:

"The whole divine mission of our Redeemer in the flesh was to restore peace to the world. For this reason He became man, suffered and rose from the dead. In such a way He brought back to the peace of God those who by offending God had incurred His anger.... The Apostle, writing about Him to those converted from paganism, says, 'And He came and preached peace to you who were far off and peace to those who were near; for through Him we both have access in one Spirit to the Father'" (Eph. 2:17-18).

Saint Methodius expresses the same thought:

"The Lamb and Son of God did all these things...so that, on our behalf, He might undergo His saving passion and be recognized, as it were, in the market-place. In such a way those who bought Him for thirty pieces of silver might recognize Him who, with His life-giving Blood, was to redeem the world. Christ, our Passover, was sacrificed for us in order that those who were sprinkled with His precious blood...might escape from the darts of the destroyer."

It is not good, however, to exaggerate in our meditations on the Savior's passion and death. They are only part of the drama of our redemption. Overemphasis on the Lord's passion and death would produce a Christianity of doom; even the youngest child knows that Christianity is a life of joy. We were made for happiness. Thus an integral part of Holy Week, the third dimension of Christian living, lies in resurrection. We shall be reminded of this thought continually during these solemn days. Death to sin is the threshold of life in Christ. Good Friday is the condition of Easter. Even among the first readings on Good Friday, when we are rightly saddened by the Savior's death, Mother Church strikes a note of joy: "The third day He shall rise again." With this thought in mind Saint Augustine observed:

"The prophet says, 'We have seen Him.' What is He like? 'He had no form or comeliness.' Why is this? asks another prophet. 'I can count all My bones.' They have numbered His bones as He hung upon the cross. An ugly sight – the sight of one crucified. But that ugliness produced beauty. What beauty? That of the resurrection, because He is 'beautiful above all the sons of men.'"

Holy Week would be folly if the resurrection were not an essential part of it. It is true that we shall climb to the summit of Calvary and stand beneath the cross of Christ, but we never forget that Calvary is the entrance to the valley of the resurrection. Thus Saint Augustine admonishes us:

"Since our Lord Jesus Christ made one day dolorous by His death and another glorious by His resurrection, let us, by recalling both days in solemn commemoration, keep sacred the memory of His death and rejoice in the celebration of His resurrection. This is our annual festival. It is our Passover, not symbolized by the slaying of an animal as in the case of the ancient people, but fulfilled by the Victim of salvation for a new people.... In our grief over His death and our joy in His resurrection we are happy because He endured sorrow and anticipated joy for our sake. We do not live in ungrateful forgetfulness but we celebrate in grateful memory."

The same saint elsewhere says: "If we unhesitatingly believe with the heart what we profess with the mouth, in Christ we are crucified, we are dead, we are buried. And with Christ we are raised from the dead on the third day."

Christ was the first to experience this leap from death to resurrection, from ugliness to beauty, from sorrow to joy. Every Christian shares the same experience at baptism. Our thoughts return lovingly and gratefully to that great day when each of us died and rose again in Christ through the life-giving water of baptism. More than any other event in our lives, baptism should make us mindful of this intimate union of death and resurrection. Considered in such a way, Holy Week is neither a tragedy nor a contest. It is our annual renunciation of sin, our annual foretaste of glory. For this reason we enter into the spirit of these days with the "grateful memory" Saint Augustine requested. This same thought was expressed by Saint John Damascene:

"Through His birth, that is His incarnation, and baptism and passion and resurrection, he delivered our nature from the sin of our first parents and death and corruption. He became the first-fruits of the resurrection and made Himself the way and image and pattern in order that we, too, following in His footsteps, may become by adoption what He is Himself by nature, sons and heirs of God and joint heirs with Him.... He gave us, therefore, a second birth in order that, just as we who are born of Adam are in his image and are the heirs of the curse and corruption, so also being born of Christ we may be in His likeness and heirs of His incorruption and glory."

The Venerable Bede draws the parallel between death and

resurrection even more strikingly:

"In what way could men be more truly encouraged to believe in the glory to come and to strive for eternal life than by knowing that God Himself had become a sharer of their humanity and mortality? In what other way could they be asked more effectively to suffer evils of every kind for the sake of salvation than by learning that their own Creator had suffered at the hands of wicked men every kind of abuse and even the sentence of death itself? For what reason could they more certainly accept the hope of resurrection than through remembering that they had been cleansed and sanctified by His sacraments and made one in His body who, tasting death for their sake, hastened to become the exemplar of their resurrection?"

The first conviction we gain from Holy Week should be a deeper appreciation of the inseparable unity of our Savior's death and resurrection. This conviction will enrich our meditations on the great liturgical events of the week; it will also afford our meditations on the need for humility a deeper well from which to draw reasons and examples. Our meditations are the condition, the Savior's death and resurrection the subject, and a God-given humility the result.

During these days we shall be spiritual beggars. Prelate or priest, religious or layman, old or young, rich or poor, not one of us can afford not to beg for the graces our merciful Savior wished to share with us these days. Saint or sinner, wise or foolish, strong or weak, not one of us can excuse himself from the spiritual exercises of this week, for as Saint John Chrysostom remarked:

"Just as soil left uncultivated by the farmer goes wild and becomes unlovely, so likewise the soul that goes without spiritual cultivation brings forth weeds and thistles. If those who each day hear the teaching of the prophets and apostles and sing from their hearts the songs of Holy Scripture have difficulty in constraining their own fiery hearts, checking their anger, freeing themselves from the poison of envy, mastering their own concupiscence, restraining all these wild beasts – what hope of salvation have they who never use these saving medicines or never listen to the divine teaching? Just as he who abandons a refuge will stray in every direction and he who forgets the fear of God will continually be tormented by cares and pains and anxieties."

Has not each of us experienced these "anxieties"? Do we not need these sacred days to rediscover the fundamentals of Christian life and thought?

The closer our union with Christ through the liturgy of the Church, the greater will be our spiritual gifts from Christ through the saving prayers of His Church. Thus Saint John Chrysostom insisted that his people take their place in their parish churches and actively participate in the ceremonies of these days. He countenanced no excuse:

"I would like to know what they are doing who neglect the assemblies of the faithful and keep away from this sacred table. I know only too well. They are either talking about vain or idle things or immersed in worldly things. In either case the time used is without justification and merits severe correction. There is no need to prove the negligence of the first group. Nor can they be excused who offer the excuse of family duties and of the needs that arise from them. It is obvious that they do not value spiritual and heavenly things above those of this world. What servant, I ask you, attends to the things of his own house before fulfilling those of his master?"

Rather than be numbered among those who keep this great week in "ungrateful forgetfulness," we should earnestly strive to "celebrate in grateful memory" the mysteries of our Savior's passion, death, and resurrection by participating in the sacred rites performed in our parish church. We should take to heart the admonition of Saint Leo the Great:

"Let us glorify God in our body so that we may show that He is dwelling in us by the holiness of our lives. Since no virtues are more worthy or more excellent than merciful loving-kindness and unblemished chastity, let us especially gird ourselves with these weapons. Thus raised from the earth, as it were, on the two wings of active charity and shining purity, we may secure for ourselves a place in heaven."

This is the purpose of our meditations these days. Holy Week points heavenward. The more ardently we enter into the spirit of this week, the more certain we shall be of entering into the glory of heaven. Saint Ambrose summarizes what our sentiments should be:

"With me and for me He suffers. For me He is sad. For me He is burned. In my stead, therefore, and in my place He grieved who had no reason to grieve for Himself. Not Thy wounds, but mine, hurt Thee,

Lord Jesus…. Just as Thy death made an end of death and Thy wounds healed our scars, so also Thy sorrow took away our sorrow."

Holy Thursday

How can we give expression to a day so full of meaning? Christ is the central figure. Two others, Peter and Judas, play minor roles.

The day begins in the early hours. We might find ourselves among the privileged few who take part in the morning Mass of the Chrism. The bishop gathers his priests and people about himself in the cathedral church to consecrate the sacred oils to be used in every church offering throughout the coming year. Gathered together in worship and service, bishop and priests recall the Lord and His apostles in the upper room. Together they worship God in the name of God's people. Together they are bound in a ministry of service, for the holy oils consecrated this morning will be used for the salvation of God's chosen people. Perhaps no utterance is given; but each, from the bishop to the youngest priest, hears again in his own heart the Master's description of His priesthood which His ministers have chosen as their way of life: "The Son of man came not to be served but to serve, and to give His life as a ransom for many" (Matthew 20:28).

These holy oils that they have come together to consecrate remind each of God's ministers of his vocation as the servant of God. Through the use of the holy oils both bishop and priests will carry out the work of the Master. Thus no pains must be spared to make this Mass of the Chrism the most solemn and sacred. Priests from far and near make every effort to take their station and exercise their ministry together with their bishop who consecrates the holy oils. No ceremony of the year can compare with the richness of this rite.

This is as it should be, for, as Saint Cyril of Jerusalem remarked, "this exorcised oil receives such power by the prayer of the bishop that it not only burns and cleanses away the traces of sin but also chases away all the invisible powers of the evil one." Guided by the vision of faith, the worshipper should look upon the holy oil and the sacred chrism as the life-giving and life-sustaining spiritual signs that they really are. Thus the same patriarch of Jerusalem admonished his flock:

"Beware of supposing this to be ordinary ointment. This holy ointment is…after the invocation the gift of Christ, and by the presence of His Godhead it brings to us the Holy Spirit. It is, accordingly, applied to the forehead and the other senses so that while the body is anointed with visible ointment, the soul is made holy by the holy and life-giving Spirit."

Every Catholic owes it to himself to participate at least once in his life in the Mass of the Chrism. At no other time in his life and in no other place will he ever share in a rite so rich in meaning. In his cathedral church, the mother of all churches in a diocese, the Catholic will discover by his own participation in these sacred rites the unity of faith that binds together the bishop, priests, and people of a diocese.

Holy Thursday is also the anniversary of the priesthood. Christ is at all times the eternal High Priest, for on this day above all others He performed his high-priestly tasks. Thus Saint Ambrose says:

"It is a priest's duty to offer something and, according to the Law, to enter into the holy places by means of blood. Seeing, then, that God had rejected the blood of bulls and goats, Christ the High Priest was indeed bound to make passage and entry into the Holy of Holies of heaven through His own Blood, in order that He might be the everlasting satisfaction for our sins."

Every priest shares in this priesthood of Christ – not for himself but for others. This day he renews his dedication by professing before the heavenly court that he, too, is willing and ready to shed his blood if necessary for his people.

Holy Thursday is the day of love, of thanksgiving, the day of God's giving of Himself in the Holy Eucharist. As we are gathered in our parish churches, we do not settle for the quick, on-the-go, almost makeshift Mass and Communion at the end of a tiring day at the office or shop; rather, we gather with our fellow members of Christ in the great, solemn liturgical evening rites. Then we are rested. Then we have time for contemplation and meditation. We come together in the evening to find ourselves, to find our real identity as members of the parish, the localized Mystical Body of Christ. This is a community feast. This night we find our unity in Christ, both in the Holy Eucharist and in the example He leaves us in the washing of the feet.

Imagine, for a moment, what this world would be like without the sacramental presence of Christ. Imagine what we would be like without the sustaining strength of Holy Communion. This is the night of our thanksgiving.

Nothing so radically uproots our selfishness as the community that was born when Christ first took bread and wine and made them the life-bearing signs of His own Body and Blood. That great sacramentalist, Saint Cyril of Jerusalem, explains the meaning of this action in these words:

"He once turned water into wine in Cana of Galilee at His own will. Is it incredible that He should have turned wine into Blood? When called to an earthly marriage He miraculously performed that wonderful work. Should He not also eagerly bestow His Body and Blood on the children of the bridal chamber? Therefore, with certain faith let us partake of the Body and Blood of Christ.... In such a way we come to bear Christ in us, because His Body and Blood are diffused through our members. Thus it is that, according to the blessed Peter, 'we become partakers of the divine nature'" (2 Peter 1:4).

We are one in God. We share the same divinity. There can be no room for selfish individualism in the life of the true Christian. The closer we approach Christ, the closer we approach each other. "When you mention Communion," says Saint John Damascene, "it is an actual coming together, because through it we have communion with Christ and share in His flesh and His divinity. Indeed, we also have communion and are united with one another through it. Since we partake of one bread, we all become the one Body and Blood of Christ and members of one another, being of one body with Christ." The Christian is his brother's keeper. For that reason we pray for all men in the celebration of the Eucharist, just as Christ Himself prayed for all men at the first eucharistic service. Saint Cyril of Jerusalem summarizes the Christian's prayer:

"After the spiritual sacrifice is perfected...we entreat God for the common peace of the Church, for the tranquility of the world, for kings, for soldiers and allies, for the sick, for the afflicted. In a word, for all who stand in need of help we all pray and offer this Sacrifice.... When we offer to Him our supplications for those who have died, though they be sinners, we offer up Christ, sacrificed for our sins, propitiating our merciful God both for them and for ourselves."

The whole wide world, with all its trouble and turmoil, conflict, and crisis, is the personal concern of the sincere Christian. His embracing love enfolds all races, all peoples, and "especially those of the household of the faith" (Gal. 6:10). This night, then, we renew our faith in the most wondrous of all God's gifts. With firm conviction we acknowledge the words of Saint John Damascene:

"The bread and wine are not merely figures of the Body and Blood of Christ (God forbid!) but the deified Body of the Lord Himself, for the Lord has said, "This is My Body," not a figure of My Body; and "My Blood," not a figure of My Blood."

Confirming our faith, Saint Ambrose reminds us:

"The sacrament which you receive is made what it is by the word of Christ.... You read concerning the making of the whole world: 'He spoke, and it came to be; He commanded, and it stood forth.' Shall not the word of Christ, which was able to make out of nothing that which was not, be able to change things which already exist into what they were not? The Lord Jesus Himself proclaims: 'This is My Body.' Before the blessing of the heavenly words another nature is spoken of. After the consecration the Body is signified.... And you say, 'Amen,' that is, 'It is true.' Let the heart within confess what the mouth utters. Let the soul feel what the voice speaks. Christ, then, feeds His Church with this sacrament and by means of it the life of the soul is strengthened."

Without faith we are impoverished, for the mind cannot comprehend the brilliance nor the heart feel the warmth that surrounds the table of the Last Supper. If our faith asks why bread and wine were chosen as the signs of Christ's Body and Blood, Saint John Damascene answers:

"Bread and wine are employed because God knows man's weakness. For, in general, man turns away discontentedly from what is not well-worn by custom. So with His usual indulgence God performs His supernatural works through familiar objects. Take, for example, baptism. Man usually washes himself with water and anoints himself with oil. So God connected the grace of the Spirit with the oil, and the water He made the laver of re-birth. In a similar manner it is man's custom to eat and drink bread and wine. Thus God joined His divinity to these and made them His Body and Blood in order that we may rise to what is supernatural through what is familiar and natural."

Saint Ambrose presents another image for our consideration. He sees the Savior hanging on the cross as an image of the precious Blood of Christ in the Holy Eucharist:

"Here is the cup you use to purify the hidden recesses of your soul. It is not a cup of the Old Testament, filled with wine pressed from that wondrous cluster who hung in the flesh upon the tree of the cross just as grapes hang on the vine. From this sacred cluster, then, is the wine that makes the heart of man glad, uplifts the sorrowful, and pours into us the supreme joys of faith, true devotion, and purity."

Let us go to the words of Saint John Chrysostom in order to apply to ourselves all that we have been saying about the Holy Eucharist. The lesson is obvious: as Christians we can do nothing better than foster our union with Christ in Holy Communion. Saint John Chrysostom says:

"Let no poor person grieve because of his poverty, for this is the festival of the soul. Let no rich person take pride in his abundance, for money cannot add to the joy of this day.... The same table is prepared both for the rich and the poor. Although a man is rich, he can add nothing to this table. Should another be poor, he shall have no less honor because of his poverty in regard to the things which are here and belong to everyone without distinction.... The same table is prepared for the poor man, sitting waiting for an alms, as for the emperor, adorned with the diadem and clad in the royal purple, who rules the world. Such are the gifts of God. He gives not according to dignity but according to the will and mind of the one who receives. Therefore, let the poor man and the emperor come with equal confidence and with equal profit to this table."

As Christians we are brothers. At God's table we are all His children. Only one distinction is worth noting: that between the worthy and the unworthy. Examining our consciences for us, Saint John Chrysostom continues:

"Let those who possess a clean heart, a clear conscience, a way of living that is without reproach, come to the Lord's table. Those who are not of this kind, let them not come even once, for they take judgment and damnation to themselves. For just as food that has the power to nourish, if it is taken by one who has a stomach infested with disease, injures and aggravates everything and becomes a cause rather than a remedy of illness, so is it with this tremendous mystery. Will you partake of this spiritual table, the table of the King, and then soil your body again with filth? Do you anoint it with ointments, and then fill it up with foulness? Do you consider that it suffices for the forgiveness of the sins of the whole year if you at each returning year partake of Communion and then at the end of the week return to your former way of life? Tell me this. If after forty days you were restored to health from a serious illness, would you return to those things that earlier had caused your illness? Would you then not squander uselessly all your former efforts? If the things of the body are spoiled in this way, how much more so the things that depend on our own free will and decision?"

Holy Thursday is the night of divine love, the love which comes into our souls through Holy Communion. For love of us the Savior will die on the cross tomorrow. For love of us the Savior will rise from the dead on the third day. For love of us the Savior gives Himself as the life of each soul that might grow weary on its journey from the death of mortality to the life of immortality. This night, then, witnesses the example of divine love. Not content with merely giving us Himself, the Master wishes to show us the limitless proportions of His love. He stoops to wash the feet of His apostles. He literally descends to the depths of humility in order to show us how we might rise to the heights of glory. With Saint Augustine we exclaim:

"What a marvel it is that He pours water into a basin with which to wash the disciples' feet who shed His Blood upon the earth with which to wash out the filthiness of sin! What a marvel it is that with the towel with which He was girded He wiped the feet He had washed who by the flesh He had put on confirmed the footsteps of the evangelists…. About to become the victim of man's hatred, He first performed the lowly services of love, not only to them for whom He was about to suffer death, but even for him who was about to deliver Him up to death…. All of us men who were damned by following the pride of the deceiver are now saved by following the humility of the Redeemer."

Our humility, like the Savior's, must be wedded to love. When stripped of brotherly love, humility can lead one down the road of self-righteous pride. Joined to Christian love, humility forces the Christian soul to empty self of self to such a degree that there can be room only for the goodness of God. From Christ's example of washing His apostles' feet, Saint Augustine draws another lesson for us:

"Let us forgive each others' sins, and for our own sins pray for each other. In doing this we shall, as it were, wash one another's feet. It is our duty to perform the ministry of charity and humility. It is Christ's pleasure to hear our prayers and cleanse us from all contamination of sin. In this way, by forgiving each other, what is loosed on earth will be loosed also in heaven."

The scenes on Holy Thursday night change swiftly. Christ leaves the upper room and converses with His apostles as they pass through the holy city, cross the brook called Cedron, and enter the Garden of Olives. He picks out three – Peter, James, and John – and goes further on to enter into the bitter prelude to His passion, the agony in the garden. Saint John Chrysostom finds a spiritual meaning in the very name of the Mount of Olives. His meaning harks back to the divine commandment of Christian love:

"Let us also go out unto the hands of the poor, for this is the meaning of the Mount of Olives. The multitude of the poor are olive-trees planted in the house of God, dropping down oil which is profitable for us. This is the oil the five virgins had, and the others who did not have it, perished. Having received this oil because of our gifts to the poor, let us enter in with lamps glowing in order to meet the divine Bridegroom."

Here on the Mount of Olives Christ suffers His bloody agony, in so many ways more painful than the blows that would be showered upon His earthly body in the coming hours. Here pass before His mind's eye all the sins of mankind until the end of time. Here He sees the sufferings of His Mystical Body, how one member would inflict suffering on another, how one member would set about to destroy himself and others. Here Christ views the sins of all mankind, the sins of the high and mighty, the sins of all the unknowns of history. Christ sees all the sins of the world, your sins, my sins. Christ sees, and His whole body perspires with great drops of blood. From the agony in the garden Dionysius of Alexandria draws these lessons for our meditation:

"By voluntarily enduring the death in the flesh, He implanted incorruptibility in it. So also, by taking on Himself of His own free will the sufferings of human nature, He set in us the seeds of constancy and courage. Thus He has equipped those who believe in Him for the mighty conflicts belonging to their witness-bearing. Those drops of sweat flowed from Him in a marvelous manner, like great drops of blood, in order that He might, as it were, drain off and empty the fountain of fear that is proper to our human nature. Also important is that sentence in the narrative which tells us that an angel stood by the Savior and strengthened Him. For this, too, is related to our salvation, inasmuch as those who are appointed to engage in the sacred struggles of conflict for the sake of religion have the angels from heaven to assist them."

The heavenly Father sent an angel to comfort Christ when His own apostles abandoned Him, and Judas heeded the Master's admonition: "What you are going to do, do quickly" (John 13:27). Saint Leo the Great explains the expression:

"This is the voice of permission, not of command, of readiness, not of fear. He who has power over all time, shows that He does not hinder the traitor in his work. Rather, He carries out the Father's will for the redemption of the world in such a way that He neither promoted nor feared the crime which His persecutors were preparing."

All this time Judas was busy performing his evil deed. In the darkness of the night he carried out his task, for so hideous was that secret mission to the chief priests that shame forbade its execution in the light of day. For thirty pieces of silver, a pittance, Judas was willing to betray the Lord of the world. Greed entered his heart. No future, unknown kingdom for him. Judas wanted power *now*. He craved glory *now*. He reached out to grasp riches *now*. To all the lesser Judases of all times who would exchange the Lord of the world for the creatures of His earth, Saint John Chrysostom gives warning:

"Hear, you covetous ones, and consider what happened to Judas. At one and the same time he lost the money, committed the crime, and destroyed his own soul. Such is the tyranny of covetousness. Judas enjoyed the money neither in this present life nor in the life to come, but at one and the same time lost both lives. Despised by the men who gave him the money, he went out and hanged himself."

Judas' tragedy did not come about in one moment. Who can say when he began to turn from Christ? Who can say when any sinner begins his downward path, turning from the friendship of Christ to the ugliness of selfish desires? When did Judas stop listening to the merciful words of a loving Savior? When does the sinner begin to turn deaf ears to the same loving words of the same loving Savior? Judas, says Saint Leo the Great, "never seriously reflected upon the proofs of the Savior's mercy. His ears had heard the Lord's words when He said, "I came not to call the righteous, but sinners," and also, "The Son of man came to seek and to save that which was lost." But these words did not pierce Judas' understanding. The mercy of Christ not only healed bodily infirmities but also the wounds of sick souls, saying to the paralytic man, 'Take heart, my son; your sins are forgiven,' and saying to the adulteress who was brought to him, 'Neither will I condemn you; go and sin no more.' In all His works He showed that He had come as the Savior, not the judge, of the world." Even from Judas we can learn lessons which will help us draw closer to the Savior he betrayed. Christ did not exclude Judas from His all-embracing love. Even though as God He knew that Judas was plotting His destruction, He loved him and had compassion on him. Up to the very last moment the Savior still hoped and prayed for Judas' conversion. Marveling at this goodness, Dionysius of Alexandria exclaims:

"How full of wonder is this endurance of evil by the Lord, who even kissed the traitor and spoke words softer even than the kiss! He did not say, "O abominable, utterly abominable, traitor, is this the return you make for so many kindnesses?" Rather than being angry with him, He simply says, "Judas," using the proper name which was the address that would be used by one who has compassion on a person.... Blessed art thou, O Lord! How great is this example of the endurance of evil that you have shown us in your own person! How great, too, the example of humility! The Lord has given us this example to show us that we ought not to give up offering our good counsel to our brethren, even should nothing remarkable result from our words."

Never-ending, never-tiring love of God and neighbor is the first lesson we can apply to ourselves from the story of Judas. Saint Basil also draws a lesson of perseverance from the traitor's sorry plight:

"Surely enough of an example for all who are living a holy life is the fall from the better to the worse in the case of Judas. After being Christ's disciple for so long a time, Judas sold his Master for a paltry sum and then hung himself with a halter. Learn then, brother, that it is not he who begins well who is perfect. Rather, he who carries the work out to completion gains God's approval."

At this very moment Peter was comfortably sleeping – Peter who boasted so proudly that he would die for the Master. Peter, chosen to be the leader, tricked by his own pride. We must agree with Saint Augustine:

"It does not please us to accuse the chief of the apostles. But in considering his action, we ought to realize more deeply that no man should trust in his own strength. What other reason had our Teacher and Savior than to show us by the example of the very chief of the apostles that no man should presume upon his own powers in any circumstance?"

To be sure, Peter was weak; he had not yet received the strength and power of the Holy Spirit. In later ages martyrs by the thousands would gladly die for the sake of Christ. But they were able to do so chiefly because they had received "power from on high." With this thought in mind we can more readily understand this comparison Saint John Chrysostom makes between Peter and Judas:

"A man's willingness is not sufficient unless he receives help from above. On the other hand, help from above will be of little value if a man is unwilling. Peter and Judas show both these lessons. Judas, in spite of receiving much help, failed because he was unwilling to contribute anything on his own. Peter, though he was generous of soul, received little assistance and thus fell. Virtue's web is woven from divine assistance and human cooperation."

Neither Judas nor Peter, however, could stop the development of events this sacred night. Christ's seizure in the garden, His scourging, crowning with thorns, buffeting, and ridicule were pre-ordained. He entered into His passion not because of the deceits, the denial, or the cunning of men, but because of the power these sufferings would have to deliver men from their sins. Saint Cyril of Jerusalem points out that even the crown of thorns has meaning for us:

"Adam received the doom:

'Cursed is the ground because of you…thorns and thistles it

shall bring forth to you.' For this reason Jesus assumes the thorns, that He might cancel the doom. For this reason also He was buried in the earth, that the cursed earth might receive instead of the curse a blessing."

The crown of thorns symbolized for many of the early Church Fathers the removal of the curse upon the earth. Just as through Adam's sin all creation suffered with man, so now through Christ's redemption all nature would be renewed and restored. In the words of Rufinus:

"It was appropriate that He who came to remove the sins of the world should also release the earth from the curses inflicted on it when the first man sinned…. Jesus was, therefore, crowned with thorns in order that the primordial sentence of condemnation might be remitted. He was led to the cross and the life of the whole world hung suspended from its wood."

It was, indeed, fitting also that on this sacred night Christ should be crowned, even if with thorns. No one knew better than He that in reality He was the victor and His persecutors the vanquished. Even during these hours of shame and blasphemy Christ remained the Master. The mockery of the soldiers who crowned Him with thorns and placed a reed in His hands and cried out, "Hail! our King!" unwittingly proclaimed the truth and fulfilled the prophecies. Thus Rufinus continues:

"In order to accomplish salvation through the weakness of the flesh, His divine nature succumbed to the death of the flesh. The reason was that, rather than being conquered by death as are all human beings, He would destroy the gates of death through the assurance that He would rise again by His own power. He was as a king who goes down into the dungeon and there throws open its doors, unties the bonds, breaks the chains, bolts and bars in pieces and leads the captives out to freedom…. In such a case the king is, of course, in the dungeon, but not under the same circumstances as the prisoners who are confined there. They are there because of their offenses. He enters there in order to free them from their punishments."

This sacred night fulfills many prophecies written about the Messiah. In order to fulfill these sacred words, Christ willingly undergoes every imaginable suffering. Tertullian comments:

"He even knows the very time that it is fitting for Him to suffer because the ancient law prefigured His passion. Thus, of all the festive days of the Jews he chooses the Passover…because He was to be "like a lamb that is led to the slaughter."… In a similar way He might have been betrayed by any stranger, but even here He fulfilled the words of the psalmist: "Even my bosom friend in whom I trusted, who ate of my bread, has lifted his heel against Me." He might also have been betrayed without a price being fixed on His head. Although this might have sufficed in other cases, it would not have been acceptable to Him who was consciously fulfilling the prophecies. It is written: 'They sell the righteous one for silver.' The very amount and the final usage of the money, as narrated in the Gospel of Saint Matthew, was clearly foretold by Jeremias."

Explaining this desire of Christ to fulfill the prophecies, Saint Leo the Great remarks:

"Things which had long been promised under mysterious figures had now to be fulfilled in all clearness. For instance, the true Sheep had to supercede the sheep which were its prototypes, and the one Sacrifice had to bring to an end the multitude of different sacrifices. For all those things which had been divinely ordained through Moses about the sacrifice of the lamb had foreshadowed Christ and truly announced the slaying of Christ. Therefore, in order that the shadows should yield to the substance and types cease in the presence of reality, the ancient observances are removed by the new sacrament, the ancient victims give way to the true Victim, the ancient blood of goats is wiped away by His Blood, and the law-ordained feast of the Passover is fulfilled by being transformed."

These are, to be sure, reasons for the blasphemies inflicted upon the sacred Body of our divine Savior. They are not, however, the chief reason. He endured all these bitter sufferings of this lonely night because He loved us. That tremendous love of the Son of God for His brothers on earth prompted Him to endure all pain, undergo all sufferings, not only willingly and freely, but even joyfully, because He realized this was the price for the salvation of all men. "Do you know why this friend of mankind did not shun death?" Saint Cyril of Jerusalem asks. Then he answers:

"It was because He did not wish to see the whole world perish in its sins. He neither surrendered His life by force nor did He die violently, but freely of His own will. For He Himself said, "I have power to lay it (my life) down and I have power to take it again." He therefore entered upon His passion of His own will, rejoicing in His noble deed, smiling at the crown of thorns, being cheered by the salvation of men, and not ashamed of the cross for by it He saved the world."

Earlier this sacred night Christ spoke tender words of love to His apostles. Now, alone and forsaken by men, even the men whom He loved above all others, He enters into the furnace of man's hatred in order to prove His love for all men, foes as well as friends. Truly, this is the night of love. This is our example: "Greater love than this no man has then that a man lay down his life for his friends."

This is the night of the Eucharist. The words of Saint Paul echo in our ears: "We are members of His Body." And as we return to our homes we will recall that other question: "Do you not know that your bodies are members of Christ?" (1 Cor 6:15).

GOOD FRIDAY

In a way, the whole world stands aghast at the tragedy of this day. We sense this grief in the stillness of nature, in the embarrassed silence of men.

We call this day simply "Good Friday" because on this day Goodness died to make all men good. The price of our virtue is the death of Him who is virtue. Terrible thought! The price of human goodness is infinite Goodness! All good men are His debtors.

In a very real sense, we caused His death. We fashioned the cross. We stood beneath that cross; our sins drove the nails deeper into His sacred flesh, pushed down the crown of thorns deeper on His sacred head. The death of our sins demanded His death. We can rise from sin only when He shall incorporate us into His resurrection.

And so today we weep. We weep for our sins because we know now what they have caused. We weep, too, for our loving Savior, not so much because He needs our sorrow, but rather because we are the guilty ones who have rebuked His love. Today we live in the shadow of His cross. Today we must remain there to satisfy infinite love, to be one with the Savior in His death for, paradoxically, His death is the threshold of our life. As Saint Ambrose told his people in Milan:

"His death is the life of all. We are signed with the sign of His death. We show forth His death when we pray. We declare His death when we offer the Sacrifice. His death is victory. His death is our mystery. His death is the annual recurring solemnity of the world."

Today we belong on Calvary, called Golgotha, "the place of the skull," by the Evangelist. Even the name has meaning for us. Here all history converges. Here time finds its fulfillment. Here each of us discovers the purpose of his life. Here Christ fulfills His own words: "And I, when I am lifted up from the earth, will draw all men to Myself" (John 12:32). Reflecting on the "place of the skull," Saint Cyril of Jerusalem draws this lesson for our consideration:

"He stretched out His hands on the cross in order to encompass the ends of the world, for Golgotha is the very center of the earth. Not I, but a prophet, has said: 'Thou hast accomplished salvation in the middle of the earth.' He who established the heavens with spiritual hands, now stretches forth human hands. They are fastened with nails to show that His humanity carries the sins of men. They are nailed to the tree so that when He dies, sin dies; and we all might rise again in holiness."

Here on Golgotha we stand today, contemplating the cruel death of our Savior. Here we belong, not because we are saints but because we are sinners. In fact, the more we have sinned, the longer we should stand here contemplating the sufferings and death of our Savior. Nor can any sinner be out of place at this holy altar of the cross for, as Saint Prosper of Aquitaine remarked,

"There can be no reason to doubt that Jesus died for unbelievers and sinners. If there had been anyone who was not one or the other, then Christ would not have died for all. But He did die for all men without exception. There is no one, therefore, in the whole human race who was not, before the reconciliation that Christ brought about by shedding His Blood, either a sinner or an unbeliever"

Standing here beneath His cross, we realize that we are not alone. At every great moment in the life of the Church, as well as in the lives of her members, we find that our companion is the Mother of God. She stands beneath Christ's cross today as His helper and ours. She offers her divine Son consolation; she tenders all her children loving solicitude.

Although she weeps (and teaches us that we too must weep), she looks to the future with holy hope and urges us to do the same. Saint Ambrose describes the Blessed Mother beneath the cross:

"When the apostles fled, she stood beneath the cross and with pious eyes beheld her Son's wounds. She did not consider the death of her divine Son as much as the salvation of the world. Perhaps because she knew that the redemption of the world would be through the death of her Son she thought that by her death also she might add something to the common good. Jesus, however, who saved all of us without a helper, did not need a helper now…. He received, indeed, the affection of His mother but sought no other's help."

With Mary we begin to comprehend the marvelous exchange as the good thief. He, too, is with us on Golgotha. He came, it is true, at first unwillingly; but now, as he contemplates the great sacrifice taking place before his eyes, he becomes the first to experience the Savior's merciful redemption. "Be of good cheer," the Savior tells him. How well he knew that his actions did not deserve to make him cheerful. Rather, he knew, as Mary knew beneath the cross, the King was here dispensing favors. He knew, too, that his request concerning the future would be answered, just as he knew that divine grace was already working in his heart. Addressing his remarks to the good thief, Saint Cyril of Jerusalem says: "Adam fell from paradise by the tree; you are brought to paradise by the tree."

Like Mary we must unite ourselves with Christ in His death, to show Him that we are willing to be His helpers in carrying out the work of saving of the world. Like the good thief we must confess our guilt; then we too shall be able to live with the holy hope that the Savior will remember us when He enters His Kingdom.

There is another exchange taking place before our eyes: Christ's return of goodness for the evil of His tormentors. Lest we judge too harshly those who actually tormented Christ in His physical body, we hang our own heads in shame, for we, by our sins, continue to torment Christ in His Mystical Body. What cruel men did here on Calvary by their own ignorance, we who are enlightened by faith continue to do by our evil deeds. This is the exchange that Saint Cyprian discusses:

"He who but a short time before had cured the eyes of the blind man with His own spittle is now covered with the spittle of His persecutors. He who now crowns the martyrs with eternal garlands is now crowned with thorns. He who now gives true palms to the victors is beaten in the face with hostile palms. He who now clothes all others with the garment of immortality is stripped of His earthly garments. He who now gives the food of heaven is fed gall. He who now offers us the cup of salvation is given vinegar to drink. He who is innocence is counted among criminals. He who is truth is accused by false testimonies.... The stars are stupefied by the crucifixion of the Lord, the elements disturbed, the earth shattered, night blots out the day, the sun withdraws both its rays and its eyes lest it be forced to gaze upon the crime of the Jews. All this time He does not speak, He does not proclaim His majesty. He endures all things, even to the bitter end, with constant perseverance so that in Him a full and perfect patience may find realization."

It is but human for us to ask why Christ the Son of God should subject Himself to these bitter offenses. Alexander of Alexandria answers the query simply: "Christ suffered that we should live forever.... For our sakes Saint Caesarius sees in the Savior's death an example of humility for all of us to follow. "If anyone wants to be a disciple of Christ," he says, "he should keep His commandments and love humility as He himself said: 'Learn of Me for I am meek and humble of heart.'" Saint Polycarp proposes the Savior's example for our imitation: "Let us become imitators of His patient endurance and, if we suffer anything for His sake, let us praise Him." Saint Leo the Great points to the Savior's willing resignation:

"Who could overcome the world's hatred, the allurement of temptations, the terrors of persecutors, had not Christ, in our name and for our sake, said to the Father: 'Thy will be done?' Let these words be learned by all the Church's sons who have been purchased at so great a price. When the shock of some violent temptation assails them, let them use the aid of this potent prayer that they may conquer their fear and trembling and learn to suffer patiently."

In His death Christ faced His finest hour. At this moment, says Saint Augustine,

"An example was given the martyrs to bear all the sufferings that persecutors would impose upon them. By concealing His aweful power for a little while, Christ commended His patience to be imitated for all time. His Kingdom, which was not to be of this world, overcame the proud world, not through fierce fighting but through humble suffering. The grain of wheat which was to be multiplied was sown in horrible disgrace and would sprout forth in marvelous glory."

All during this time He remains our Leader, Savior, Sovereign, the Lord. So Saint Cyprian draws this lesson:

"If it can be done, let us follow Him. Under His sacrament and sign let us be counted. He opens for us the way of life; He leads us back to paradise; He guides us to the kingdom of heaven. Having become sons of God through Him, we shall always live with Him. Having been restored by His Blood, we shall always rejoice with Him."

Expressing the same thought, Saint Augustine says pointedly: "Crucify your sins, that you may die to sin. He who dies to sin lives for God. Thus you should live for Him who spared not even His own Son. For Christ died for us that we might live in His revivified Body."

His consummation is our commencement. He gladly hangs on the cross today because He knows He shall rule from the same cross for endless ages. *Crux infama, crux gemmata*: The cross of shame becomes the cross of glory! Today He willingly endures all sufferings and blasphemies because these are the price of our salvation. He hides His divinity so that through His humanity He may draw all of us closer to His divinity. His love embraces even those who are now reproaching Him. "He overcame evil by goodness," says Saint Amphilochius. "He defended even those who put him to death, eager to gather them into His net. He cancelled their offense and pleaded their ignorance. Made the sport of their drunken frenzy, He submitted without bitterness. He suffered their drunkenness and in His love for all men called even them to repentance. What more could He do?"

He would leave nothing undone. He would spare nothing to deliver us from the slavery of sin. Only when He has accomplished this will He surrender His life. When it was accomplished He cried out, "It is finished!" In that cry He let all men of all time know that He surrendered His life, not because death had power over Him, but because He had the power to lay down His life of His own accord. "He gave up His spirit," says Saint Augustine, "in humility with a bowed head. With uplifted head He will receive it again in the resurrection."

This is an awesome moment. Shocked, nature stands still. Then, revolting at the hideous crime, nature is seized with fits of violence. "The powers were astonished," says Alexander of Alexandria, "the angels wondered. The elements trembled. The whole created universe was shaken. The earth quaked and its foundations rocked. The sun fled away and the light of day withdrew. They could not bear to look upon their crucified Lord. All creation in amazement cried out, 'What is this awful mystery?' The astonishment, however, does not prevail long. Immediately it gives place to victory, the greatest victory: love conquers death. Saint Peter Chrysologus describes how death is vanquished:

"Death is now judged. Death which seizes guilty men, now meets its Judge head on. Death, which held dominion over its slaves, now rises up against its Master. Death, which was victorious over men, now encounters God. In this conflict the dominion of hell perishes and its laws are blotted out. The power of death is destroyed, and in punishment for its rashness in attempting to harm its Judge it must bring its victims back to life.... Man is fashioned anew, his life restored, and now everything holds together through forgiveness because the condemnation of death has been swallowed up by the Author of life."

Expressing the same sentiments, Saint Cyril of Jerusalem exclaims:

"Death was struck with dismay when it beheld a new Visitor descending into hell who was not bound by the fetters of that place.... Death fled and his flight betrayed his cowardice.... All the holy ones of old whom death had devoured were ransomed. In such a way it was fitting for the King who had been heralded to become the Redeemer of His noble heralds. Then all the holy souls cried out... 'O death, where is thy victory? O death, where is thy sting?'"

It was right that the loving Savior of all mankind should release the souls of the just of the Old Testament. They had lived in hope of His coming and now He had come to make them sharers in His glory. This Saint John Damascene explains:

"Just as the Son of holiness rose for those upon the earth, so likewise He brings light to those who sit under the earth in darkness and in the shadow of death. Just as He brought the message of peace to those upon the earth, releasing prisoners, restoring sight to the blind and being the Author of everlasting life for those who believe in Him, so now He goes down to be the same deliverer for those who hoped for His coming."

By His descent into the limbo of the just, the Redeemer threw His mantle of love over all those who had waited for His deliverance. With the same loving mercy He provided for the men and women of countless ages to come. At the moment that His spirit went forth to deliver the holy souls of the Old Law, His Body became the fountain of redemption for all men of the New Law. The soldier pierced His side with a lance, and at that moment the Church of the living was born. The parallel is striking. "Just as Adam was a figure of Christ, " says Tertullian, "Adam's sleep foreshadowed the death of Christ. As Christ slept a mortal slumber, the wound was inflicted in His side. In the same manner as Eve was formed, the Church – true mother of the living – was formed from Christ's side." Rufinus continues the parallel in these words:

"If you ask why He is said to have shed water and blood from His side and not rather from some other part of His body, my answer is that His side with its rib mystically signifies a woman. The source of sin and death, you know, came from the first woman, who was the rib of the first Adam. Thus the source of redemption and life comes to us from the rib of the second Adam."

Saint Augustine continues the same comparison: "Without a doubt, the blood and water which poured forth from His side, when pierced by the lance, represent the sacrament by which the Church was formed, just as Eve was formed from the side of the sleeping Adam."

Over and above every consideration, the cross of Christ stands out this day. That very same cross stands out every day in a Christian's life. Our lives as Christians are intimately woven around the cross. We cannot escape it. It is a part of our thinking, a part of our being. It is, first of all, a reminder of the Savior's infinite love; it is also a promise of our salvation and a pledge of our future glory. No wonder, then, that we should make the cross the symbol of our faith. With it we live; we have value. Without it we die, we are nothing. It is good for us, then, this day above all days, to meditate upon the cross of Christ.

At the very dawn of creation the cross was foreshadowed by the tree of good and evil. Just as that tree in paradise was the battleground between preternatural life and natural death, so the tree on Calvary was the battleground between supernatural life and eternal death. "Since death was by a tree," Saint John Damascene says, "it was fitting that life and resurrection should also be bestowed by a tree." Saint Irenaeus, relating the tree of paradise and the tree of the cross more closely, says:

"The disobedience caused by one tree was blotted out by the obedience of the other tree. Obedience to God was fulfilled when the Son of Man was nailed to the tree, destroying the knowledge of evil and conferring the knowledge of good. For evil is disobedience to God and goodness is obedience to God…. By hanging on the tree He obeyed even unto death and thus blotted out the old disobedience caused by the first tree."

If the cross of our Savior recalls the tree of paradise, it equally foretells all the graces that will come to man through the Church until the end of time. For both reasons the cross is to be considered much more a symbol of victory than an instrument of shame. This consideration prompted Saint Leo the Great to exclaim:

"O wondrous power of the cross! O unspeakable glory of the passion which became the Lord's tribunal, the world's judgment, and the power of the Crucified! From Your cross You draw all things to Yourself, O Lord! When You stretched out Your hands to an unbelieving people that mocked You, the whole world was finally brought to confess Your majesty. When all the elements combined to pronounce judgment upon the crimes of the Jews, when the lights of heaven were extinguished and the day turned into night – You drew all things to Yourself, Lord…. In this way type gave way to truth, prophecy to revelation, the ancient law to the gospel. You drew all things to Yourself, Lord, so that what previously was performed in the one temple of the Jews in mystic signs is now celebrated everywhere by holy men in every country in revealing rites…. Your cross is the font of all blessings, the source of all graces, and through it the believers receive strength in return for weakness, glory in return for shame, life in return for death."

Saint Methodius is even more explicit in hailing the cross as the sign of victory: "The cross is the confirmation of victory, the way by which God descended to man, the trophy against the spirits of the world, the repulsion of death, the foundation of the ascent to veritable brilliance." Rufinus sees the cross as a victory over three kingdoms at one and the same time. "Consequently, a form of death was devised which symbolized this subjection. He was raised aloft in the air, thereby conquering the powers of the air and gaining a victory over the heavenly rulers. His outstretched hands He held out day long to the people who were on earth, rebuking unbelievers and welcoming believers. And He subjugated the underworld through that portion of the cross that was buried in the earth."

Holy Mother Church emphasizes the glory of the cross in her liturgy today. She holds it high as the standard of salvation, the symbol of Christ's eternal victory. Like her divine Master, she can see in the cross only a claim to glory. "Every deed of Christ, " says Saint Cyril of Jerusalem, "is a boast for the Catholic Church, but her greatest boast is the cross." For this reason Mother Church today asks her children to venerate the cross in a special way. She beseeches them to come forth and kiss the feet of the image of the Savior hanging on the cross. She urges them not to forget for a moment the cross and its values for the salvation of their souls. Little wonder, then, that the cross should be the sign Mother Church employs in all her sacred rites, for as Saint Augustine says:

"What other sign is the sign of Christ but the cross of Christ? Only through this sign are rites duly performed when it is applied on the brows of the believing, or over the water out of which they are reborn, or to the oil by which they are anointed with the chrism, or during the Sacrifice in which they are fed. Now who can say that no good is accomplished by what evil men do? We are signed with the cross of Christ (which evil men fashioned) in the celebration of His sacraments and thus we receive every good."

We can neither forget nor escape the cross. We see it on our buildings; we wear it on a chain around the neck; we engrave it on the covers of our books. But even if none of these signs were used, we could not escape the image of the cross. If evil men were some day to try to erase every man-made image of the cross, nature herself would preserve the sacred image of our salvation. This Saint Methodius explains when he says:

"Every creature has been marked with this sign for the sake of his own freedom. The birds which fly on high form the image of the cross by the expansion of their wings. Man, too, with his hands outstretched, represents the same sign of the cross. When the Lord fashioned man in this way at the beginning of time, He made his body form the sign of the cross to teach him that he would be for all time consecrated to God, freed from all discord and lack of harmony."

Such considerations on the cross of Christ should prompt us to make the sign of the cross reverently and frequently. It is our public confession of faith in our Savior. It is the weapon we use when the devil tempts us or the world tries to allure us. It is a reminder of our dignity and the price that was paid for our salvation. Saint Cyril of Jerusalem admonishes us:

"Let us not be ashamed to confess the Crucified. Be the cross our sign made with boldness by our fingers on our brow and on everything: over the bread we eat, the cup we drink, in our coming and going, when we lie down and when we awake, when we are on a journey or remain at home. The cross has no price, for the sake of the poor. The cross demands no effort, for the sake of the sick. It is the sign of the faithful and the horror of the devils, for when they see the cross they are reminded of the Crucified and flee from us."

Death and life, triumph and tragedy, sorrow and joy, defeat and victory: these are the paradoxes of Good Friday. All center around the cross of Christ. Our lives, too, must center around the cross of Christ. "We should glory in the cross of our Lord Jesus Christ, in whom is our salvation, life, resurrection; by whom we are saved and delivered."

The Vigil of Holy Easter

You walk out into the night. The air is fresh and crisp, full of expectancy. You drive to church with your family. You greet your neighbors as you enter the church. Although no one says it, you know you are going to participate in one of the great events of the year. This is the night of the great vigil, the Easter vigil. Saint Augustine tells us why it is so great:

"How eagerly we should keep watch during this vigil, the mother of all the sacred vigils.... On this sacred night the whole world keeps vigil, both the world that hates Christ as well as the world that has been restored by Him. The latter, now delivered from sin, watched because it wants to praise its deliverer; the former, now condemned, watches for an opportunity to blaspheme its judge. The latter keeps watch with a fervent and loving mind; the former with weeping and gnashing of teeth. Love inspires the latter; hate moves the former. Thus, unwittingly, even our enemy teaches us how we should keep watch tonight, for he who envies us keeps watch in order to ensnare us…. Let us, then, watch and pray so that both externally and internally we may fittingly celebrate this vigil."

Why do we assemble in our parish church with friends and neighbors tonight? "We prolong our singing tonight," Saint Augustine says, "because He in whose honor we sing will grant us to reign with Him in eternal life."

It seems long ago that we heard the dreadful cry, "It is consummated." Our Savior has rested in the tomb. He has, to be sure, suffered the penalty of death. But for Him this was not so much a penalty as a prologue. Now we gather together to share in the glory of His resurrection.

Again the scenes have changed swiftly. Penitence and sorrow are things of the past. Holy hope and confidence fill our hearts and souls tonight. We come together in joy to begin our celebration. "This celebration," Saint Augustine reminds us, "has made this night the most important of all nights in the whole world." This is our great moment precisely because it was, and continues to be, the Savior's greatest moment. We watch and wait to see the Man of Sorrows transformed into the Victor who comes to make us sharers in His victory. Saint Peter Chysologus explains the meaning of this mystery for us:

"You have seen that He was buried so that no one could say His death was only imaginary…. Christ devoted the three days of His burial to the three abodes He was going to deliver, namely, the region beneath the earth, the earth, and heaven. He was going to restore all the things in heaven, repair the things on earth, and redeem those beneath the earth by this period of His three days' rest. In this way He opened the grace of the Blessed Trinity to all men for their salvation."

The contrast is striking. It seems almost impossible that such transformation and transfiguration could happen in so short a time. If it seems shocking, it is so only to those who have no hope. For us Christians, however, this is the great feast of hope. It embodies the conflict between light and darkness, between the glory of heaven and the damnation of hell. With this thought in mind Saint Amphilochius cries out:

"Death has seized our Lord Jesus Christ but shall not keep its hold on life. It swallowed Him not knowing Him and, in returning Him to life, restores all of us to life. Of His own free will He is now held by death. Tomorrow He shall rise again and hell shall be emptied. Yesterday, on the cross, He darkened the sun's light so that in the middle of the day it appeared to be night. Today death has lost its power and appears almost to have died itself. Yesterday the earth mourned and in sadness clothed itself in a garment of darkness. Today the people who walk in darkness have seen a great light."

The feast of light! How the Church dwells on the image! The paschal candle, symbol of Christ, is lighted and carried into the church. The great paschal hymn, the *Exsultet*, is sung by the deacon in praise of the great light that now shines in the house of the faithful. The comparison is evident: sin hides in the darkness of confusion; life delights in the brightness of the great light. Again we perceive the admirable exchange: we walk from the darkness of death into the brightness of life because the Savior has prepared the ground and given us sure footing. The Venerable Bede explains it in this way:

"From the beginning of earthly creation until now the course of time has been so divided that day preceded night. This was so because man got lost in the confusing darkness of this world after he fell from paradise because of his sin. But now day fittingly follows night, since through faith in the resurrection we are, through the mercy of Christ, brought back from the shadow of death and the darkness of sin into the light of life."

The riches of this night are here for all of us to make our own. There is little need for human words or pious exhortation. The symbolism of every action performed tonight should be obvious to all. "God does not call us," explains Saint Hilary of Poitiers, "to the blessed life through arduous investigations. He does not tempt us with the studied arts of rhetoric. The way to eternity is plain and easy: believe only that Jesus rose from the dead through His own power and confess that He is the Lord." All great events, like all great mysteries, are simple. Tonight we need only to confess our belief in the simple fact of the resurrection. With this truth as a starting point, the whole meaning and purpose of our salvation is evident. The Venerable Bede spells out what this belief implies:

"We must believe that our bodies also shall be endowed with heavenly glory after their resurrection. They shall have power to do what they please and shall be free to go wherever they wish.... The children of the resurrection shall have no other food or drink than true life and salvation, joy, peace, and every good."

This is the holy hope of future joy that our faith now promises us. This is the assurance that each of us receives tonight because our Savior has prepared a place for us. He is the first-born of the new creation effected by His resurrection. We are His brothers and with Him sharers in a new life. This simple truth is brought home to us tonight with a renewed force and vigor. Our faith is strengthened, our hope renewed, our charity rekindled because we have come together tonight to return with the Christian community to the very foundation of our religion. Tonight, above all other times in the year, are the words of Saint Ambrose fulfilled in our lives:

"We have seen how serious an offense it is not to believe in the resurrection, for if we do not rise again, then Christ died in vain and – in fact – Christ Himself never rose again from the dead. For certainly, if He did not rise for us, He arose for no one, since He had no need to rise only for Himself. We know, however, that the universe rose again in Him, heaven rose again in Him, and the earth rose again in Him, for there shall now be a new heaven and a new earth."

Everything about the prayers and rites tonight is oriented to the sacrament of baptism, in which we received the three great virtues of Christian living. Christ dies – to rise with newness of life; in baptism we too die – to rise with newness of life. The new members of our parish community are brought forward to be baptized. We ourselves are asked by our father in Christ to renew our baptismal promises. Saint Leo the Great states succinctly the effect of baptism:

"Passing from the old state into a new life and casting off our earthly image in exchange for a supernatural identity is a sort of dying and rising again. Thus he who is received by Christ as well as he who actually receives Christ is not the same after he comes to the font as he was before. His body now becomes the flesh of the Crucified."

The sacred actions performed before us and for us tonight move swiftly. We pass quickly from the blessing of the baptismal water to the renewal of baptismal vows until we stand before the altar of the Lord to join in the great hymn of eucharistic praise. This is the Mass of the resurrection. We gather about the altar tonight, as the holy women gathered about the tomb. From them we should learn how we should act on this most sacred of all nights. Saint John Chrysostom draws these lessons from the behavior of the holy women:

"These holy women spent a great deal and exposed themselves to many dangers in order to care for Him whom they thought was dead. But we neither feed Him when hungry nor clothe Him when naked, and when we see Him begging, we pass Him by…. It is not nearly such a great deed to feed Him when He appears to you in His own person as it is to serve the poor, the maimed, and the down-trodden for His sake…. In the latter case we show Him greater reverence, since by following His words and serving our fellow man we refresh Him in all things."

As the women approached the tomb, the earth quaked and they heard a mighty roar. "The earthquake," says Saint Hilary of Poitiers, "signified the power of the resurrection. Hell is now shaken with alarm because the sting of death is crushed and the dark places are filled with light through the rising of the Lord of hosts." Entering the tomb, the holy women see an angel sitting near the place where they had laid His sacred Body. The Venerable Bede sees a hidden meaning even in the very posture of the angel:

"Rightly did the angel stand who foretold the coming of the Lord into the world. The angel's stance showed that the Lord would come to wage war against the prince of this world. But the herald of the resurrection is sitting to show that the Lord, having overthrown the author of death, would now ascend to the throne of His Kingdom. He sat upon a stone rolled back from the entrance of the tomb to show that the Lord had thrown open the gates of hell by His own power.

The night encompasses all the paradoxes of Christian living. Rather, Christ the Conqueror embodies in His own person all the seeming contradictions of all who strive to lead good Christian lives. What happened on this night? Why were the tables turned? Saint John Chrysostom offers this answer:

"Those who previously seemed to have conquered were above all others put to shame, defeated and ruined. He who seemed to have been defeated on Good Friday now arises in brilliant and mighty conquest.... Thus it is for each of us. He who is dragged to martyrdom conquers by being bound, beaten, maimed and slain. Nowhere do we overcome by doing harm. Everywhere we triumph by enduring unjust punishment. This shows that true victory is from God.... Knowing these things, then, let us pursue the true victory which is gained by suffering unjustly and fleeing from all wrong-doing. In such a way we shall live this present life in all tranquility and at the same time receive all the good things of the future life through the grace and love of our Lord Jesus Christ."

His victory is ours; His glory is ours. He has lifted us up, drawing us to Himself; and in Him we have found our new life. So tonight we shout, "Alleluia!" We shall continue to sing our "alleluias," then, we cry out ceaselessly, "praise God," and thus encourage all creation to join in our hymn of praise.

We leave the church and go back out into the cool spring air. The strains of "alleluias" ring in our ears. New Easter clothes are but an outward manifestation of the new life that has come to us through the resurrection of Christ. We greet our neighbors more warmly, now understanding better our oneness in Christ. Even the world looks better, brighter. We exchange greetings with everyone; and no matter what words we use, they echo our "alleluias." We are dedicated anew, incorporated again, in the life of the risen Savior. We are commissioned by Him to offer with Him and in Him an everlasting "alleluia." We were made to praise God. This is our joy. This is our glory. This is our resurrection.

We slowly begin to make our way back home. As we depart, Saint Leo the Great gives us a final admonition:

"We must keep these thoughts in mind, dearly beloved, not only during this Easter festival but for the hallowing of our entire lives. We should consider these present religious exercises and all the delights that we have experienced during this short observance but a prelude to an entire life of goodness. If any fault creeps into your lives, destroy it immediately through sincere repentance. Since the curing of deep-rooted diseases is a slow and difficult process, apply remedies early, when the wounds are still fresh. Thus we shall continually rise from our faults and merit to share in the everlasting resurrection of our own glorified bodies in Christ Jesus our Lord, who lives and reigns with the Father and the Holy Spirit forever and ever. Amen."

EASTER SUNDAY

Joy and glory. We cry out "Alleluia," praising the Lord who is risen and with us, soon to return to heaven and then to be even more closely with us. "Alleluia," is more than a word tacked on at the end of a prayer: it is even much more than an expression of our joy and glory on Easter morning and throughout the Easter season. "Alleluia" is a state of existence; it expresses what the Christian life truly is. St. Methodius extends the Church's invitation: "Sing a new hymn of conquest and a new song of peace to Christ who gained the victory. Come, everyone, and rejoice in the Lord!"

Easter candle and Easter water, Easter eggs and Easter breads all are expressions of the new life that has risen in our midst. The world rises from death to greet the Son of the resurrection. All men are restored; all men are reborn; all men are charged with the spark of glory from the glorious One who draws each of us into the joy of His resurrection. This is more than history, infinitely more than a pious remembrance. The resurrection continues to happen. Christ continues to be the unvanquished Victor. He continues to speak every Easter dawn of every Christian's life: "Have confidence; I have overcome the world."

Today holy Mother Church uses Saint Methodius's exhortation to his people long ago:

"Come, beloved, and let us with willing hearts and open minds listen to what the Lord our God shall say…. He will speak to His people and His saints and to all who open their hearts to Him. Today the trumpet blast of the prophets has aroused the world and has filled with joy and gladness the churches of God scattered among the nations."

This is Easter, the day of the Lord. "Let us rejoice," the psalmist cries out, "and be glad in it" (Ps. 117:24). Enraptured by the joy and glory of this day, Saint Gregory Nazianzen exclaims, "O Pasch! Great and holy, purifier of all the world! O work of God, light and life, wisdom and power! I rejoice in all your names! O child of that great mind, His desire and His image!" Have we lost our capacity for wonderment? Have we forgotten in the dreariness of living the freshness of a child's joy? Our sophistication might have dulled us. Our learning might have made us deaf to the sound of spiritual joy and have blinded us to the sights of Christian gladness. If so, we have made ourselves paupers by seeing only half of the canvas. Forty days we spent, devotedly and sometimes drudgingly, following the Savior up to Calvary's summit. But we cannot stop there. Calvary is only the beginning. Christ suffered crucifixion as the condition of resurrection. The Man of sorrows of Good Friday is the King of glory for all times. A Christian must suffer, but suffering is only his passport to glory. Joy is the essence of Christianity. Glory is the result of Christian living, but this joy and glory and alleluia of praising God begins on earth.

The Church teaches the same lesson in her liturgy. Saint Augustine explains that lesson when he says:

"These holy days which are celebrated after the resurrection of the Lord signify the life that is to come after our resurrection. The forty days before Easter symbolized the life of suffering in this mortal life. Now, however, these joyful days point to the future life when we are destined to reign with the Lord. The life signified by the forty days before Easter we are living now. The life symbolized by the fifty days after Easter is not yet possessed, but it is hoped for and loved all the while we are awaiting it. That very desire is our way of praising God who promised us eternal life – and our praises are alleluias."

The accent must always be on joy and glory. Our life is one of joyful service to God and His people. Our efforts are works of glory when they are united to the glorious works of God. The Eastern mind understands this better than our departmentalized Western mind. The earlier Christians, too, gave witness to the resurrection by the glorious joy of their lives. Their joy was contagious, giving us an example of the spirit we must restore to our muddled and confused world. Saint Proclus gives testimony to the joy of his people:

"Glorious is our paschal festival! How splendid is this great assembly of the Christian people! In this holy mystery are contained many things, both old and new. The celebration – rather, the joyfulness – of this week is shared by such a multitude that not only man rejoices on earth but even the heavenly powers join us in the joyful celebration of Christ's resurrection. The angels and the hosts of archangels make holiday, standing in attendance as they await the triumphant return from earth of Christ our Lord, the King of heaven. The multitude of the saints also rejoice, bearing witness to Christ who was born before the day star rose. The earth rejoices, for she has been washed by divine Blood. The sea rejoices, for it has been honored by His feet upon its waters. Above all else, let every soul rejoice!... By His resurrection Christ fills our hearts with great joy this day. He makes us glad today because He has saved us through His passion, given us immortality through His death, healed our wounds and lifted us up by His resurrection!"

"O Pasch! great and holy, purifier of all the world." Saint Gregory's words echo throughout the day, throughout the season, throughout the Christian life. Saint Leo the Great explains the word for us:

"Since you are celebrating the holy Pasch, you should know, brethren, what the Pasch is. It means the "crossing-over".... On this day the children of Israel crossed over from Egypt to the promised land and the Son of God crossed over from this world to His Father. There is no profit in celebrating the Pasch, then, unless you imitate the Lord whom you worship. That means you must cross over from Egypt (that is, the darkness of evil-doing) to the light of virtue. You must cross over from the love of this world to the love of your heavenly home."

Easter and resurrection, ascension and heaven; neither can be separated from the other. Passing from death-to-sin to life-in-Christ is but the first step of the passage from earthly joy to eternal glory. Easter points heavenward, as surely as our new life in Christ is already the beginning of heaven on earth. The resurrection prepares us for our own ascension; we trace the footsteps of the glorious One. Examples from the story of the resurrection point our way to heaven.

The evangelists tell us that the women came to the tomb "very early in the morning." From this phrase the Venerable Bede draws this application:

"Mystically, this gives us the example of how, scattering the darkness of vices and turning our face to the light, we should be earnest in offering the Lord the odor of our good works and the sweetness of our prayer."

Speaking more directly so that none of his people could possibly miss the lesson, Saint Ambrose asks the question:

"What were these holy women seeking at the tomb, if not Jesus our Savior? If you wish to find Him, come as these women came when the sun is risen. Let no darkness of evil be in your hearts, for the desires of the flesh and evil deeds are darkness. Those whose hearts are filled with this kind of darkness cannot see the light and cannot understand Christ, for Christ is the light. Therefore, brothers, drive the darkness from you (that is, all sinful desires and evil deeds) and secure sweet spices (that is, earnest prayer). Then cry out with the psalmist, 'Let my prayer be counted as incense before Thee.'"

At every great moment in Christ's life on earth, angels were present. An angel announced His coming and a host of angels proclaimed His glory the night of His birth. An angel strengthened Him in the lonely hour of His passion and an angel announced His resurrection. The holy women at the tomb, says Saint Severianus, "see a young man in order to understand the age of our resurrection, for resurrection knows no old age." Saint Jerome comments on the white garment worn by the angel:

"He appeared clothed with a white robe because he has announced the joys of our great feast. The shining whiteness of the garment proclaims the splendor of our festival. The enemy has been put to flight and the kingdom is restored. The shining white garment expresses great joy; the King of peace was sought and found and shall now never be forsaken."

Angels also appeared at the ascension. "And while they were gazing into heaven as He went," says the sacred writer, "behold, two men stood by them in white robes." The Fathers of the Church were fascinated by the white garments of the angels. Saint Gregory the Great says the white garments symbolize "a festive state of mind"; observing that the angels of the nativity had no white garments as did the angels of the resurrection, he goes on to explain:

"…there was great rejoicing among the angels when the Lord entered heaven. At His birth divinity seemed to have been humiliated. At His ascension humanity was exalted. White garments are more fitting for exaltation than humiliating."

For the early Church, moreover, the white garments had a

deeper meaning than they have for us today. The early Christians saw this as the season of rejoicing for the growth of the Mystical Body since the catechumens had been baptized and now wore their white garments as a sign of their joy in sharing Christ's glory. Although we no longer wear the white robes of the neophytes, we too have renewed our baptismal promises on Holy Saturday night. Accordingly our souls are clothed with the mystical white garments of baptismal innocence and Christian joy. The word, then, that Saint Augustine directed to the neophytes of Hippo long ago apply with equal force to all of us today:

"Listen to me, you who have been baptized and reborn in the Blood of Christ…. I beg you not to imitate your former companions so that the holy grace of Him who refused to descend from the cross but willed to rise again from the tomb may be in you always! Turning to the Lord our God, the almighty Father, let us give thanks from the bottom of our hearts and ask Him by His grace to drive evil from our thoughts and deeds, increase our faith, direct our thoughts, grant us His holy inspirations, and lead us to everlasting joy."

How much more deeply the neophytes of the early Church understood the likeness, or image, of Christ implanted in the soul of the Christian! They had a better grasp of the totality of redemption than we. They understood the role of the resurrection in mankind's salvation. Expressing this thought, Saint Augustine says:

"Christ is our salvation. he is our salvation when He was wounded for us, fastened with nails to the wood, taken down from the wood and laid in the sepulchre. But He also rose from the sepulchre; though His wounds were healed, the scars remained. He felt this to be necessary for His disciples for by the scars He kept He is able to heal the wounds of their souls."

This, then, is the principal theme of the days of Easter: we rejoice because our glory is assured, not through our own merits but through the victory of Christ our Head. He has drawn us to Himself, caught us up in the infinity of His glory, and in a way made us sharers in His own divinity. Surely, then, we have every reason for rejoicing. We would not, in fact, be true to our Christian vocation if we did not rejoice. Saint John Chrysostom exhorts us:

"Let us celebrate this greatest and most shining feast in which the Lord has risen from the dead. Let us celebrate it with joyful devotion. The Lord has risen! He has lifted up the whole world with Him. The Lord has risen! He has shattered the chains of death."

Our joy reflects the joy of the Savior. We are born again in the likeness of His image, and this image is the shining brilliance of divinity. "Let us become like Christ," says Saint Augustine, "since Christ became like us. Let us become gods because of Him, since on account of us He became man."

Christian joy demands faith as much as future glory supposes hope. A time of joy, Easter is likewise a season of faith. The apostles themselves give us an example of the faith that should mark the Christian. Saint Ignatius of Antioch expresses the thought in these words:

"For my part, I know that even after His resurrection He was in the flesh and I believe this to be true. When He came to those who were with Peter, He said to them: 'Handle Me, and see; for a spirit has not flesh and bones as you see that I have.' As soon as they touched Him and felt His flesh and pulse, they believed. For this reason they later despised death and even showed themselves superior to death."

Holy hope, too, is assured by Christ's resurrection. The resurrection is the beginning of Christ's triumphant return to His heavenly Father. Because we are conformed to the likeness of His resurrection, we too are beginning our glorious return to the land of our spiritual birth. Thus Saint Augustine says:

"He rose again to give us hope that what dies will also rise again, lest death should cause us to despair and deceive us into thinking that our whole life has ended. As a matter of fact, we were anxious about our soul; by His resurrection He has now given us assurance about our body.... He came down from heaven to heal you; He returns to heaven to lift you up."

In another sermon the bishop of Hippo confirms our faith by stressing the unity of the Mystical Body of Christ: "He is the Head of the Church and the Church is His Body; the whole Christ is both the Head and the Body. He has already risen from the dead. Our Head, therefore, is in heaven." Then, boldly, Augustine concludes: "Where the Head is, there are the rest of the members. Let us not despair, for we shall follow our Head."

Follow our Head: these are words of faith and hope. No Christian doubts them; all Christians hope for their fulfillment. Saint Augustine continues:

"He has risen and ascended into heaven. There He must be followed. Heaven was far away from us before our Head had gone there. Now why should we despair if we are members of that Head? Who would be unwilling to follow Christ where there is supreme happiness, supreme peace and everlasting security?"

Faith, Saint Paul tells us, is "the assurance of things to be hoped for, the conviction of things not seen" (Heb. 11:1). The resurrection caused consternation; the ascension turned bewilderment into confirmation of the fact that Christ lives; Christ reigns, and "of His kingdom there will be no end" (Lk. 1:33). Trying to probe the feelings of the apostles during these forty days of Easter, Saint Leo the Great explains:

"The blessed apostles, who had been encouraged by many miracles and instructed by many discourses, were still terrified by the cruelty of the Lord's passion. Only with great hesitation did they accept the reality of His resurrection. The Lord's ascension, however, gave them a new lease on life, turning fear into joy. They now directed their attention to His divinity, seeing Him enthroned at the Father's right hand. His bodily presence no longer prevented them from contemplating the Lord. He descended to earth yet did not leave the Father; now, ascending to heaven, He has not left His disciples."

Christian faith is strengthened rather than weakened by Christ's triumphant return to His Father's house. Saint Augustine puts these words into the Savior's mouth: "You do not wish to let Me go, for every man is reluctant to part with his friend.... But it is better for you that you no longer see Me in the flesh because then you will be able to contemplate My divinity. Externally I am leaving you; internally I shall fill you with Myself."

As it was with the apostles at the dawn of Christianity, so it is with us today. All that Christ did, He did for all men. As He conformed the apostles to the image of His resurrection, so today He incorporates us into that same likeness. As He strengthened the apostles' faith through the overpowering majesty of His divinity, so today he strengthens our faith. "He ascended into heaven," writes Saint Peter Chrysologus, "not to take Himself back into heaven (for He always remained there), but rather to lead there all of us whom He freed and snatch us from the powers of hell. Understand, then, that God has raised us up, planting our feet firmly in heaven and removing us from the slippery roads of the earth on which we are liable to fall." Although faith employs material signs and symbols, the more we detach ourselves from materiality, the stronger our faith becomes. No one understands this better than Christ Himself. Before His resurrection He was the man of the people, Jesus, the son of the carpenter of Nazareth. After His resurrection He withdraws from the mob. He is seen only by His intimate followers. Today He reigns as a hidden God, not seen by human eyes but known and loved by divine faith. "He became," says Saint Leo the Great, "more present to us in His divinity to the extent that His humanity became more removed from us."

Although we do not see His glorified Body, we live as members of His Mystical Body. The glorified Christ has no need of our service; the mystical Christ is always in need of love and service. During His life on earth Christ said to Nathanael, "You will see heaven opened, and the angels of God ascending and descending upon the Son of man" (Jn. 1:51). In a lengthy passage Saint Augustine makes an application for all of us:

"He would not say "ascending unto the Son of man" unless He were in heaven. Nor would He say "descending unto the Son of man" unless He were also on earth. At one and the same time He is both above and below; above in the unity of the Trinity, below in the needs of His people. He is above with the Father; He is below in us.... Fear Christ above; recognize Him below. Here He is poor, there He is rich. Rich, indeed, as the Son of man who has ascended into heaven and sits at the right hand of the Father. Yet He is still poor on earth in the poor, the hungry, the thirsty."

All that Christ did, He did for our instruction. Our present joy and future glory would be empty, indeed, if we did not profit from gladness in preparation for glory. Saint Gregory the Great exhorts us:

"Dearest brothers, we must follow Him in our hearts to where we believe He has ascended in His body. Let us turn away from earthly longings. Nothing here on earth can truly satisfy us. Reflect seriously on this fact. Although mild in countenance when He ascended, He shall be terrible when He returns. Now He commands with gentleness; then He shall exact with sternness. So let nobody waste this time of repentance which is granted us. Let nobody neglect to do all he can for his salvation."

The devout life leads to the glorious life. So faith tells us, hope promises us, charity assures us.

We repeat over and over, "This is the day which the Lord has made; let us rejoice and be glad in it" (Ps. 117:24). The day is great because it is already a foretaste of heaven. We rejoice and are glad because our King is enthroned, our Lord is glorified, our Head has imprinted the image of His glory on our souls. Little wonder, then, that Saint Jerome exclaims:

"A day of happiness now shines forth. It holds the primacy among all other days for the first light has shone upon it. On this day the Lord rises triumphant from the dead!" ❧

1964

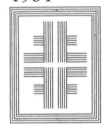

OUR BANNED THEOLOGIANS

During the second session of the Second Vatican Council in the fall of 1963, I conducted this interview in the Pensione Sitea, Rome, with the four theologians who were banned from speaking at The Catholic University of America. They were Fathers Godfrey Diekmann, O.S.B., Hans Küng, John Courtney Murray, S.J., and Gustave Weigel, S.J. It appeared in the Spring, 1964, issue of American Benedictine Review.

F *ather Yzermans:* What does this entire discussion concerning the Church and the episcopacy going on during Vatican Council II mean to the American layman or laywoman?

Father Murray: Admittedly, many of the things discussed in the second session of the council do not directly apply to the laity, except, of course, the reforms prescribed by the Constitution on the Sacred Liturgy. However, behind these discussions is a principle which I do believe affects the laity a great deal. As the process of decentralization goes on, the principle of freedom becomes more and more obvious. First the principle of freedom for the pope to deal with his bishops directly and not through the medium of a bureaucracy must be established. Then the same principle must be established concerning the priest in relation to his bishop and the same for the laity in relation to the clergy. All this is going to take an awfully long time.

THE CHURCH AS COMMUNITY

Father Diekmann: But don't you think, Father Murray, that these discussions have another practical value for the people of the Church?

Most Catholic people have come to regard the bishop as their "boss." He represents the Church for them. This also seems to be the way the average bishop regards his own calling. He is in charge of a certain area, a certain territory. Now, perhaps for the first time, these discussions on the collegiality of bishops are bringing about the realization that bishops have a responsibility to the Church universal. This idea is coming alive, first of all in the minds of the bishops themselves as well as others. There is an opening out to the needs of the Church which simply was not the normal procedure for the average diocese in the past. This very basic theological principle of responsibility toward the Church universal is now being established. Bishops of dioceses are beginning to realize they have a responsibility, shared by all their brother bishops, for the entire Church.

This is one of the most important effects these discussions could have in American dioceses. Priests and people in a diocese will come to realize more fully that a diocese is not a self-enclosed, independent unity, subject through historical circumstances to parochialism, in the bad sense of that word. When the Catholic world captures this sense of collegiality a broader sense of responsibility will certainly become the normal part of the Christian experience.

Father Weigel: Collegiality does bring home in ordinary language an insight which theologians who have thought about the matter have developed during the past thirty years. This insight includes a spiritual vision of the Church, and this vision indicates that the Church's power and strength is in the dwelling of the Holy Spirit. He works not only on individuals but likewise in an orderly fashion on the whole Church. His power, his direction, his holiness is rendered external in the Church by an in-built system of power. This power is resident in the Spirit and through the Spirit reaches out to the whole Church.

This in-built system of power the council identifies with the episcopacy. It is not only the power by which the pope rules the whole Church; it includes that. It is not simply the power of a bishop in his own diocese; it includes that, too. Both these seemingly distinct powers are one and the same. We call it simply episcopacy. The bishop governs the local church; the episcopacy governs the Church universal. It is the action of the Holy Spirit on every Catholic.

We also speak of the Church's magisterium, a big word which means the Church's teaching office. For some time this has been identified only with the episcopacy. This is a mistake. Everyone teaches. My mother taught me. The sisters in grade school taught me. The parish priest taught me. In fact, the bishop himself taught me very little. The whole Church is a teaching Church. The episcopacy directs and authenticates what is the right teaching either for the local church or the Church universal.

Father Diekmann: Isn't this actually the great contribution of Cardinal Suenens' talk during the second session? His talk was not only one of the great talks of the Council but also, perhaps, the most ecumenical talk insofar as it was a recognition of the insight of the Protestant Reformation. The Cardinal spoke of the pneumatic Church, the Church in whom the Holy Spirit lives. This is the basic concept of the Church as presented in the New Testament. Only after this concept of the Church being guided by the Spirit is clear can you speak of a structuring of the Church, of a hierarchy, a clergy and a laity.

Cardinal Suenens made this point clear and in so doing stated the recognition that Protestants were wrong insofar as they rejected the hierarchy, but that they did have a very important, clear insight into something which has been obscure for centuries. They always insisted on this pneumatic character of the Church, the Spirit guiding the Church in all its parts. I was thrilled by that speech.

Father Küng: You know, of course, our whole vision of the Church takes into consideration only one dimension. It is like a human being who has only one eye and is unable to see the perspective or the profundity of the Church. We have only the present discussion on ministry, or hierarchy. But there is a much more profound and difficult discussion than this. Such a discussion would be one that deals with the Church's charismatic structure. This is much more important than the organizational aspect of the Church, even though as a Catholic I know this is absolutely essential for the Church. But it is a secondary thing in relation to what is ultimately important. Even for a member of the hierarchy, the important thing is whether or not he is really in the right spirit, that is, the Holy Spirit. This is the decisive factor in each man's life, be he bishop or barber. If he does not have this right spirit he will lose his soul; he will lose his Catholicity; he will lose everything.

In heaven we will have no ministry or hierarchy. We will have no popes, no bishops, no priests. We will have only God who is all and in all. That means that the Church today already possesses what is said in Scripture, namely, the armor of the Spirit. This is the essential principle of the Church's life today which will become fully revealed in eternity. The Spirit, then, is much more important than all the organization, even though in this world we do need organization in the Church.

Father Diekmann: Also, when we speak of the episcopacy as receiving the Holy Spirit, we must understand this in the context of the rite of episcopal consecration. The bishop receives the Spirit, not as if he himself has a special right to this gift but insofar as he must now be the servant of the Spirit in this body of the Church where he is constituted a leader. All this must be seen as a ministry of the Spirit, with the Spirit ruling the whole body composed of bishop, clergy, and laity.

Father Küng: That very notion makes the idea of collegiality much more comprehensible if we would use the word "community." Collegiality is a very curious word; it is a legal term. It is too new. It is under suspicion because it is new. If we would use the word "community" it would be clear that collegiality is not only proper to the episcopacy but is really an essential principle of the whole Church. If a parish is not a community, then it is really not what a parish should be. If a pastor and his assistants in the parish house are unable to form a community, then it is not truly a presbytery in the sense of the early Church. If a diocese is only an administrative unit and not a community, it is really not what a local church should be. If the Church universal is only an external organization and not really a community, it is not really what Jesus intended his apostles and disciples to be.

Father Diekmann: You know, in spite of all the weakness of the schema on the Church, it has certain strong virtues. One of these that struck me most of all is that any talk of monarchial hierarchy is completely eliminated. The concept of the bishop is presented as pastor and pater, shepherd and father. These are magnificent terms. They involve the whole idea of charity and the power that comes from love.

Father Weigel: I agree with you. But an even more fundamental thing for our day is that we are moving away from the notion that the structure of the Church can only be expressed in legal terms. This was, after all, Pope John's idea in convoking the council. The acttual decrees or constitutions that are written in this council will be important insofar as they stress this notion that the Church is an ontological reality and not merely a legal organization. The emphasis on the Church as a living body, it seems to me, would have great influence in further discussions on the relations between the Church and civil society.

CHURCH AND SOCIETY

Father Murray: Certainly in the past all relations between Church and state were conceived in juridicial terms. At the South African Bishops' Conference somebody asked me about the books on public ecclesiastical law. Should they not, the asked, all be rewritten? I had to say yes. What you find in them has nothing to do with theology on the one side and politics in the high sense on the other. The problem of Church and society is an enormously complicated one, but it basically has to be conceived in terms of theology first and good political philosophy secondly. The fact is that you do not find any good political philosophy in the books on public ecclesiastical law at least I never found any.

Father Weigel: The reason is that they are considering a political situation which was long ago dead.

Father Murray: True, they have no concept of what the genuine nature of a political relationship is at all. They conceive it in a completely paternal fashion, a relation of father to child; or in an absolutist sense, a relation of ruler to subject. The notion of the citizen who is himself a bearer of political power the so-called democratic development – has not got into the books on public ecclesiastical law.

Father Küng: From the theological point of view I would even say the relation of Church to society was an egocentric view, the view of a man who is completely concentrated on himself. It has never been sufficiently thought out that the Church is really at the service of the world. Precisely, we have lost the concept of the universal plan of salvation. We are not capable of seeing that the Church has no goal for herself. The Church is a sign and a help to the world and not for herself.

Father Weigel: The reason for this is the fact that the whole system of such thought derived from the time when Church and state had no meaning whatsoever. The notion of the state is a seventeenth century one. Most of these ecclesiastical laws derive from a period when there was no notion of society as we know it today. A society being controlled by a central legal authority was just not known. In those days society was actually managed by a number of different organizations and not all concerned the state. We have not measured up to the times we are now living in. We are still judging our situation according to norms of the past, and now we find that the present situation cannot possibly conform to these norms.

Father Diekmann: Precisely because of that, Father Murray, might it not be better to avoid complications and misunderstandings and not use the phraseology of Church and state?

Father Murray: Those very words are a terrible handicap in discussing this enormous problem. Pope Leo XIII did the best he could to break through, but he did not succeed. He tried to change the position of the problem by employing the terms "Church" and "human society." What happened, unfortunately, was that the best elements in his thought were distorted in the tradition of the manuals concerning ecclesiastical law written in the nineteenth century. These books neatly figured it all out in the midst of a highly polemic situation when the Church was faced with laicism and consequently in the position of conflict with the world. That world was Europe at the time, a small world, and consequently the whole problem was completely distorted.

Father Küng: However, the roots of the problem go back further than that. The first treatises of lawyers against the civil powers, specifically the particular quarrel between Pope Boniface VIII and King Philip IV of France. The treatment of the Church in these works was quite different from the view expressed by the early Fathers of the Church.

THE ROLE OF THE LAITY

Father Weigel: One of the major anachronisms of this council, showing that it is already out of date, is a group of bishops discussing the laity without their being present or consulted during the discussions. Monsignor George Higgins is quite right in advocating a greater voice for the laity. If it is the purpose of this council to develop the self-awareness of the Church as Pope Paul said, it is not possible for the bishops to discuss the self-awareness of the laity in the Church. No layman as yet has had a voice in the council and only to a very minor extent have the commissions given the layman a voice. The lay apostolate must be the result of the layman's own self-awareness of the Church, granting, of course, that he follows the guidance of the episcopacy. This failure makes me think there is a time lag in the whole matter.

Father Diekmann: This anachronism, as you say, Father Weigel, was very keenly felt in the Liturgical Commission. All of us in that preparatory commission were aware of the contradiction of a group of clerics deciding among ourselves exclusively the worship of God's people. Yet it is characteristic of the liturgical movement that it has in some ways tried to keep the rights and needs of the laity in mind. We wanted laity on our commission and we did not presume to speak for the laity. This feeling has helped to make the constitution on the liturgy somewhat successful.

Father Murray: To go back to this doctrine of collegiality, I believe that the bishops themselves do not really believe in it. I do not believe that they have any full consciousness of it, not to mention experience. The council, it is true, has opened up the possibility of acquiring this experience by the extraordinary manifestations of collegiality which the council itself presupposes. I fear, however, that the bishops will go back to their dioceses and, since the doctrine is not sustained by any genuine experience, it will die a-borning.

Father Weigel: However, the bishops were never unaware that this episcopal college was something that Christ himself put into the Church. They did not know precisely what this episcopal unity meant, perhaps, but the bishops understood that they were rulers of more than their own little sections.

Father Murray: But practice has shown that the individual bishop considered his own vertical line to the Holy Father rather than anything like a horizontal line of unity with his fellow bishops in governing the Church.

Father Küng: We have to distinguish between the sphere of theological reflection and the sphere of vital experience. Even if people did not realize exactly what collegiality meant on the level of theological reflection, in the realm of vital experience there really always was a community of the episcopacy.

The Constitution on the Sacred Liturgy

Father Murray: Of course, there has always has been a certain sense of freemasonry among the bishops, just as there is among the clergy and also among the laity. But I am not at all sure that this freemasonry is what is really meant by the theological doctrine of collegiality. The development of true collegiality in the United States, for instance, is going to be extremely difficult. In the matter of the liturgy, we are not going to have any uniform, even regional, much less national, liturgical reform before we are all long since dead.

Father Diekmann: I am not so sure, Father.

Father Küng: I also am not that sure.

Father Diekmann: The episcopal liturgical commission in the United States, which was appointed in 1958, has not take any decisive steps. Therefore, the bishops do not feel bound in any way. Of course, they were not really bound; but I mean to say, many of them ignored the suggestions that were made. Now, however, after the experience of the council and after the collegiality of the bishops will be declared....

Father Weigel: But not defined.

Father Diekmann: Not defined, but nevertheless declared. I think this will actually bring about an organ by which the liturgy can be made a national movement. There will be so much pressure, so much good public sentiment, that each bishop will necessarily go along with the declarations of the body of bishops.

Father Küng: The trend of the times is a great thing. The trend in the Church because of this council will make many good things which were not done before actually reach their fulfillment.

The Ecumenical Trend

Father Weigel: An ecumenical trend became quite clear during the last year. There was no solid hostility to ecumenism in 1962, but neither was there enthusiasm. In 1962 the council publicly manifested, and without possible refutation, a great and deep interest in ecumenism. The bishops all over the world, and especially in the United States, upon returning home from the first session showed great favor for the ecumenical meetings; they were anxious to found ecumenical institutes, and Protestants were speaking in Catholic church halls. All this was possible because of the council. It may seem a bit shallow, but nevertheless it happened.

Father Küng: Perhaps we theologians are asking for too much deep reflection. The Church is not only thought. It is enough for a man, priest or layman, to experience what has to be done here and now even if he does not realize all the intellectual implications. If everybody would realize all the intellectual implications I am sure nobody would act.

Father Weigel: There are very few theologians who are capable of action. Perhaps I am wrong, but we do not have to ask for too much reflection. We need the Holy Spirit. Complete understanding of an action inspired by the Spirit is not necessary. Often understanding comes only later.

Father Küng: Precisely. In the matter of the liturgy it is not necessary for everybody to go through the same steps of historical research and fully understand the development of the Mass throughout the centuries. Of course, it would be very nice if it were done but it is not necessary. It is enough if they come to realize that this is what God is asking at this time and this is the manner to be followed in doing so. This would be a living experience, founded of course on historical research, even though all do not understand the intellectual steps of that research.

Father Murray: I am sure, Father Küng, that you do not wish to minimize the importance of intellectual research.

Father Küng: Of course not.

Father Murray: As long as action remains in the realm of conformity to fashion, the mood can change overnight. For instance, throughout the world expectations of the council have been built far too high. People are expecting too much and there is not going to be that much coming out of the council. It is a very slow growth.

Father Weigel: They tell a very funny story that happened recently. When they were preparing for the Mass in commemoration of the anniversary of the election of Pope John, the master of ceremonies rushed in to the Secretariat of Unity's desk and wanted to know how many of the observers were going to receive communion. He was most excited and the unity secretary said to him: "They are not going to Communion."

"Oh, yes," said the master of ceremonies, confusing the Protestant observers with the Catholic lay auditors, "I was told last night that they are going. I want to know how many hosts to put on the paten."

Overhearing this exchange, a photographer of the council said: "Well! if they are going to Communion the council is ended!" The photographer was pretty sharp.

Father Diekmann: Aren't we doing less than justice to the Holy Spirit by taking for granted that the ecumenical change that has taken place during the last year is nothing more than a matter of going along with what is fashionable?

Father Weigel: I don't think so.

Father Diekmann: I do think so. Basic to this whole ecumenical problem in the United States is the unwillingness, let us say, of most Catholic priests to take seriously the Christian dedication of their Protestant minister brethren. This unwillingness is based on a completely false understanding of what theology actually is. We have to a certain extent brushed aside Protestant ministers because our own theology was presented to us in a manual fashion. We thought of it as a logical system so reasonable that anybody with any intelligence must see its logic. Therefore, many Catholic clerics concluded their Protestant brothers were either stupid or in bad faith. The very fact, then, that in one or two years' time this seriously talking theology with Protestant ministers has come about makes this change in outlook more than just a matter of fashion. Here too was the "new Pentecost" of which Pope John spoke.

Father Weigel: I agree, Father Diekmann. But there was also something else. While the clergy generally had this very narrow view, the people did not. The people never supposed, especially in a place like America where we are living with Protestants and Jews, that all these other people were condemned to hell.

Father Diekmann: I know that. And the Catholic sense of faith was and is strong in the people. Therefore, the willingness manifested now to deal with Protestant ministers as equals in the sense of dedication to Christ means a real change of outlook. This is one of the most important things that has happened to the Catholic Church in the United States.

Father Küng: If you are inside the council and witness the whole procedure there are many reasons for pessimism. However, the entire new trend is greater and stronger than the council. Events have borne out my original thesis that I stated even before the council opened. What has been stirred up in the Church by the convocation of the council is vastly more important than the council itself. As Cardinal Suenens said, this new ferment is the beginning of a new period in the life of the Church.

Father Weigel: That is true. I was especially happy when Cardinal Suenens mentioned that someone else, Pope Paul perhaps, can make reality out of what Pope John saw intuitively. An example of this happened recently in the council. Instead of quoting St. Thomas, a bishop quoted Christian Skydsgaard, the Danish observer delegate of the Lutheran Church. I looked then at Dr. Skydsgaard, sitting next to me in the observers' tribune, and said: "Now it's not St. Thomas; mind you, it's Christian Skydsgaard!"

Father Küng: You know, several weeks ago I expressed a certain pessimism. Although I might have a certain pessimism in the theological field, I am not pessimistic in the realm of reality. After all, that is where true progress is being made.

Father Murray: If by the realm of reality you mean the run of the mill American, I am very skeptical.

Father Weigel: I am not.

Father Diekmann: I have great confidence in youth.

Father Weigel: That is not the question. I am not completely sold on youth.

Father Küng: Youth, you must remember, is not a question of years. The future of the Church is always in the hands of youth. ✢

1966

 ARDINAL ALBERT MEYER

Cardinal Albert Meyer of Chicago died on April 9, 1965. He served as one of the ten presidents of the Second Vatican Council during its first session. He emerged at that time as a leader of the American bishops. After his death Father George Dyer, editor, invited me to submit an article to Chicago Studies *as a tribute to the deceased Archbishop of Chicago. It appeared in that publication.*

"Since my strength is coming back only gradually, I must confess that I am not exactly looking forward with anticipation to the next session of the Council, although I will do my best to prepare for it."

On February 16, 1965 Albert Cardinal Meyer wrote these words to his friend of many years, Rev. Barnabas Ahern, C.P. The following day he was taken to Mercy Hospital with a malady which would be calmed only by the merciful hand of death fifty days later. His words to Father Barnabas in many ways epitomized his entire life. He was reluctant to exert leadership, with the self-effacing humility of a genuine Christian. Against nature's inclination, he would force himself to perform his duty because he loved the Church.

Those close to the Cardinal knew his natural shyness, his love of learning, his deep spirituality. He was happiest with his books and throughout his life remained a scholar. In the early days of his priesthood he confided to a friend that he resolved from his youth never to commit a deliberate venial sin. His nature prompted him to shy away from crowds and he appeared the happiest when he could be alone with a few close friends in a boat on one of Wisconsin's numerous lakes.

His early life in Milwaukee was led in the shelter of a German home noted for its solid piety and respect for authority. From his early days in the seminary he was recognized by teachers and fellow students as highly gifted. His postgraduate studies in Europe (1927-1930) brought him into contact with the best biblical scholars and theologians of that period. All this was providentially preparing him for his role as a distinguished, although reluctant, leader of the American hierarchy at the Second Vatican Council.

Ecclesiastically he was also being molded over the years for this task. First as seminary professor and later as seminary rector of St. Francis Seminary, Milwaukee, he came to know and love priests as few others could. As bishop of Superior, Wisconsin, he learned the problems of a small diocese through the intimate association of his priests and people which only a minimum of administrative details can allow. He was happy when appointed Archbishop of Milwaukee in 1953 for, as he said, he then felt he was returning to his own home, to the family and friends of his boyhood, to former classmates and students. With some understandable natural reluctance he followed the coastline of Lake Michigan southward in 1958 to become the ninth spiritual leader of the Chicago archdiocese. When elevated to the College of Cardinals in 1959 he knew better than most that the honor was Chicago's even more than his own. His honesty and simplicity demanded that he allow no public receptions on that occasion.

His role as the Archbishop of Chicago placed the Cardinal in positions of influence in the Church universal. Successively he became a member of the Congregation for the Propagation of Faith, the Congregation of Seminaries and Universities, the Congregation for the Fabric of St. Peter's, and the Holy Offce. He was also appointed to the Biblical Commission and the Commission for the Revision of the Code of Canon Law. When the Council met he was among the twelve presidents.

Cardinal Meyer, however, felt these titles were mostly *honoris causa* and did not expect to be consulted very frequently. He said on one occasion that he had only been consulted once by the Biblical Commission. After the Council's first session he was appointed a member of the presidency. He felt, too, that after the appointment of the four council moderators the presidency was of relative unimportance. He served, however, because his love for the Church forced him to accept these positions.

These observations are made by way of preface to the theme of this article, namely, Cardinal Meyer's interventions at the Second Vatican Council. Understanding the man helps in understanding his thinking. His words at the Council were heeded precisely because he was Cardinal Meyer. One leader of the Council put it this way: "Meyer is a very good man. What he says ought to be listened to."

Meyer, the "good man," comes through in his interventions. Meyer the biblical scholar, Meyer the theologian, Meyer the priest, Meyer the bishop are all reflected in his words at the Council. Precisely because he was Meyer he became the outstanding American leader at the Second Vatican Council. He did not seek leadership. It was thrust upon him because he was what he was. Several incidents bear testimony to that fact.

SUBTLE LEADERSHIP

In the summer of 1963 Cardinal Meyer realized that the American hierarchy needed instruction on the contents of the schemata before the Council. After the first session he realized how ill-prepared the Americans were for the theological implications of the conciliar discussions. As a brother he invited his brother bishops to an August meeting in Chicago for study and discussion. In no way did he intend to dictate or dominate, nor did he do so in fact. He would never push. At the Chicago meeting, as at other meetings of the American hierarchy, he was simply one of the bishops. Since he had no mandate to lead he held back from imposing himself on his colleagues. He did not desire to lead, but unconsciously his colleagues were already making him their leader. He was aware at all times that three American cardinals took precedence to him. Many often said that Cardinal Meyer would lead the American hierarchy only if he had a mandate from the Holy Father himself. At the same time they felt that once given that mandate, he would assume the leadership. Even now some say that if he had lived he would have *de jure* received the leadership that he *de facto* assumed during the Council's third session.

The American bishops at the Council gravitated towards Meyer. In their conversations they would seek to discover what he was thinking.

In their promenades up and down the side aisles of St. Peter's they would seek him out and put their questions to him. In their meetings they respectfully listened when he rose, ever so unassumingly, to state his view. Bishops would ask him for copies of his interventions in order to make them their own. Wrote one American bishop: "My interventions…merely followed the same position as those by Cardinal Meyer on religious liberty, ecumenism and the priesthood."

CHURCHMAN OF THE WORLD

At one Monday meeting of the American bishops during the second session Meyer's leadership not only carried the day but saved the American hierarchy from a good deal of embarrassment with their brother bishops. At this particular meeting, an American bishop asked for a show of hands to support him in an intervention he intended to give. His intervention was aimed as an attack upon many Italian ecclesiastical customs. Before the show of hands Cardinal Meyer rose. Calmly, gently and pleasantly he said, "Bishops, I am really wondering about the prudence of this intervention. I myself know that the bishops in Italy are very jealous of these things. I am afraid if we begin trying to dictate to them they could easily retaliate by dictating to us. I think it is better if we just leave the whole matter drop." With that the bishops' vote went the other way. He was their leader even though he did not sit in the president's chair.

The incident also reveals the outlook which helped make the Cardinal a true churchman. While many bishops unfortunately are confined by the boundaries of their own nations or experiences, Meyer was not. As a student he associated with men from many countries. He came to know their manner of thinking and was simpatico even though he himself might not agree with their positions. His attitude was summed up by a close associate who said, "Meyer's thinking was simple: Let America be what America is and let other people work out their own problems in their own way. Let us not try to interfere." Thus the Cardinal reflected the sturdy, midwestern conservatism of his youth.

On this particular occasion Meyer manifested his own acquired love for the Italian people. He loved them and he understood them. On two occasions he preached in their language during his time at the Council. His congregation loved him for it and not a few remarked that he preached better than many of their own priests. He was very proud that he could speak his Latin and his Italian well.

His leadership was revealed too in the work of the conciliar commissions. He served as co-chairman on the subcommission of chapter four of the schema on divine revelation. The other co-chairman was not adept at Latin and quite willingly turned the leadership of the commission over to the Cardinal. In that position his leadership qualities came to the fore. He spoke very clear, facile Latin. He was not only understandable but was gifted in drawing out the opinion of each member of the commission. He scrupulously followed the agenda. He gave each member the feeling that his opinion was important. He would keep the discussion to the point. Said a *peritus* associated with this commission, "He had very clear-cut ideas of where we were going and how we were going to get there. He was the perfect chairman."

On no occasion, perhaps, did Cardinal Meyer so forcefully emerge as a leader in the public's eye than on that "Black Thursday" during the last week of the third session. Journalists, present and otherwise, have painted the Cardinal in all sorts of hues, shapes, movements and moods. Removing all exaggerations, one fact stands out. At the moment it was learned that no vote on religious liberty would be taken, literally hundreds of bishops turned to Meyer as their leader. This was a personal tribute as well as recognition of his stature among his colleagues.

If, as some reporters remarked, the Cardinal on that occasion was "furious," it was explainable. He had already been personally assured by Cardinal Cicognani on Thanksgiving Day that there would be a vote on religious liberty. Now, Cardinal Tisserant, dean of the board of presidents, approached him and asked for his affirmative vote in shelving the vote on religious liberty. "This is perfect travesty," said Meyer; "under no condition." Tisserant replied, "Well, Your Eminence, it really does not matter. We already have enough affirmative votes." Those present knew that Cardinal Meyer was angry, very angry.

Reluctantly, he assumed a certain degree of leadership during the Council, even though he himself never truly accepted as much as his colleagues were willing to confer. He was at all times conscious of the burden he carried as the Cardinal-Archbishop of Chicago. He once remarked that the influence exerted in the Council often came from the position one had in making his intervention. He felt that on many occasions the cardinals had the psychological advantage because they could always speak first. He spoke, conscious of his own responsibility to the Church. This sense of responsibility forced him to assume the leadership offered him; and towards the end of the third session he himself appreciated more fully his ability to lead.

A keen observer of the Council, Mr. Sidney Hyman, paid tribute to Meyer's leadership in an article that appeared in the *Washington Post* at the end of the Council. A member of the Jewish faith, Mr. Hyman wrote: "It is true that Albert Cardinal Meyer of Chicago, before his untimely death while the Council was in progress, grew daily in stature as a man who had done his intellectual homework. He seemed to have both the mental powers and the strength of character to emerge as the post-Council leader of the American branch of the Catholic Church."

Spiritual Life

His sense of satisfaction at his growing influence in the Council in no way contradicted the Cardinal's humility; in fact, it arose from his humility. He never sought preferment, yet he always accepted a fact. The fact, whatever it was, was a truth and his humility was deeply rooted in truth. He accepted in real joy the fact that in his position he could perform a service to the Church.

His humility, as a matter of fact, in some way explained his shyness. He was the first to admit that he had difficulty in mingling with people. Nonetheless, he would never shirk his duty in being among people. But he always wanted real people, people who needed him as a priest, people whom he could serve.

He was, nonetheless, committed to people and the things they represented. One of the very fine things about his character was his willingness to serve all people. During the second session he was invited to a doctoral defense at the Biblical Institute. He wanted very much to go, just as the hosts wanted very much to have as many cardinals present as possible. This he knew. When extended a personal invitation he replied, "You know I would very much like to attend the reception but it falls on the feast of St. Cecilia, the patronal feast of my titular church, and I am committed to offer Holy Mass there that evening. But I know you need the support of the college of cardinals, so I will ask Cardinal Ritter to represent the American cardinals." He asked, and Cardinal Ritter was present.

The Cardinal knew what people often overlook, namely, that knowledge is also a virtue. This was part and parcel of his entire life. He knew eight languages. He was familiar with the very latest in theological and biblical scholarship. For him study was more than a virtue; it was a way of life. When the Council was announced, he immediately prepared himself to take intellectual charge of the situation. Every day the Council was in session he prepared himself through study and prayer.

On one occasion he gave evidence of the prayer that accompanied his studies. This appeared, seemingly unconsciously, in his intervention on the sources of revelation. In the middle of his address he declared, "Having thought the matter over before God, therefore, I must express my own view in accord with what Cardinal Bea has already said." He *must* because of his sense of duty; he "thought the matter over before God" as a true Catholic scholar.

He was very serious about his preparation for each session of the Council. Even though his meeting with the American hierarchy in August, 1963 might have left much to be desired, he still continued to prepare himself personally. He conferred with Father Barnabas Ahern frequently both in Chicago and Rome. He asked for a position paper on religious liberty from Father Robert Hartnett, S.J., of Loyola University. Father Francis McCool, S.J., of the Biblical Institute spent time with him in Chicago between the second and third session.

As a scholar he knew his limitations as well as his areas of competency. He knew that he could speak with some authority on the priesthood as a seminary rector, on Sacred Scripture as a biblical scholar, on the liturgy and the modern world as a bishop. Although others urged him to deliver an intervention on the laity, he submitted only one. He felt that on this topic Bishop John Wright could speak with greater authority. He would speak only on the truth that he knew, as he knew it. He recognized that truth, when already crystallized through an authentic and authoritative source, is always a truth that can be – and must be –

uttered with perfect liberty. He had a tremendous respect for the truth.

COURAGE AND THE SPIRIT

This may explain why papal teaching, and especially that of Pius XII, played such a great role in his writing and preaching. For him the pope's statements crystallized the truth. For the same reason he respected divine revelation. God's word was the last word. On practical matters he was often unsure of himself because he knew, intellectually, the limitation of human existence. In these areas he was always willing to listen, deferring to the judgment of others, readily substituting another's opinion in place of his own. Nor did this mean a putting off of decisions. After mature deliberation, he made his decision because he knew decisions must be made by authority. Again, his sense of duty always won the day.

The wisdom he developed through prayer and study also produced in him a profound respect for the Spirit. He would often say that his proposals came not from him but from above. He would be willing to experiment even though naturally it frightened him at times. His total principle of action could be summed up in the words: "Do not extinguish the Spirit." His confidence in the workings of the Spirit overcame his natural reluctance for action.

He looked upon both thought and action as manifestations of the Spirit. At all times the practical problems of administration were approached from this supernatural view. In conversations with friends he would frequently refer to the stirrings of the Spirit. Quite naturally then, he was very happy to hear the discussions about charisms in the Council. His respect for the Spirit, perhaps, was also rooted in the background of his own family life. Coming from a German family, very conscious of the role of *Der Alte*, he was prone to defer at all times to a higher authority. When he himself was placed in a position of authority, He looked to the Spirit as a higher authority. He accepted his responsibility under the authority. He performed his duty only after consulting that authority.

His respect for the workings of the Spirit, however, caused him not a few doubts. It is no easy task to ascertain true and false spirits as Paul reminded the Corinthians. He had a very difficult time in seeing how the spirit of the Council would ever become a living reality. Not a few times he expressed his concern about the misinterpretation of the Council by the intemperate, the imprudent and misguided.

A friend called on him shortly after the third session. As he entered the Cardinal's room Meyer exclaimed, "What is it that we have let loose in Rome?" The Cardinal was terribly preoccupied about the uprooting influence the Council was having on those who did not understand it. In order to survive in his position the Cardinal had to have a great confidence in the Spirit.

One and all attest to Meyer's great charity. This comes through not only in the actual words of his interventions, but for those who listened to him in the Council, in the very manner of his presentation. At no time did he attack anyone. Even those whom he consulted in drafting his declarations attest to the fact that he would invariably soften the tone of his sentences. He refused to believe that there could be squabbles and factions in the Council because he could not conceive of serious conflict among Christian brothers.

One of his own priests, closely associated with him throughout his years in Chicago, says simply, "He hated to offend anyone. If he even so much as thought he might have hurt someone unintentionally, it would bother him all night. He would literally lose sleep over the thought." No one, perhaps, better expressed the dimensions of the Cardinal's charity than one of his own associates in Chicago. Referring to Meyer he said, "He had a great bigness about him rooted in his deep respect for the individual. At all times he was a priest's priest and a people's bishop." A fine tribute, indeed!

COUNCIL INTERVENTIONS

All this is a long way of coming to the issues we are discussing, namely, Cardinal Meyer's interventions at the Council. It is a long way, but a necessary one. They cannot be understood apart from the man. Nor can we even now give a full treatment of the topic we have set out to record. Perhaps the Cardinal offered other interventions to the commissions of the Second Vatican Council that we may not even know about for many years. We have here for our examination and study only the eleven interventions he delivered on the floor of the Council.

We do know, however, of one written intervention that was submitted to a commission, and even this has an ironic twist. Shortly after the end of the third session the Cardinal called Father John Courtney Murray, S.J., to Chicago. He wished to discuss the subject of religious liberty with the distinguished American theologian. For two hours the two men discussed this and related issues of the Council. The Cardinal was, at that time, drawing up a written intervention to submit to the Secretariat for the Promotion of Christian Unity, which was concerned with the subject.

After their conversation the Cardinal did, in fact, submit an intervention in writing on the subject of religious liberty. According to Father Murray, the intervention was carefully considered by the special theological commission during its February-March meeting the following year. The irony of the fact, however, is this: The Cardinal had reproduced his intervention and sent it around to some other members of the American hierarchy. When it was presented for the consideration of the commission, it appeared as the observations of an American bishop from only the Lord knows where! Nonetheless, the Cardinal had consulted with Father Murray, both on that occasion and other occasions in Rome, leaving us to speculate on how differently the American hierarchy might have appeared during the Council if it had made more effective use of the American consultants!

The Cardinal's oral interventions are indications of his leadership and at the same time assure him a respected place in the history of the Second Vatican Council. That observation is made neither because he spoke the most frequently (Ernesto Cardinal Ruffini lays claim to that distinction) nor most eloquently (in my opinion, Josef Cardinal Frings merits that honor). Cardinal Meyer, however, deserves a niche of honor because repeatedly and consistently he voiced the most representative and theologically progressive thoughts of the Second Vatican Council. Another writer, on another occasion, must examine how effective his interventions were in the ultimate formulation of the conciliar constitution or decree. That remains outside the scope of this article.

"Better Consult Meyer"

It was nonetheless, quite generally recognized that Meyer's was a voice to be heeded. On more than one occasion members of other hierarchies approached him after his intervention to ask for copies of his address. In one commission meeting an American consultant overheard a group of French bishops remark, as they were discussing a crucial issue: "We had better consult Meyer on this. His judgment would be most valuable." It is a known fact among those closely associated with the Council that both Cardinal Suenens and Cardinal Alfrink diligently made efforts to cultivate the friendship and the subtle influence of Cardinal Meyer among the Americans.

Cardinal Ottaviani, too, was a friend of the Chicago cardinal, even though he referred to the latter as *uomo freddo* (a cold man). Cardinal Meyer's actions, however, in no way deserved the epithet. During the first session the Cardinal-Secretary of the Holy Office was quite anxious to have Cardinal Meyer speak. It must be remembered that Cardinal Meyer had great respect for Ottaviani. One night they were both dinner guests in the apartments of Cardinal Cicognani. At the end of the dinner Meyer drew Cardinal Ottaviani aside and said: "Your Eminence, I have decided to speak in the Council and have handed in my name." He referred to his intervention of November 19, 1962 on the sources of revelation.

"That is fine," said Ottaviani, "I am glad to hear it."

"But, Your Eminence," replied Meyer, "I do not think you will like what I am going to say concerning divine revelation. In conscience I cannot accept the position of the schema as it is."

The reply came fast. "That is all right with me, Your Eminence. Just as long as you speak."

Cardinal Meyer, in usual charity, went on: "But I want you to realize, Your Eminence, that nothing I will say tomorrow should ever be interpreted by you as indicating any reflection on you, either personally or on your dignity as a cardinal."

On the occasion when Cardinal Meyer related this incident he went on to quote this passage from the prayer to the Holy Spirit recited at the opening of every working congregation of the Council: "Let us not disturb order, You who love absolute justice. Let not our ignorance betray us into evil, nor let favoritism influence us, nor respect for high office or persons corrupt us." This opening Council prayer, incidentally, had a deep effect on him. He referred to it frequently. In a way, he felt it was almost a divine seal of approval on his actions. It did not really matter much to him who liked or disliked what he would say. Once he was convinced, under the assurance of the Spirit as he saw it, he was absolutely fearless.

The Cardinal's interventions were, in the final analysis, of great moment and respectfully received because they were from the very depths of his own soul. He strove mightily to give honest expression to his deepest convictions. He worked diligently over each intervention. His work made him seek out the best minds he could assemble in drafting his interventions. Those who worked with him estimate that he spent at least five intense hours in the actual drafting of each intervention. This in no way takes into consideration the many hours of remote preparation and thought he gave to each subject between and during the sessions of the Council. In his presentations he was always concerned with the positive approach. In this sense he followed Pope John's admonition to the letter. He was not concerned with condemnations. He wanted the Church to speak to the modern world in a language modern man would understand.

His interventions fall easily into five categories. As a pastor he was concerned with the liturgy; thus his first two interventions in 1962, on October 24 and November 9, were on the liturgy. With the same pastoral approach he spoke on the Church of sinners on October 21, 1963. As a bishop he spoke to his colleagues on episcopal conferences on November 12, 1963. As a priest and one close to young men becoming priests he spoke on the priesthood and seminary training during the third session on October 13 and November 12 ,1964. As an American he became the champion of religious liberty and the Jews in his interventions of November 20, 1963, September 23,1964 and September 28, 1964. He revealed his love for Scripture in his interventions on the schema of divine revelation on November 19, 1962 and October 5, 1964. He was the pastor, the bishop, the priest, the American and the scholar.

An Intellectual Round-robin

For Cardinal Meyer his interventions were not only a matter of teaching the faith but also of witnessing the faith. For that reason he felt that he was the instrument of the Spirit and strove mightily to be as humanly worthy as possible to reflect that Spirit. His interventions usually began with consultation. He would invite Father Barnabas Ahern, C.P., and Father Francis McCool, S.J., to his residence in Rome. The three would visit, the Cardinal first telling them what he would like to say and asking for their ideas. Together they would examine the entire document under discussion on the council floor, pointing out its good and bad points as they viewed them. The Cardinal would then state what he would like to say. That, in turn, would evoke further discussion.

"It was all very thought-provoking," said Father McCool, "sort of an intellectual round-robin."

After several hours of discussion the Cardinal would present the points he would like to make and ask the two priests to present him with a draft. After some time they would return with the draft and again the "round-robin" approach would begin.

"The Cardinal," said Father Barnabas, "had a sixth sense in knowing what was crucial and what was peripheral. He would use his theological knife and cut the intervention down to the exact and precise ideas he wanted to express. Even though in the discussions each of us would have our say, he would always revise the draft so that it would say only what he wanted it to state."

"Even after we thought we had helped him in drafting an intervention," Father McCool added, "he would never quite deliver the intervention the way it was written the night before. He would often simplify the Latin. he would say, 'I want to talk American Latin, not Ciceronian rhetoric.' He would always put his interventions in his own words."

"Then, too" said Father Barnabas, "We would sometimes try to state a point very forcefully. He would always smooth it out. He would almost always change an imperative to a subjunctive. It just was not his character to speak vehemently."

The Cardinal would never be quite satisfied with his interventions until he actually arose to deliver them. This is borne out by examining the actual copy he used in delivering an intervention. Words are crossed out; at time whole sentences are deleted. Phrases are inserted, modifying clauses scrawled in. Each time he rose to speak he grew in the awareness that he was being listened to, that his words were important as a witness of the faith as learned and lived in the United States.

In seeking the assistance of Ahern and McCool, the Cardinal either consciously or unconsciously bore testimony to another truth of faith. He knew what a bishop should be as the chief witness and judge of the faith. At the same time he also knew that no bishop can fulfill these essential roles alone. He needed others to help him crystallize his ideas, form his judgments and supply him information. Ultimately, of course, he had to make the decision. He had to formulate the words.

OBSERVATIONS ON HIS INTERVENTIONS

It is impossible at this time to make definitive statements on the Cardinal's interventions because we do not yet have ready access to all the documents of the Council. Certain things, however, can and should be recorded here.

The Cardinal's love for Sacred Scripture is well known. Little wonder then that the decree on divine revelation aroused his deep interest at the Council. He worked closely with the commission drafting this decree. He felt very strongly on the whole notion that revelation is a "dynamic communication" between God and man. He also had a great deal to do with getting across the idea that tradition is a continual reality in the whole living Church. Yet he was most careful in making the distinctions between authentic tradition in the Church and that type of tradition which would identify itself with the superstitious practices that many people indulge in. Thus in his intervention he insisted that in the matter of tradition everything must be controlled and directed by a higher authority. The distinction he drew was basically that between apostolic tradition and the conservation, preservation and embodiment of that tradition in various forms. Tradition, thus understood, echoes through every person in the Church but not including everything that every person in the Church is doing. This is the meaning of the expression in his intervention of October 5, 1964 that "tradition is something living, dynamic, all-embracing." As a Scripture scholar he won the hearts of the Protestant observers at the Council. They were deeply impressed by his scholarship and knowledge of Scripture. He went to several of their meetings and each time impressed them by his familiarity with the latest advances in biblical scholarship.

Cardinal Meyer emerged among the American hierarchy when he rose to speak on the nature of episcopal conferences. In this intervention of November 12, 1963 he struck the middle ground between those who would vest all authority and those who would invest no authority in a national episcopal conference. His words echoed the sentiment of the majority of the American hierarchy.

On that occasion he said: "I propose...the general principle be done over and indeed somewhat in this fashion: ...'Let the common deliberations of the bishops legitimately united in a national conference have this principal objective that the residential bishops after an exchange of information in a fraternal spirit may better tend, according to their consciences, their own parts of the flock of the Lord and, at the same time, remain in communion with the bishops of the same region.'" He had a deep abiding respect for the episcopacy. He had learned from his own experience how to use power and, undoubtedly, he had seen cases where power was abused. He was insistent on the role of the bishop in his diocese as the true shepherd, as the link between God and God's people.

Speaking to one of his associates he said: "I do not want a strong national episcopal conference. It would be nothing but a new bureaucracy." He cited, for example, how little northern bishops would know in determining how southern bishops should conduct their affairs. "I would not want," he said, "a bishop from Wisconsin telling a bishop from Mississippi how to run his see."

His Finest Hour

The Cardinal's love of the priesthood was proverbial. Seldom did it shine through so splendidly as in his intervention of October 13, 1964 on the schema of priestly life and ministry. The fact that today the Catholic world possesses a refined decree on this subject is eloquent testimony to his leadership. This schema was presented to the Council in the form of propositions which, unfortunately, did no more than reflect the spirituality of a bygone era. Here the Cardinal was confronted with a document that belied everything his entire priestly life represented. He was almost a "new breed" priest in St. Francis Seminary, Milwaukee, decades before the term was coined and some of his priests in Chicago were considered such. He was the seminary professor, the seminary rector, the bishop most vitally concerned with the priests-to-be and the priests under his care. He could not, he would not, settle for half-a-loaf. Thus he rose and spoke: "In all sincerity I should confess that the schema of propositions in all it encompasses is not very satisfactory.'

At no time in the Council did he ever rise so magnificently to the task. This was, all agreed, his finest hour. It was his most eloquent intervention. He had written the text completely by himself, working it over and over on the very night before he delivered it. It was a surprise to all his associates. No one knew he was going to give it. No one expected it at the time. Only now, upon reflection, all his friends and associates realize that this was his great moment in the Council. He spoke well, from the heart, and not a person in the Council chambers who listened doubted for a moment that here was a priest among priests speaking of his dearest love – the priesthood.

He was at his best when he talked about the priesthood. In fact, the priesthood was his whole life, his whole spiritual life. He seemed to possess an intuitive sense about anything concerning the priesthood. His whole heart was in it. And he had very definite ideas about the priesthood. Frequently he would say, "The Mass is the only unity of the priesthood." Precisely because the schema of propositions ignored this unity he was against it. One day he remarked, "What is the unity that binds all priests together? For me there is only one unity, be they priests in the chancery, in the parish, in the cloister, in the school. The only thing that binds all of us together is the Mass. The Mass, in fact, is the priest's whole life." Precisely what he wanted to see in this schema was the simple statement that the priest's life is unifed in the Mass and the Eucharist. On another occasion he said, "For me the Mass has been my whole life."

The Cardinal also had practical concerns. Frequently he worried about the morale of a priest who would never become a pastor. He felt the present situation as existing in many large dioceses was unwholesome. He could not see how it could survive. "I do not see what we can do," he said, "but we have to somehow or other change this particular situation or at least strengthen the spirituality of priests so that they will be able to lead a full priestly life even though they remain assistants for a long period of time."

THE EPISCOPATE OVERSTRESSED

His love and reverence for the priesthood, likewise, prompted him to feel that the Council overstressed the role of the bishop to the detriment of the priest. He was keenly aware of that fact and continually insisted on a stronger statement from the Council concerning priests. In this connection it is interesting to note that Bishop Ernest Primeau of Manchester referred to Cardinal Meyer during the fourth Council session. In his written intervention concerning curates he said: "His Eminence Albert Cardinal Meyer, of happy memory, often used to say that the more serious problem concerning parishes and priests in his own diocese as well as in many other areas of the United States arose from the fact that priests did not become pastors before many years passed, sometimes twenty and even thirty years."

The same love of the priesthood was carried over into his intervention of November 12, 1964 on the education of priests. Here again he spoke from the years of his experience at St. Francis Seminary. He spoke from the heart. He approved the principle that episcopal conferences should establish the norms of seminary training in their respective areas. His own sense of duty to the church is reflected in these words he uttered: "The priesthood, although conferred in a sacrament, is first of all a grace freely given to an individual for the good of the Church." Even on the floor of the Council the Cardinal could not, would not, forget his origins. His sense of duty compelled him to be first, last, and always the servant of the Church. In this intervention Meyer was arguing that we must first have good Christians before we will develop good priests. The priesthood serves the Church. Goodness is the presupposition; generosity is the determinant.

Another intervention throws an interesting light on the

Cardinal's own personal life. On September 23, 1964 he bore witness to the American religio-political experience in the United State by speaking "in the name of almost all the bishops of the United States" on religious liberty. In that address he presented five reasons for the approval of the declaration. The Cardinal sat at the table of the presidency next to Cardinal Ruffini of Palermo, who was opposed to the declaration. Yet, the Cardinal-Archbishop of Palermo was not only a former teacher but also a close friend of the Cardinal-Archbishop of Chicago. When Meyer sat down after delivering his intervention on religious liberty, his former teacher said: "It is all right when you Americans speak that way, but if you were in Palermo you would sing another song." Cardinal Meyer smiled, as he always smiled. He was not cynical. He was sincere. His smile captured Ruffini. They respected each other in spite of differences which would never disrupt friendship. One day Meyer said: "Ruffini was a good teacher. None of them was better than he. None of them."

The Church in the Modern World

A later theologian, philosopher or environmentalist might say that Meyer's greatest intervention has been given scant attention. That remains to be seen. His intervention of October 20, 1964 was, without a doubt, a moment to be remembered. He spoke on the Church in the world of today in a language that would have caused Teilhard de Chardin to stand up and cheer. The address was both historical and futuristic. At one and the same time he attacked all forms of dualism in Christian philosophy and approved a cosmic concept of redemption. "It seems," said Cardinal Meyer, "recourse should be had to St. Paul's teaching on the economy of salvation." That, perhaps, is the key sentence. He hinted at an eschatology of the Church in the modern world that theologians for several generations will strive to develop. He stood opposed to the old and unsavory dichotomy between the spiritual and the temporal. It was, many thought, straight and simple de Chardin. However, those who knew the Cardinal well protested. It was, they said, Pauline, sinking roots in the eighth chapter of the Epistle to the Romans. Others said it was no more than a throw-back to the Old Testament in which God's revealing word admits no separation between the temporal and the spiritual.

Albert Cardinal Meyer, an American prelate at the Second Vatican Council, was the reluctant leader who shone magnificently for one, brief shining moment. His spirit compelled him to serve the Church at all times and, perhaps, at no time so well as during the days of the Council. We are all the richer because of his gracious presence among us. ∾

1966

EW PENTECOST IN THE CHURCH

This address was delivered to members of the First Friday Club of the employees of the U.S. Senate in February, 1966. It was well received at that time and for that reason is published in this volume.

entecost Sunday marks the proclamation of the Church to the world. This Pentecost Sunday marks the end of the jubilee Pope Paul proclaimed at the end of the Council. The jubilee was intended, during these past six months, to prepare all our hearts and souls for the "new Pentecost" launched by the Second Vatican Council.

So many changes have happened to all of us during the past five years that we will never, will it or not, be the same again. Many of these, admittedly, have been unsettling to those rooted in their tracks. Other events, unfortunately, have been alarming to those in a position of authority in the Church. Most changes and events, however, have thrust upon each of us a demand for maturity, the mark of a deeply and truly Christian man or woman in our world today.

Now, as we mark the end of the Council jubilee we might, with profit, reflect on the major and immediate effects the Council has brought about in each of us. Understanding these changes will enable us to be the type of Christian the Church wishes us to be in the years ahead.

Almost five years ago good Pope John convened the Second Vatican Ecumenical Council. In his opening address to the Fathers of the Council he quoted, not without reason, the words Peter addressed to the lame beggar: "Silver and gold I have none; but what I have, I give thee. In the name of Jesus Christ of Nazareth, arise and walk."

Since that historic October 11, 1962, the Church has been meditating on these words of Peter, the Prince of the Apostles. She has been applying these words to her own life and striving through prayer and meditation to instill in her children throughout the world the same generosity, the same spirit of love and service that prompted Peter to perform a miracle for the lame beggar who sat at the temple gate called Beautiful.

This spirit unleashed by the Second Vatican Council has captured the imagination of the world. More than that, this spirit has become part and parcel of the spiritual life of all those who call themselves Christians. The Fathers of the Second Vatican Council have fostered this spirit through their four years of prayer and study during the time of the Council. Theirs has been a prophetic voice thundering across the continents of the world and finding echoes in countless men and women of goodwill who eagerly await a new day in a better world.

This battle-scarred and pleasure-plundered world has been the concern of the Second Vatican Council. We who glory in being Christians are truly in the world and thus it will be no better or no worse than we are ourselves. We are all together Christ's little flock. We are God's people, gathered together as children of the Father, brothers of the Son and instruments of the Holy Spirit. We are the Church, each one of us, and as such the world and the Church will be not better, no stronger, no holier than each of us in our living and thinking.

Good Pope John told us how we as the members of the Church must live. We must live in such a way, he said, that all men will see through us that the Church is "the loving mother of all: benign, patient, full of love and goodness." In our lives we must reveal the compassionate tenderness of the Church. That quality of love and commitment must be so real, so evident, so sincere that the world about us will recognize through us all the love, all the concern and all the anguish of the Church for all men in our world today.

What, then, might we ask is the image the Second Vatican Council has given us of our holy Church? What are the qualities of the Church in the world today that each of us should reflect in our daily lives? What must be the virtues we practice today and tomorrow that our

Holy Father Pope Paul VI wants us to manifest as "the light of the world" and "the salt of the earth"? We will know how we must live by reflecting on the nature of the Church, for if we are proud to be the members of that Church we must live our lives as the Church seeks to live her life in the world today.

1. Ours is a Church of *worship*. We have been made for no other reason than to render praise and glory to our Heavenly Father. The Church was born, the Church lives and the Church will be ushered into glory for the same reason: to give praise and glory to the holy and undivided Trinity. The "Constitution on the Sacred Liturgy" reminds each of us of this, our most essential and fundamental obligation as Christians and human beings. "Every liturgical celebration, because it is an action of Christ the priest and of His Body which is the Church, is a sacred action surpassing all others; no other action of the Church can equal its efficacy by the same title and to the same degree."

We may perform many great and generous deeds. We may be engrossed in important political, educational or social work, We are, to be sure, burdened down with the cares of making a living, minding a family and serving our country. Nothing, however, absolutely nothing, is so vitally important to our lives as our duty to worship. We serve mankind best, we reflect the image of the Church best, when we are a praying Church, a worshipping family of God. We must worship God because we are human, because we are Christian. If we do not worship God, or if we pay Him only slight attention, we end up in the most dismal of all frustrations by worshipping ourselves.

2. Ours is a Church of *witness*. When Our Blessed Savior laid down His blueprint for Christian living in the Sermon on the Mount he admonished his followers in these words: "So let your light shine before men that they may see your good works and glorify your Father who is in heaven."

The Council has taught us that the Church is the witness, the sacrament, the sign of Christ in the world. The Church does not exist for herself; the Church lives among men to be a witness. Her martyrs bore witness to Christ by the shedding of their blood. Her holy virgins and confessors and pious men and women throughout the centuries bore witness to Christ by their lives of heroic virtue. Countless millions of

Christians today bear witness to Christ by the examples of virtue, goodness, love and sacrifice they offer their friends and neighbors.

Our witness of Christ must be such that our lives would not
make sense if God did not exist: "The joys and the hopes, the griefs and
the anxieties of the men of this age, especially those who are poor or in
any way afflicted, these are the joys and hopes, the griefs and anxieties of
the followers of Christ."

We must identify ourselves with all those who suffer, all the
downtrodden, all the afflicted, in order to reveal to them the love and the
joy and the peace of Christ. Our hands must be Christ's hands. Our
words must be Christ's words. Our love must be Christ's love. The neighbors with whom we live, the people with whom we work, those who are
most ugly, most unloved, most unwanted – all these people must see
Christ in us. They must see Christ in us so clearly that they can truly say,
"What you are thunders so loud I can't hear what you're saying." Let our
light shine so all can see in us the shining image of Christ Jesus.

3. Ours is a Church of *service*. Shortly before His passion and
death on the Cross our Blessed Savior told his apostles: "The Son of man
did not come to have service done him; he came to serve others, and to
give his life as a ransom for the lives of many." Nothing has been so
highly dramatized by the Second Vatican Council than the Church's
desire to be the servant of all mankind. The "Constitution on the
Church in the Modern World" tells us: "Christ entered this world to
give witness to the truth, to rescue and not to sit in judgment, to serve
and not to be served."

In his address to the Fathers of the Council Pope Paul VI
declared: "The Church looks upon the world with profound understanding, sincere admiration and the firm conviction to serve, not conquer, it.
She does not despise it, but appreciates it. She does not condemn it, but
hopes to strengthen and save it."

As the Church desires, so each Christian must desire. We must
serve the world – the whole, wide, wonderful world. We serve the world
by serving one another. We cannot rest as long as poverty and disease,
hatred and strife, rivalry and jealousy, wickedness and sin exist among us
and within us. We cannot be content to live only our own lives. We
must share with everyone we meet: all of us are brothers and sisters

because we are God's family. Our consciences can give us no peace until we have done all in our power to help our brother in need. The corporal and spiritual works of mercy are not just a catechism answer. They are a way of life that each must follow or else be a failure as a Christian.

To follow Christ means to serve all those that Christ wants us to serve. That service demands love, for in each man and woman we must see the image of Christ Himself. That service demands sacrifice, for we must find our Calvary in a total, selfless emptying of self, counting no costs, taking all risks and being willing to lay down our lives for another: "Greater love than this no man has than to lay down his life for a friend." In a word, we serve God best, we witness Christ best, we worship the Blessed Trinity best when we give ourselves, everything we have and everything we are, for the love of others. This is the supreme joy. This is the fullness of the truly Christian life.

Our Church is like Peter's little boat on the Sea of Galilee. Our Church today has launched out into the deep and sometimes dangerous waters of our world. Just as the waves sometimes vent their fury against the shores, so the world today and tomorrow will rock and sometime imperil Peter's boat, the Church. Our Church will weather the storms because we will be at the helm to direct Peter's barque to the safe harbor of "a better world willed by God."

We will be good sailors on Peter's boat if our worship of the living God will be intelligent and active; if our witness of Christ will be bold and courageous; if our service of humanity will be sacrificial and loving. Our hope and consolation will be, today and tomorrow and always, the presence of Christ in us and with us. He gave us this assurance when he said: "Have confidence, I have overcome the world." ∞

1967

HALLENGE TO CHANGE

The phenomenon of change in the world and the Church has held a fascination for the writer at least since the day of his ordination to the priesthood. "Change" has often been the subject of his writings and addresses. This essay expresses this fascination. It was published in the Spring, 1967, issue of Chicago Studies.

Years ago this February the late Emmanuel Cardinal Suhard penned a prophetic pastoral letter entitled *Growth or Decline?— The Church Today*. The late Archbishop of Paris wrote: "Something is dead on the earth which will not rise again. The war therefore assumes its true meaning. It is not an intermission but an epilogue. It marks the end of a world.... The confusion, the feeling of maladjustment which results in all fields, justifies the feeling so often expressed in the ambiguous phrase: 'The world is in revolution'."

About this same time another prophetic voice was sounded from quite a different area of the world. The Jesuit scholar, Teilhard de Chardin, an unfortunately quiet man in his lifetime, wrote in one of his many notebooks, "Today something is happening to the whole structure of human consciousness. A fresh kind of life is starting."

From yet another quarter the same sentiments were voiced. Speaking to a throng of people in St. Peter's Square on February 10, 1952, Pope Pius XII exclaimed: "The whole world must be rebuilt from its foundation, transformed from savage to human, from human to divine, that is to say, to make it as God would have it. Millions of men plead for a new way."

More recently, the same message was uttered by Pope John

XXIII in his dramatic address on the occasion of the opening of the Second Vatican Council. He said: "In the present day Divine Providence is leading us to a new order of human relations. By man's own efforts, and beyond the greatest expectations, we are being directed towards the fulfillment of God's higher and inscrutable designs."

These are the voices of the prophets, if you will, that have pointed out for us the change that is upon us. One aspect of this change, as it affects the youth of the United States, was detailed in *Time's* "Man of the Year" article last January. Commenting on the nature of the "Now People," *Time's* editors wrote: "For better or for worse, the world today is committed to accelerating change: radical, wrenching, erosive of both traditions and old values. Its inheritors have grown up with rapid change, are better prepared to accommodate it than any in history, indeed embrace change as a virtue in itself. With his skeptical yet humanistic outlook, his disdain for fanaticism and his scorn for the spurious, the Man of the Year suggests that he will 'infuse the future with a new sense of morality, a transcendent and contemporary ethic that could infinitely enrich the empty society.'"

The adjectives in that quotation are most revealing and, at the same time, somewhat disconcerting. To repeat: Change is "radical, wrenching and erosive." The Man of the Year is endowed with a "skeptical yet humanistic" outlook, a "disdain" for fanaticism and a "scorn" for the spurious – and he will infuse the future with a *new* sense of morality. It need not be pointed out that this description of the "Now People" is not so much evaluative as it is reportorial. We might not like it; we might very much be disturbed by it. Nonetheless, this is the world in which we find ourselves. This is the challenge to the Church which some have called a challenge to change and others have described as an upheaval of consecrated values.

The challenge to change has, I fear, caught most of us unaware. We have lived too long and too comfortably with the established Church, with its traditional thought patterns, its latent and sometimes obvious mistrust of "the world," with its protective ideological walls against the "new," the "different," the "unusual." We have, as the religious men and women of the Christian tradition, built our fallout shelters too safely and securely. Perhaps we have never denied that the

Christian life is a risk, a leap into the dark, but actually we have lived in such a manner that we refused to recognize the fact.

As the philosopher Leslie Dewart has pointed out, we deluded ourselves as Christian leaders and people into a false security attached to an outmoded system of philosophy, an outmoded cultural form and an outmoded language. The denial of the drastic need for accommodation and renewal in our philosophical, theological and sociological thought and actions has left us not only irrelevant but largely ignored.

Certain writers claim that the reluctance of the Church to accept change has brought into being the "death of God" theology. Bishop John T. Robinson, author of *Honest to God*, expressed it bluntly in the headline to one of his articles, "Our Image of God Must Go." Thomas J. Alitzer, in his essay, "America and the Future of Theology," stated his position by saying "the American who is in quest of a deeper form of existence must look forward to the future, not a future which is simply an extension of the present, but a future that will shatter all that we know as present." Although some theologians are already preparing their answers by embarking on "the living God" theology, both approaches converge remarkably on three points. There is a complete breakdown of the traditional, supernatural notion of God for an ever-growing number of people. The study of "the secular meaning of the Gospel" leads to the life, teaching and death of Jesus as the center for Christian life and faith. There is a revolutionary openness to the possibilities of the present and the future.

At the same time it must be pointed out that both schools represent a change from our traditional approaches to Christian theology, and consequently, our daily thinking and living. We have, I believe, already come to that day described by Leslie Dewart as "one day" when he wrote: "The price that the Church would one day have to pay for resisting gradual change would be the need to undergo sudden, painful and traumatic change. The accumulated pressures in the Church were bound to find a sudden avenue of escape as soon as a crack in the monolith would develop."

I submit for your consideration, therefore, that the present state of change within the Church and within society (the one working on the other constantly) has been sudden, radical and painful. This state of change is, as I see it, the challenge to the Church today.

Philip Scharper, recently describing this change, remarked that "the fact of change is indeed characteristic of our time, but not change as a transition to a more stable order. What characterizes our time is change leading to change leading to change." It is a challenge in itself as well as in the tensions that it is producing among all of us.

THE PILGRIM CHURCH

This change produced in all of us a state of crisis. We are, in fact, members of a Church in crisis. Nor is the situation necessarily unfortunate. We are, after all, members of a pilgrim Church, and what pilgrim has not had difficulties along the way? We are, too, members of a suffering Church, and the present status is perhaps God's way of purifying his Church. We are, finally, the followers of Christ and like him as individuals and members of the community we must pass over the Mount of Calvary before we enter into the valley of the Resurrection.

We know that the Church today is suffering a crisis of authority, not only between superiors and inferiors, between a philosophy of blind obedience and rational assent, but also a questioning of the very nature of authority itself. Few Christians would deny the Pauline maxim that all authority comes from God, but that is not really the basic question. Many thinking Christians are asking about the very teaching authority of the Church, the immutability of doctrine, the difference between a development of doctrine and the total negation of a doctrine, the intellectual foundations of ecclesiastical infallibility.

The Church, too, is undergoing a crisis of knowledge. Modern science and research have brought about profound insights into Christian teaching, insights that have shattered the simple faith of some as well as bolstered the more intelligent faith of others. The knowledge explosion outside the Church has outstripped the knowledge explosion within the Church, in some cases causing a serious credibility gap and in others a sophisticated write-off of the Christian catechesis of a previous era. Some have called this a crisis of faith. I am of the opinion, however, that the crisis of faith is an effect of the abstract manner in which the traditional Church has defined its dogmas. Looking at the question historically,

Jeffrey Burton Russell observed: "The Christians' interest in abstract truth ever goes enchallenged, the inevitable companion of orthodoxy is dissent." The current dissent of the "Now Society" has brought about the crisis of theological knowledge.

There are, to be sure, many crises within the Church today. We need not enumerate them all here, but one more should be mentioned, one which I would consider to be the most serious. This is the crisis of Christian love. If it be true that orthodoxy generates dissent and dissent generates repression, it is even truer when the orthodoxy is questionable, dubious or ill-defined. The repression that takes place in the Church is even more despicable than the repression exercised by other societies precisely because the Church is called to be the loving family of a holy God. This repression, perhaps beginning with suspicion and climaxing in hatred, is presently taking its toll among us. Sometimes without even recognizing it we are pitched into alien camps, we are drawing lines too straight, we are issuing ultimatums which are quite literally injuring the entire body of Christ. The Christian mark of love is sometimes so blurred that our fellowmen cannot see, much less understand, that ours is a community, a chosen people of God, a mystical body of Christ. This is ultimately the greatest crisis of the Church today. This is our most shameful scandal.

AN ANSWER: COMMUNICATION

Up until now I have been writing as a journalist and have pointed out a few of the crises in the Church that this almost universal and almost apocalyptic change has forced upon us. The change, unfortunately, has found most men in the position described by Walter Lippman. He wrote: "The ideas and issues we have been so hot and bothered about during my lifetime have in these days become largely irrelevant.... The kind of life men are living today was not even imagined when they were still at school. Therefore, they are not prepared for it. Because their ideas are out of date while their lives are being changed so rapidly...they have had to become 'pragmatic' in the sense that they deal with the details of living and making a living and have put aside the great issues of the world. They do not have the ambition to participate in history and to shape the future. They are preoccupied with the more immediate things which may help or hurt them. Their state of mind is marked by a vast indifference to big issues, and in this indifference there is a feeling that they are incompetent to do much about the big issues."

This spirit of indifference is definitely to be reckoned with even if it is not the spirit of the "Now Society." This group is determined not only to "make a better world" but in the majority of cases, "a better world willed by God." They are questioning his image and his relevancy, but theirs is precisely the challenge to change that we must answer. If we do not project an intelligible image of God and if we fail to explain his relevancy then I fear we are doomed to be ignored. Nevertheless I believe that we have a providential opportunity to meet the challenge through communications.

It is a rather startling fact that all of us have lived and are continuing to live through a communications revolution the likes of which has never been witnessed before on earth. This revolution – and by no means have we come to its end – ranks in importance with the discovery of fire, the invention of the wheel and the perfection of the steam engine. A few figures might be presented for our reflection. In the world today there are printed each day 300 million newspapers; 200 million copies of periodicals appear either monthly or weekly. 170,000 movies theatres attract over 17,000 billion spectators each year. There are over 6,000 radio stations and over 400 million receivers. There are over 1,000 television stations transmitting to over 120 million people who spend 2,000,000 billion hours each year before their sets. The figures are staggering and admittedly quite incomprehensible. I cite the figures, however, to point out that the communications media are not only part of our life but, in reality, for the greater part of mankind, the central part of daily existence.

THE COMMUNICATIONS LAG

For far too long the Church has lagged behind in the understanding, appreciation and application of communications because, quite simply, "the cult of secrecy" has prevailed from the highest echelons down to the smallest parish. This "cult of secrecy" has literally choked communications process on all levels. It would take an historian to document how and why "the cult of secrecy" was developed in the Church. It may be, as Dr. Russel insinuates in his book, *Dissent and Reform in the Early Middle Ages*, that secrecy was one means of repression. It may be, too, as Leslie Dewart suggests, that the Church's concern for doctrinal rigidity could silence the opposition secretly and thus cut off those who would dissent from its traditional doctrinal formulations. So firmly entrenched within the Church is this "cult of secrecy" that even today it is most diffiicult for us to escape traditional thought-patterns in the area of communications. The effect has been disastrous for, in the long run, it has hurt nothing more severely than the Church itself.

That, I know, is a strong statement and therefore needs both explanation and documentation. The immediate by-product of healthy communication is the formulation of public opinion; the better the communications the healthier the public opinion. The Church cannot live and develop without this opinion. Pope Pius XII called opinion "a natural echo, a more or less spontaneous common resounding of acts and circumstances in the mind and judgment of people who feel they are responsible beings, closely bound to the fate of their community." In his address on February 17, 1950, he called public opinion "the mark of every normal society" and added that "by her attitude towards public opinion, the Church places herself as a barrier against totalitarianism." Finally, he said, "Because the Church is the living body, something would be wanting in her life if public opinion were lack...and the blame for this deficiency would fall back upon the pastors and the faithful."

Karl Rahmer, in his essay entitled *Free Speech in the Church*, directing his remarks to all who hold official posts in the Church, speaks more to the point. He writes: "If they do not allow the people to speak their minds, do not, in more dignified language, encourage or even tolerate, with courage and forbearance and even certain optimism free from anxiety, the growth of a public opinion within the Church, they run the risk of directing her from a soundproof ivory tower, instead of straining their ears to catch the voice of God, which can also be audible within the clamour of the times."

Public opinion must be able to grow side by side with laws and institutions, acting somewhat in the nature of a collective ombudsman of the community. Public opinion is born out of a desire and need of man to meet his fellow, to understand him and to communicate with him in active participation in the life of the community. It must be spontaneous and free. This freedom will assure diversified opinions which may present complementary truths and values and thus assure a balance and an enrichment to the entire community. Thus Amleto Cardinal Cicognani in a significant letter to the French Social Week last July summed up these thoughts when he wrote: "This is to say that public opinion, in order to establish itself sanely, needs a true climate of liberty, outside the pressure of myths and all constraint which would strive to impose a uniformity whose appearance is the humiliating signal of dangerous regression."

One of the conclusions drawn up by the participants in that French Social Week emphasized the responsibility of Christians in forming public opinion within the Church. It reads as follows: "The Christian's function is not confined to his presence in the world. Public opinion has a place – in fact and of right – in the very life of the Church. Opinion is no more infallible in sacred matters than in secular ones, but it is just as useful in so far as it is the reflection here and now of the people of God. Many of the faithful have as yet a conscience that is too little aware of their responsibilities of forming an opinion within the Church and speak too often without the necessary knowledge and reflection. A considerable effort of education must be accomplished among Christians so that individuals and groups alike may contribute to the formation of an informed and enlightened opinion. This presupposes that responsible authorities provide the faithful with the information they need and at the same time guarantee them freedom of expression within the Church."

The point is simple: We must have communications within the Church in order to foster a healthy public opinion which will enable the Church to come to know itself better. This knowledge will help the Church resolve the crisis we have already mentioned. Furthermore, public opinion, serving as an ideological yeast within the Church, will also help all the members of the Church see more clearly the need to re-define roles and modify processes within the Church.

QUALIFICATIONS FOR COMMUNICATIONS

The first of these is patience. If it is true that "the cult of secrecy" developed over many centuries, no one will achieve the complete and universal practice of communications within the Church overnight. Sometimes a small success is better than a total victory. Sometimes it is better to listen than to speak; and we must not forget that listening is at least half the process of communication.

The good communicator's second virtue is prudence. He will choose a rifle instead of a shotgun, setting his sights on one object rather than ranging all over the field. He will see that a word of encouragement is better than a book of condemnations. He will know that understanding another's problem is more effective communication than the presentation of his own arguments.

The third virtue of a good communicator is knowledge. Personality wears thin; competency is solid gold. Communication demands that something be taught and something learned; someone must inform and someone must be informed. Knowledge demands a respect, a reverence for truth and beauty and the two always go together. Knowledge makes not only the communicator but also his communication relevant. And knowledge is a gift of the Holy Spirit.

The final virtue of a good communicator is a sense of humor. The tension and strife found frequently in the Church today could be less bitter if all of us indulged in a bit more humor and less intensity. I believe that all of us could profit by laughing at ourselves more often, by realizing that no one individual is so important that he must be taken that seriously, by recognizing that hope is still a Christian virtue and Christ's promise is with the Church until the end of time. Chesterton wrote, "All jesting is in its nature profane, in the sense that it must be the sudden realization that someone who thinks himself solemn is not so very solemn after all." He also wrote, "A sad saint is a sad sort of a saint."

Most of us welcome the changes taking place around us for we recognize that through them "a fresh kind of life is starting." This attitude is perhaps our heritage as a nation. For as Henry James said: "The new world grasps me with its irresistible power of assimilation and creative courage. I saw the American courage to go ahead, to risk failures, to begin again after defeat, to lead and in action, to be open toward the future, to participate in the creative process of nature and history."

Nor do we fear for the Church, for we share the feelings of Pope

Paul in his opening words to the Vatican Council: "Let no other light be shed on us but Christ the light of the world. Let no other truth be of interest to our minds, but the words of the Lord, our only Master. Let no other aspiration guide us, but the desire to be absolutely faithful to him. Let no other hope sustain us, but the one that, through the meditation of his word strengthens our pitiful weakness: "Behold I am with you all days, even unto the consummation of the world.'" ᴗ

1969

IGNS OF HOPE

This editorial is the last one I wrote for The Priest *magazine, published by Our Sunday Visitor, Inc., Huntington, Indiana. It appeared in the August, 1969, issue.*

In the introduction to his masterful study, *Theology of Hope*, Jurgen Moltmann makes the following observation: "From first to last, and not merely in the epilogue, Christianity is eschatology, is hope, forward looking and forward moving, and therefore also revolutionizing and transforming the present."

During the past few weeks we have been studying Moltmann's great theological contribution on the virtue of hope. We have been trying to apply some of his observations concerning hope to the contemporary scene of the American clergy. We also have reflected on the words one of our readers addressed to us several months ago: "As priests we must be filled with a great hope, for it seems to me that we have stumbled into the pit of despair."

We grant that there are some signs that might lead us into the chasm of despair, but to go that route would be neither Christian nor human. We firmly believe that we as priests must be the ambassadors of a great hope for all people. We further believe that we must be the living witnesses of a holy hope, rooted in a deep spirituality, that will enable our fellowmen to rise above the insecurities, the uncertainties and the confusion of our times.

For this reason we have jotted down four points that are, at least for us, signs of hope. They are, admittedly, no more than the bare skeleton of a much more detailed study that may follow sometime in the future. They are, nonetheless, at least a beginning of what might be a profitable discussion among all of us.

1. The Progress of This Century

We have, in the history of the Church in the United States and Canada, come so far so fast that it is somewhat staggering. From a poor immigrant Church we have become a firmly established People of God. From a Church that was part and parcel of a reactionary establishment (contrast St. Pius X's decree, *Lamentabile Dei*, with Pope Paul's *Populorum Progressio*) we have emerged as one of the leading forces in the world for social progress. Compare the instruction of the Biblical Commission in the first decade of the century with the conciliar constitution on Divine Revelation. Compare the militarist stance of the Church in North America in 1917 and its present pacific trend in the Vietnam war. Compare the presidential campaigns of Alfred E. Smith and John F. Kennedy. Compare the pope as "prisoner of the Vatican" and the pope as pilgrim traversing the world. Compare the conditions of the workingman before and after the American Bishops' Statement *On Reconstructing the Social Order* of 1919. Compare the intellectual status of the Catholic community before and after World War II.

For these, and so many other movements of progress (such as the biblical, liturgical and social action apostolates) we must not only be grateful to our predecessors but must also interpret these movements as joyous signs of hope.

2. Young Clergy, Religious and Laity

For at least a decade we have suffered from listening to conversations among priests who cared more about football scores than midrashes. For the same length of time we suffered from listening to reports from lay people who were more concerned about the hot lunch program than the control of the catechetical program. Happily, these days are dead – or at least dying.

We are proud to be a priest and to be associated with young priests. Quite honestly, they put us middle-aged priests to shame for they are, for the most part, so much more alert and alive intellectually and apostolically than we are. We are happy to be associated with young lay-men and women who seem many times more concerned about the future of the Church than many clerical colleagues of our own vintage.

We interpret the zeal, concern and commitment of these young priests and lay people as the one – and perhaps the greatest – hope of the Church in our times. Of course, we are free to criticize their excesses, and we suspect that they are among the first to welcome such valid criticism. But we can neither ignore nor negate the fact that in these priests and lay people lies the great hope of the future of the Church.

3. OPENING TO THE WORLD

During the time of the Council Karl Rahner wrote that the Church was no longer a citadel, secure upon a rock, with slots in its walls for taking pot shots at the world. The Church as a "mighty fortress" died the day the Fathers of the Second Vatican Council subscribed to this simple, yet poignant, statement:

"The joys and the hopes, the griefs and the anxieties of the men of this age, especially those who are poor or in any way afflicted, these too are the joys and hopes, the griefs and anxieties of the followers of Christ. Indeed, nothing genuinely human fails to raise an echo in their hearts.... That is why this community realizes that it is truly and intimately linked with mankind and its history."

In recent years we have come to realize that the role of the Church is to be *in* the world. The Church's stance has changed. We no longer attack the world. We no longer reject human values. We no longer look out upon the world as "the enemy."

On the other hand, somewhat like a new bridegroom, we go out to meet the world. Of course, we are embarrassed. Of course, we know that we are uncomfortable. Of course, we also know that we have sinned by neglect. But – and indeed, this also is a sign of hope – we are at least willing to put an end to the dualism of body and soul, spiritual and material, temporal and eternal, and come to accept man not only as man but also as that creature created in the image and likeness of God.

4. Challenge to Change

We have moved into a new era of not only human but also Christian values. This is not to say that the essentials have changed, but it does admit that the externals not only can but actually have changed. This surely is what Pope Paul reiterated in his speech on June 23, 1969, when he said he was "disposed to modify existing positions which are purely legislative, not doctrinal, when it is reasonable to do so" as well as "desirous...of continually and interiorly renewing the spirit of canon law for better service to the Church."

This is part of "the big leap forward" that Pope John predicted. Now a leap forward is always a dangerous thing. It leads us into unknown and uncharted territory. It is unsettling because it recognizes so many of what we thought were the tried and true programs and policies as inadequate. It makes us stop and think, reconsider structures, reexamine positions, and in some cases not only play the role of the historian who studies the past but also the prophet who prepares the future. All this creates a certain degree of tension that makes each of us more than a bit uncomfortable.

However, thank God, we now find ourselves accepting, in varying degrees, the fact that we must change simply because we belong to a Church whose motto now is *ecclesia semper reformanda* the Church must be in a continuous state of renewal. We are no longer members of a static Church. We no longer are mere archivists of the past but prophets of the future. We find ourselves, like it or not, accepting as a *fait accompli* these words spoken by Pope Pius XII on February 11, 1952:

"The whole world must be rebuilt from its foundations, transformed from savage to human, from human to divine, that is to say, to make it as God would have it. Millions of men plead for a new way of life. They look towards the Church of Christ as to the only strong pilot who...can grasp the helm in so vast an undertaking."

This is the challenge of our times. Such an opportunity might never come our way again in many centuries. We are not only the molders of the present, but, quite literally, the heralds of a better Church and world willed by God. Seldom in the history of the Church has God given so many men and women so great an opportunity as He has given us.

An Extraordinary Drama

In the concluding paragraph of his book, Dr. Moltmann writes: "This is an age of diaspora, of sowing in hope, of self-surrender and sacrifice, for it is an age which stands within the horizon of a new future." That horizon, we believe, must be pointed out by priests who will to be the prophets of a new future.

Prophecy is always a dangerous exercise, but it is, at the same time, always a necessary one for the life of the Church. Prophecy, too, is closely associated with contemplation. Hence, the priest who exercises a prophetic role must also practice a certain degree of contemplation. This we were told by Leon Bloy when he wrote at the turn of the century:

"Present events are certainly hideous, but not vulgar as to their tendencies.... I therefore again think that we are at the prologue of an extraordinary drama, the like of which has not been seen for twenty centuries, and I invite you to a certain degree of recollection...." ❧

1972

GOOD LIFE IN A SMALL TOWN

This article appeared in The New York Times, *Sept. 15, 1972. It expressed my sentiments when I served as pastor of St. Rose of Lima Church, St. Rosa, Freeport, Minnesota. Senator Walter F. Mondale had it published in the Sept. 25, 1972 issue of the* Congressional Record.

I suppose you can start with a softball game. Young men watching young ladies competing against New Munich or Freeport or Melrose. Young mothers with young husbands and two young children on the hood of the car. The cheering, the yelling, the laughter – and sometimes, tears – as spectators scream for their favorite team. It is a good way of life.

And, again, we might start with a visit to a nursing home. It might be Pine Villa in Melrose or Albany Nursing Home. Grandma and Grandpa are here. They lived the good life. They are rich with memories. They know more about life and living – and even dying – than all of us put together. They are the depository of the wisdom of over one hundred years.

Then, too, you might take that third grader on his bike. He rides it back and forth, long into the hours of the dark. What thoughts pass through his mind? What dreams? What visions? He, too, is part of this good life.

What, then, when you sit down and try to put all the pieces together, is this very elusive and abstract thing we call "the good life?" We know it is not war – we are far removed from it. We know it is not national scandal – we are far removed from that, too. We know it is not envy, greed, or jealousy – happily most of us are spared these tiresome, tedious sins.

We do know what we have. Good land and good climate. Shopkeepers and farmers, children and households, husbands and wives, teachers and pastors. We look at times for a cloud on the horizon and at other times for a rainbow in the sky. We mark time not so much by the letters on a sheet of paper as by the wind and the rain, the snow and the heat. We are a hardy people. Land and family, faith and nature, have all combined in making us what we are, for better or for worse.

We are a close-knit people. Our families mean a great deal to us. Our community is our social, cultural and religious center. We really don't care too much about what goes on in New York or Washington or Rome. We belong to each other. We have created a happy, wholesome way of life. We do our work. We say our prayers. We love our families, friends and neighbors. When all is said and done, is there really too much more to life and living that matters?

Our joys are simple. Our needs are few. We look forward to a barn dance, a shower dance, a neighborly visit over a glass of beer at the local pub. We mark births, weddings and deaths with a celebration, seeing in each a sign of life here and hereafter. We don't easily express our feelings; we take them for granted. We know how we feel, we don't have to advertise it.

Sometimes the outer world impinges upon us. We are sometimes upset by the folly and the madness of that world that seems to lose its sense of balance. It might be Vietnam or Watergate or Papal directives on First Holy Communion. But, really, nothing disturbs us too much. We do, however, take pride in the fact that many sons and daughters of our area have answered the call of church and state throughout the years. They have served as missionaries and public officials, if these words are still in fashion, in every corner of the world – bringing, we like to think, the good news of our good life to people less fortunate.

We must admit, we are not much interested in politics. We have never produced from our area a high-ranking politician, such as Senators Hubert H. Humphrey and Walter F. Mondale. We do lay claim, however, to the fact that a Congressman was born and reared in Melrose. By the same token, however, we are very proud that our area has contributed to the service of the Church many priests and sisters.

We do have, when all things are considered, the good life. Some people may call it culture. Be that as it may. We fear, however, one fact. Our schools today are not contributing to our culture. On the contrary, they are despoiling our Christian rural culture. We do have a problem here. How can we make educators understand that there is a regional culture and how can we persuade them to preserve it? This is not our problem; this is the problem educationists have created for us. How can we educate the educationists?

Sometimes we wonder, as we look over our fields and hills, how we can preserve this for our children. We know that they really do not know the bounty that is theirs. We hope, and even pray, that some day they will. We even think, and sometimes say among our relatives and neighbors, perhaps this current shortage, these current high prices, will bring all of us – city cousins and country cousins – back to a more simple, hearty and wholesome way of life. ∾

1974

UR LADY'S JUGGLER

This rendition of a medieval legend appeared in a limited edition of 1400 copies as the Christmas book of North Central Publishing Company, St. Paul, Minnesota in 1974. I re-wrote the legend at the request of the company's president, Mr. Alfred G. Muellerleile, giving the juggler the name of "Barnaby."

Some stories are so worthwhile that they belong to every age and every generation. The medieval tale, Our Lady's Juggler, is one of these. Barnaby was a native of Peigne, a busy market town of thirteenth-century France. There he learned the juggler's art which he performed in towns and villages during the weeks of the fair. Often the country audiences would greet Barnaby's simple tricks and feats with indifference. But when, head down, balancing on his hands, he threw high into the sky six copper balls that glistened in the sunlight and then caught them with his feet, they knew he was an acrobatic genius.

In spite of the acclaim he earned, Barnaby was sick of the world. He had traveled far and wide; he owned his own horse; he had the finest clothing. And yet he was not a happy man.

He had a strong devotion to Mary and this gave him the desire to become a monk. One day while visiting the famous Cistercian Abbey of Citeaux, a monk said to him:

"Friend Barnaby, take care. There is no more beautiful vocation than the monastic profession. It is one that proclaims the glories of God, the Blessed Virgin and all the Saints. The life of a religious is an eternal canticle to the glory of God."

So Barnaby became a monk. He fulfilled his novitiate, he took his vows, he was an obedient and humble religious. But he was not happy. The others could go to chapel, sing the Pater and Ave and the Divine Office. Poor Barnaby did not know Latin. Well he knew how to leap and jump, but he did not know those strange words in so foreign a language. So he worked in the dining room and kitchen, serving as best he could.

"Dear Lady, Mother of God," he prayed one day, will you give me the grace to praise you as best I can?" Barnaby waited. He received no message. So he prayed again. "Queen of Heaven, I want so much to be your servant. Will you kindly tell me what I should do?" Again there was no answer. So Barnaby continued to wait for a word from his Lady, the Immaculate Virgin of Nazareth.

Barnaby waited – and waited. He said his prayers. He did not lose hope. He fulfilled his religious duties. But no message from his Lady. No word was spoken. No special direction was given by Father Abbot. Barnaby continued to wait and to pray.

Soon he began to worry. He was at a loss physically and mentally. He questioned his vocation. He was not sure of his spiritual progress. What could he do? What service could he render the Church? Would it be best for him to go back to the village fairs since he had nothing to give his God and Lady. Soon he received his answer.

One evening as the monks were engaged in leisurely discourse, Barnaby heard one of them tell the story of a monk who had known nothing more than to recite the Ave Maria. He had been despised for his ignorance but, upon his death, a rose had blossomed from his mouth in honor of each letter in the name of Mary, and his holiness henceforth became manifest.

Then Barnaby said, "I will go to the Immaculate Virgin." And Barnaby went to the Chapel. He was alone, with not a soul in sight. He removed his habit and undressed himself to his leotards. He stood before the Virgin's Altar and made his prayer:

"Dearest Lady, I am not a very good monk. I am not a very intelligent man. I am no more than a simple juggler, and not even very good at that. But I will give you the best I can. I pray that you will accept my humble art as a prayer for your honor and the salvation of all."

With that Barnaby began to perform his art in front of the

Virgin's altar. At first he juggled three of the copper balls, then six, then ten. In spite of his own humble admission, he was a genius at his craft. While he prayed in his own simple words, for the poor souls in purgatory, for the poor people of the world, the most Holy Father, and his brother monks of the abbey, he performed his art so strenuously that he worked himself into a sweat. Then exhausted, he fell to the floor.

"My blessed Mother," he said in a prayer of love and confidence, "there is no more that I can do for you. This is the best gift I have to offer, and this is all that I can give. Please accept it as an honor to your Divine Son." With that Barnaby clothed himself in his religious garb, and went back to join his brother monks in their evening recreation period. He sat silently, listening to their learned conversations and tried to absorb as much as he could from these wise scholars and professors.

As Barnaby sat and listened there was joy in his heart because he knew he had performed the best prayer he was able to give. He still did not understand the high-sounding phrases and the technical, theological terminology that his brother monks were speaking. But he knew he loved God and Our Lady. So much of this talk seemed little related to his own concern, but, as a good monk, he kept his silence.

Barnaby was unable to write a treatise on sacred liturgy or theology. He was never asked by Father Abbot to teach the young men who came to the monastery. He was assigned to work in the monastic garden. This he did with great pleasure in the company of several of his brother monks.

He lived according to the Holy Rule of Saint Benedict from sunrise to sunset. He lived by this Rule of work and worship and found joy in his heart as a monk of Citeaux. Barnaby took pains to be prompt when the bell called and was always most careful to practice charity with his brother monks. He never forgot the lessons he learned as a novice, and he daily crossed his knife, fork and spoon in a triangle in honor of the Holy Trinity.

Barnaby's greatest joy, however, came after evensong. Devoutly he listened as the monks of Citeaux sang Vespers. Although he could not understand the words they sang, he knew they were words in honor of God the Father, Son and Holy Spirit. So he prayed in his own heart with his own words and, perhaps, his own words were a better prayer than all the psalmody sung so piously by his brother monks.

Then when all had left the great white-washed abbey church, Barnaby offered his own prayer. At this moment of the day he was the happiest man. He stood before Our Lady's altar, made a reverential bow, took off his religious garb, and then, in his own best way offered his prayer. On some days he would juggle three spheres, other days six oranges, other days ten apples. He would exhaust himself in performing his art, but all the while he would pray:

"Dear Mother of God, I am your son. I belong to you because you are my mother. Please watch over, guide, and direct me. I will do the best I can to do the will of your Divine Son. Help me to serve you and all poor people. Help me to grow in grace."

After performing his act in honor of the Virgin he would some-times fall exhausted to the floor. Needless to say, his brother monks thought poor Barnaby was somewhat unusual. A curious monk watched him one night as he performed his prayer in front of the Virgin's altar.

Scandalized, the monk ran in haste to the Abbot's cell. "Father Abbot," he cried, "come to the chapel. Brother Barnaby is desecrating the holy place with barbarous orgies." The Abbot and the monk hur-riedly made their way to the Abbot's balcony of the chapel.

Peering down in the dimmed light they saw Barnaby in the midst of his performance. Throwing the copper balls almost to the vault of the chapel he leaped high in the air catching them before his feet touched the ground. With reckless abandon he pirouetted around the altar, flashing the copper balls aloft and catching them, first in one hand, then in the other. The flowing movements of his body, the graceful ges-tures of his arms and the lightness with which his feet touched the ground gave him an ethereal appearance.

Filled with shock, indignation and righteous rage the two left the balcony and proceeded to the nave. Cautiously peering from behind a column they saw that the niche that held the Lady statue was empty. "The idolatrous simpleton has destroyed the statue," whispered the monk. Emerging from behind the column the altar suddenly became flooded with light so brilliant that the surrounding area was as bright as midday. Barnaby was lying on the floor, his limbs outstretched. And standing beside his prostrate body was a most beautiful lady. She was

clothed in flowing robes of white. Her hair, black as ebony, was irides-
cent as if studded with a thousand diamonds. Her face shining in the
brilliant light, seemed to reflect all of man's nobler virtues – love, beauty,
hope, kindness, compassion, tenderness, goodness, truth.

The sweet and noble Queen took a white cloth, and with it she
very gently fanned her minstrel-before-the-altar. And the beautiful and
gracious Lady fanned his face and neck and body to cool him, and lovingly did she concern herself upon the care of him. And the holy angels
who remained with him paid him much honor. The noble Lady made
the Sign of the Cross over him and the Lady and the angels waited for
the hour when God would call him from this vale of tears.

Suddenly the brilliant light was gone. Darkness came upon the
chapel. The Abbot and the monk moved to where Barnaby lay and
found him dead. And leaving the chapel they set about making arrange-
ments for his burial.

Several days after the funeral the Abbot was deep in prayer
before the Virgin's altar. Looking up to the niche he gazed at the statue.
"Strange," he mused, "I do not remember a smile on the Virgin's face
when Brother Luke first carved the statue." ～

1976

N LEAVING A PARISH

After I resigned as pastor of St. Rose of Lima Church, St. Rosa, Freeport, Minnesota, I lived in San Francisco and undertook research on the Apostleship of the Sea. I missed the People of God of St. Rose of Lima Church. This article appeared in the pages of The New York Times *on May 23, 1976.*

I am sitting by my window overlooking the city by the bay. Sheer beauty! My colleagues have given me the dubious title of "writer in residence." A decade ago my colleagues then called me simply "a refugee from the tractor." *Sic transit gloria mundi.*

Six months ago I lived next door to Main Street, Sinclair Lewis' Sauk Centre, Minn. There I lived six years, a proud and happy pastor of 115 families and 761 people. We were a rural parish ("over the river and through the woods" and that bit). We were small, closely knit, lovers of farm and family. We were proud of our solid Catholic German ethnicity and the rich black soil among the rolling hills of central Minnesota.

I am doing research on a slice of Americana along the port of the Golden Gate. However, I am stuck. I left my heart not here, as Tony Bennett sings out, but in Saint Rosa, Minn.

During the six years I had been pastor there I came to know and deeply love these good people of God. I had baptized 74 children, witnessed 32 marriages, laid to rest in God's holy acre 24 members of the parish. As statistics go, minimal; as love goes, infinite.

Pastors come and go. This we take for granted. People remain, members of a community, of a city or village, of a parish. We might talk until the cows come home about changing structures in the Church. One fact remains: The parish is with us and will continue for generations yet unborn to be a fact of religious life here and hereafter. No American institution has endured throughout our national life as firmly as the parish. It is haven and home, the stamp of spiritual identity.

I have seldom heard my colleagues talk about a pastor's leave-taking of a parish, nor have I read an article or book on the subject. The people will come and pay the usual tributes, for they are "the faithful." But the life of the parish goes on without this pastor or any other pastor for that matter. Another one will always come along next Sunday.

But *this* pastor left a bit of his heart in *that* parish. He also stamped his brand on that parish, for better or worse. I suppose that is the best expression, after all. As husband and wife, so pastor and parish, take each other "for better or worse." They might not remember your name, but in years to come they will say, "We once had a pastor who...."

When all is said and done, that is the best tribute one can and should expect. It recognizes a pastor, any pastor, for what he is, or should be – a man of God. Who thinks of Junipero Serra along the freeways of California? Who thinks of John Wesley in the cotton fields of Georgia? Who recalls Jonathan Edwards on the village greens of New England? One fact remains: There once was a pastor who did his work and passed on to labor in other fields of the Lord.

How, too, does a pastor let his people know how he feels? He is expected to be a rock – solid, stolid and steady. He is not expected to let his emotions hang lightly on his sleeve. He is to be father and brother to one and all and intimate to none. He is a man set apart. St. Paul said it: He is "chosen from among men" and "appointed to act on behalf of men in relation to God."

So a pastor looks back over the years after his departure. He wonders, at times, how "chosen" he was for he is made of the same common clay. He wonders, too, how he related himself and his people to God by going to baptismal dinners, wedding receptions, wakes, graduations, anniversaries and the other hundred occasions in the course of the year.

This pastor looks back over the last six years. Did he keep and spread the faith? Did he make his people better and happier by his presence among them? Did he preside over a worship that was meaningful, relevant and grace-filled for "his" people?

Neither pastor nor people can live all day in the sanctuary. Both must be concerned about the problems of the world. Did this pastor make his people oriented, disturbed, committed to the crucial social problems of war and peace, poverty and hunger, injustice and denial of human rights? He tried, at least. Only time – and lest we forget – the grace of God will tell.

This pastor would not be honest if he did not admit that at times he was curt and impatient. (Why do people always have to call at the dinner hour?) He must also admit that he could have – should have – given better sermons if only he had the time to prepare. (Why didn't he turn off the TV?) He could have – should have – visited the hospitals, the jails, the schools more than he did. (Why didn't he skip that weekly golf game once in a while?)

Such are a few of the thoughts that give insights into the life of a pastor and his people. At night he puts out the cat, turns off the lights and climbs the stairs. He heaves a sigh, whispers a prayer and says more to himself than his Creator, "At least I tried."

Pastors are really not too important. People are. As long as there are people there will be a parish – and a pastor.

Pastors are like ships that pass in the night. Here today gone tomorrow.

The lights are going out upon the hills of San Francisco. Tomorrow is another day. ❧

1979

 MAN AHEAD OF HIS TIMES

This essay was written as an assignment while I attended the University of Alaska – Anchorage in 1979. Professor Will Jacobs, who taught a course on the Philosophy of History, was intrigued by John Emerich Edward Dalberg, Lord Acton. He urged me to write this assignment as a term paper. This is its first publication.

"What alienated him from his Victorian contemporaries...is what may endear him to the present generation, for whom salvation lies not in a choice between liberalism or conservatism, between religion or atheism, but in some reconciliation or transcendence of these irreconcilables. It was the genius, and the ultimate paradox, of Acton's mind to effect this reconciliation or transcendence by importing religious values into secular affairs and secular values into religious ones. Into politics he brought the moral fervor of the prophet, into religion the humanism of the liberal statesman; and to both he carried the message that power, whether religious or secular, was a degrading, demoralizing and corrupting force."[1]

John Emerich Edward Dalberg, Lord Acton, was born in Naples, Italy, Jan. 10, 1834, and died in Tegernsee, Bavaria, on June 19, 1902. The future baron was the son of Sir Richard Acton and Marie Louise Pellini de Dalberg. Upon his father's death in 1837 he succeeded to a baronetcy in England. His mother brought the child to his estate at Aldenham shortly after that time.

During his youth he received the finest education in Paris, St. Mary's College, Oscott, and under a private tutor, in Edinburgh. The bitterest disappointment of his youth was his rejection as a student at

Cambridge University because of his Catholic faith. Ironically, in the evening of his life (1895) he was appointed by Queen Victoria as Regius professor of modern history at Cambridge and there drew up his plans and acted as director for the *Cambridge Modern History.*

His rejection at Cambridge proved to be the turning point in his life and thought. He enrolled at the University of Munich in 1850 and there became the pupil, traveling companion and intimate friend of John Ignatius Dollinger, one of Bavaria's leading Church historians. Under his already famous mentor the young man developed a passionate love for history and critical scholarship. His title, cosmopolitan background and fluency in four languages opened the doors of the most noble statesmen, prelates and scholars on the continent.

He returned to England in 1859, determined to open the vistas of liberal intellectual thought to the provincial, conservative Catholics of his own country. He sat in Parliament as a representative of County Carlow, Ireland, from 1859 to 1865, but practical politics did not interest him. During this period he became a close friend and confidant of William Gladstone, the liberal Prime Minister of the late nineteenth century. In 1858 he became part-owner of the Catholic journal, *The Rambler* (the previous editor was John Henry Newman); the review's name was changed to *The Home and Foreign Review* in 1862. The years between 1859 and 1864 were the most prolific period of his life as a writer.

His liberal stance brought him into open conflict with the conservative Catholic hierarchy in England, whose leader was Cardinal Henry Edward Manning. His insistence that Catholic scholars should be free of all ecclesiastical restrictions to discuss religious questions, his opposition to the temporal power of the papacy and his opposition to the definition of papal infallibility caused him to be suspect by the English hierarchy and Roman officials. His frustration caused him to withdraw from public attention and retire to his library at Aldenham, making frequent journeys to Bavaria, the native country of his wife. In 1869, upon Gladstone's recommendation, he was raised to the peerage, serving as lord-in-waiting to Queen Victoria.

He was in Rome during the First Vatican Council, serving as informant to Dollinger and leader of the group called "the minority" by the "infallibilists." (In reality, the "infallibilists" were the minority, representing only about one-fifth of the fathers of the Council.) He was opposed to the definition of infallibility, but after its definition he proved his orthodoxy satisfactorily to his local bishop, even though rumors abounded at the time that he was excommunicated. To the present day scholars debate whether or not he sincerely accepted the dogma and in what manner, if he did so. The greatest shock of his life, a traumatic experience from which he never fully recovered emotionally, occurred when he heard that Dollinger had been excommunicated by the Church.

He withdrew more and more from public affairs, became vehemently opposed to the growing spirit of ultramontanism within his Church, although he held firmly till his death the principle he taught his son in 1890: "A Church without a pope is not the Church of Christ." He was a man of exceptional piety, which not even his bitterest enemies gainsaid. In the later years of his life he was estranged from his wife, for reasons unknown; she lived in Bavaria and he in England. Perhaps more than anything else, his piety spared him from censures that many of his enemies in Rome and among the English hierarchy would have liked to impose upon him. Herbert Cardinal Vaughan, Archbishop of Westminster, tried in later years to offer Acton signs of reconciliation on the part of the Church. The latter accepted these tokens piously and gratefully.[2]

In April, 1901, Lord Acton suffered a paralytic stroke and shortly thereafter retired to Tegernsee, Bavaria. The following year, on June 19, he died. He died peacefully, firm in the conviction that he expressed many years previously in a letter to Gladstone: "All I write and all I think, and all I hope is based on the Divinity of Our Lord – the one central hope of our poor wayward race."[3+]

Owen Chadwick, in the Creighton Lecture of 1975 entitled "Acton and Gladstone," made this observation: "The mystery that hung about Acton should rather be sought in his sense of isolation from his fellow men; the Englishman who because of European life and background never felt quite at home in England; the member of a Bavarian family who, after the death of the little daughter Lily in October 1881, never felt at home in Bavaria; the international and aristocrat whose roots were dissipated so widely that he had no roots, and spent years living in a villa at Cannes; the Catholic who felt out of step with the

Catholicism of his age; the born scholar who knew too much to write; the nearly bankrupt baron who must keep appearance and act milord to the world; the Liberal politician at home only with the one Liberal leader who started as no Liberal – the solitariness of Acton's personality is enough to account for the sense of mystery which he imparted."[4]

HISTORY OF LIBERTY

In the mid-1870's Lord Acton removed himself from ecclesiastical controversies, devoting his time chiefly to work on what he envisaged to be his *opus magnum*. He had traveled extensively, spent countless hours of research in the leading archives of Europe, made voluminous notes and continued to purchase books which he thoroughly annotated in pursuit of this goal. His work was intended to be entitled the *History of Liberty*. As early as 1880, however, he confided to Mary Gladstone that he felt he would never fulfill this ambition and fifteen years later in his inaugural lecture at Cambridge he intimated the same to his students.[5] The *History of Liberty* is, as some historians have pointed out, the greatest book that was never written.

During this time he was an optimistic historian, believing that "the history of mankind could be understood as a tortuous yet persistent advance towards liberty."[6] In his *Lectures on the French Revolution*, Acton expressed the same optimism with regard to the continually expanding archival deposits: "In a few years all these publications will be completed and all will be known that ever can be known... In that golden age our historians will be sincere, and our history certain. The worst will be known, and then sentence need not be deferred."[7]

Scholars have offered various explanations why Acton did not complete his great work, even though as early as 1877 he outlined the direction he intended to take. He imposed upon himself such rigid demands in following the proper historical method that he was unable to fulfill them. The more he searched for documentary evidence the more he realized the many gaps in completing a thorough examination of liberty. Finally, age brought a wisdom that youth does not enjoy and the sage of Aldenham gradually realized that the inherent viciousness of man prevented his arrival at the golden age of liberty. McNeill also suggests that

Acton was caught in the conflict between what he felt *should* be morally right and what actually was the fact. This in later years filled him with a degree of frustration and pessimism.[8]

Lord Acton, however, did use a broad brush and painted the perimeters of what his *History of Liberty* might have become. This is found in two lectures, one entitled "The History of Freedom in Antiquity," delivered on February 26, 1877, and the other entitled "The History of Freedom in Christianity," delivered on May 28, the same year. In the first Acton expressed his own reservations concerning the attainment of perfect freedom: "No obstacle has been so constant, or so difficult to overcome," he wrote, "as uncertainty and confusion touching the nature of true liberty."[9] He offered several examples from the history of modern states to support this thesis. Then he hastened to define his term, a definition that he adhered to in these writings on the subject. It is an all-embracing definition he wrote:

"By liberty I mean the assurance that every man shall be protected in doing what he believes his duty against the influence of authority and majorities, custom and opinion. The State is competent to assign duties and draw the line between good and evil only in its immediate sphere. Beyond the limits of things necessary for its well-being, it can only give indirect help to fight the battle of life by promoting the influences which prevail against temptation – religion, education, and the distribution of wealth."[10]

He proceeded through a survey of Hebrew and other Eastern nations and the Teutonic tribes to show how despotism reigned in the person of rulers who claimed a mandate from God or the gods. He claimed Athens as the nursery of liberty, pointing out, "It was a momentous step in the progress of nations when the principle that every interest should have the right and means of asserting itself was adopted by the Athenian Constitution."[11] He briefly surveyed the history of Rome from the Republic to the despotic Diocletian and concluded: "The ancients understood the regulation of power better than the regulation of liberty. They concentrated so many prerogatives in the State as to leave no footing from which a man could deny its jurisdiction or assign bounds to its activity."[12]

Even Socrates, Plato and Aristotle were more concerned with intelligent government than with liberty, fearing the effects of a misguided insistence upon liberty. They opted for a strong administration which would concentrate on making men happy and prosperous – but not free. Acton reiterated his thesis in another manner at this point: "A generous spirit prefers that his country should be poor, and weak, and of no account, but free, rather than powerful, prosperous, and enslaved."[13] After this survey of antiquity Acton concluded that three ingredients were lacking, namely, representative government, the emancipation of slaves, and liberty of conscience. On these counts he faults the nations of antiquity in not measuring up to the definition he had earlier given liberty.

His summation of this lecture served as a suitable introduction to the one he gave three months later: "The liberties of the ancient nations were crushed beneath a hopeless and inevitable despotism, and their vitality was spent when the new power came forth from Galilee, giving what was wanting to efficacy of human knowledge to redeem societies as well as men."[14]

Lord Acton's companion lecture, "The History of Freedom in Christianity," was delivered before the same group, members of the Bridgnorth Institution in the Agricultural Hall, London. The attainment of liberty was a pot of gold at the end of a long, shifting and most often elusive rainbow. In Acton's view, the first centuries of the Christian era extending from Constantine to Justinian were, in spite of all the wisdom acquired in man's journey before the time of Christ, no more than the Empire making "the Church serve as a gilded crutch of absolutism."[15] The first stirrings of liberty were not in the conquered states of the East nor the dying Roman Empire but in the migration of nations: "to the institutions of these barbarians, not yet crushed by despotism, the future of the world belong." He continued:

"This primitive Republicanism, which admits monarchy as an occasional incident, but holds fast to the collective supremacy of all free men, of the constituent authority over any constitutional authorities, is the remote germ of Parliamentary government."[16]

A major portion of this essay was devoted to his defense of that position. He demonstrated how this torch of liberty was kept burning, be it at times dimly, through the constitutional assembly in Visigothic Spain, in the representative governing body (be it ever so limited) of the Holy Roman Empire and in the writings of those representatives of the Guelphs

(Church) as opposed to representatives of the Ghibellines (State). Liberty was alive in those areas of Europe almost in direct proportion to where the "barbarian" immigrants held strongest sway (Spain, Saxony, northern Germany, England). For Acton, feudalism (especially in France) was a step backward and while acknowledging the necessity of a strong papacy in order to be a unifying power in an emerging Europe, he regretted that the Vicar of Christ was in fact a despot. The Magna Carta was a major victory for liberty, "...it was in conformity with the public law to which all monarchs were held subject, that King John was declared a rebel against the barons, and that the men who raised Edward III to the throne from which they deposed his father invoked the maxim *Vox populi Vox Dei*."[17]

Remarkably, about this same time Thomas Aquinas was teaching a doctrine of liberty at the University of Paris which Acton approvingly quoted: "A king who is unfaithful to his duty forfeits his claim to obedience. It is not rebellion to depose him, for he is himself a rebel whom the nation has a right to put down. But it is better to abridge his power, that he may be unable to abuse it. For this purpose, the whole nation ought to have a share in governing itself; the Constitution ought to combine a limited and elective monarchy, with an aristocracy of merit, and such an admixture of democracy as shall admit all classes to office, by popular election. No government has a right to levy taxes beyond the limit determined by the people. All political authority is derived from popular representatives. There is no security for us as long as we depend on the will of another man."[18]

There were, however, other impediments blocking liberty during the emergence from the medieval to the modern age, which Acton places at the beginning of the sixteenth century, citing as examples such men as Columbus, Copernicus and Luther. He viewed with abhorrence the disastrous effects of Machiavelli's teaching of monarchical absolutism; he lamented the fact that the clergy, so often on the side of liberty in the feudal period, were now mostly identified with the interests of absolute monarchy. He saw little effect of the Reformation on behalf of liberty, for he said: "The direct political influence of the Reformation effected less than has been supposed. Most States were strong enough to control it."[19] If anything, despotism of the ruler was strengthened by the formation of the church which for all practical purposes became a department of the state. He viewed the France of Louis XIV as the epitome of tyranny: "...the admiration with which he inspired the most illustrious men of his time denotes the lowest depth to which the turpitude of absolutism has ever degraded the conscience of Europe."[20]

Surprisingly, he found the splinter groups of Protestantism as the strongest haven of liberty by their insistence on being free from the control of the state. This movement began about the beginning of the seventeenth century. "Many years before the names of Milton and Taylor, of Baxter and Locke were made illustrious by their partial condemnation of intolerance, there were men among the Independent congregations who grasped with vigour and sincerity the principle that it is only by abridging the authority of States that the liberty of Churches can be assured."[21]

Lord Acton's concluding words not only gave expression to the optimism he possessed at this time but also lyrically supported his theory of the tortuous, upward advancement of mankind in its quest for liberty. He said:

"But I have fixed my eyes on the spaces that Heaven's light illuminates, that I may not lay too heavy a strain on the indulgence with which you have accompanied me over the dreary and heart-breaking course by which men have passed to freedom; and because the light that has guided us is still unquenched, and the causes that have carried us so far in the van of free nations have not spent their power; because the story of the future is written in the past, and that which hath been is the same thing that shall be."[22]

RELIGION PURE AND UNDEFILED

In the lectures we have discussed in the preceding pages we can see Lord Acton as a man of patience and compassion, as much an apologist for the Catholic Church as for liberty, as a man with the deep spiritual conviction that Divine Providence guides humankind along the "tortuous" (one of his favorite words) path to liberty, confident that God and his goodness will triumph over the tyranny and despotism of fallen man.

From another essay we gain further insight into Acton's thoughts and feelings. He remains a deeply religious man, but is hurt and angry by the despotism and arrogance he sees in his own Church, chiefly because intellectually he cannot reconcile his theology of the Church with the flagrant tyranny he finds among the contemporary leadership of the Church. He is not the apologist as he was in the above lectures; he is now the propagandist, using his pen to refute the grandiose claims (plots and schemes, as he will discover six years later during his stay in Rome at the time of the First Vatican Council) of the "infallibilists."

His essay appeared under the title "Ultramontanism" in the July, 1863, issue of the *Home and Foreign Review*. In it he reveals the profound influence that Dollinger had upon his pupil as well as the genuine conviction he held throughout his life that Germany represented "the pure spirit of scholarship and truth."[23]

In the first paragraph of this lengthy essay (approximately 19,000 words) Acton expressed an ecclesiology excelled in the English-speaking world of that time only by that of John Henry Newman. He wrote:

"The Church must teach all nations; but she has no special promise that any one will listen to her. She must watch over those within her fold, but she knows not whether her vigilance will avail. No divine protection insures her against losses by persecution, dogged unbelief, neglect of her law, or apostasy from her creed; and there is no assurance that the means of grace which she dispenses will effect by degrees the moral improvement of our race, or that sanctity will gain in intensity or in extent as time goes on. There may be diminution in the area of Christendom, and decline in the virtue of Christians. But there must be some exception to the possibility of retrogression, or Christianity would be inferior to Judaism; nay, if stagnation could paralyze every function of the Church of Christ, His works would be less perfect than the works of men."[24] It is difficult to determine if his opponents in England and Rome feared him more for his piety or his learning!

Acton then proceeded to describe Ultramontanism as "a designation to indicate the esoteric spirit of Catholicism, the real essence of the system [Protestants] oppose."[25] He compared Ultramontanism with Gallicanism, noting that both claimed to profess liberty, while they were two sides of the same coin: "One system was the instrument by which absolute monarchs extended their power over the Church, whilst by the other the same principle of absolutism was introduced into the Church herself. Both were expedients by which ecclesiastical liberty was curtailed, and authority made superior to law."[26]

Acton traced the origins and tenets from the lofty philosophy of Comte de Maistre, the romanticism of Chateaubriand, the liturgical pietism of Guéranger – all who exalted the supremacy of Church over State, the absolute authority of the Roman Pontiff in matters temporal and spiritual and the rejection of the scientific method and higher criticism in any matters pertaining to faith and doctrine. Popular ultramontanist writers of the time descended to the level of imputing base motives to their opponents, ridiculing science as the enemy of faith and when they were unable to gloss over any truth that detracted from Roman absolutism, they simply denied it.

This was too much for Acton. He answered the ultramontanists by documented historical facts, pointing out that "their labour would be in vain if it could be shown that the pontifical power had manifested itself in various degrees at various times, or that there had been serious vicissitudes in its spirit."[27] He was particularly distressed by the implicit, underlying fallacy in their literature, namely, the denial of any truth or fact that in the least way impinged upon the absolute prerogatives of the papacy. To Acton this was a denial of the unity of truth and he saw behind it the shadow of William of Ockham. He offered a word of advice:

"There are two things which it specifically behooves every Catholic engaged in controversy to observe in his treatment of adversaries: that the discussion ought to be a means of converting them from error, instead of repelling them from truth by the fault of its defenders; and that no bitterness or personality should scandalize them by occasions of sin. The course enjoined by the Church is to win over opponents by considerate, gentle, generous and affectionate treatment, joined to the most uncompromising and relentless exposure of their errors."[28]

Then Acton dealt a crushing blow when accepting as his own conviction these words of no less a personage than Pope St. Gregory the Great: "It is the devil who takes away from certain persons the desire of mastering secular sciences, because he knows how much they serve us in religious questions."[29]

In opposition to the ultramontanists, Acton held up those scholars of northern Europe who sought to employ the scientific method and higher criticism to ecclesiastical disciplines. "The strength of this school was necessarily confined to Germany," he wrote, "where its most eminent representatives were the divines Mohler, Dollinger, and Kuhn, the metaphysicians Baader and Molitor, the political writers Gorres and Rasdowitz, and historians such as Movers and Gfrorer."[30] Acton cites Gugler of Lucerne as the originator of the group of scholars opposed to ultramontanism. He quotes these words of Mohler as the spirit guiding the northern European opposition: "It is obvious that the student of history must not pervert facts; and one may suppose that Christianity expressly prohibits falsehood. From the Christian point of view most of all, therefore, we are forbidden to be partial, to alter facts, to omit one thing, to be silent on another, or to add anything which we have not found."[31]

The primary purpose of Acton's essay was not unfolded until the closing pages. His readers knew well the author's firm opposition to any doctrine of infallibility. The entire essay was a preparation and a defense of the firm conviction held by the author. Acton left no room for even the slightest shadow of a doubt. He wrote:

"It is necessary to notice briefly an opinion held by some who are either ignorant of the Catholic system or especially hostile to it, that an arbitrary authority exists in the Church which may deny what has hitherto been believed, and may suddenly impose upon the faithful, against their will, doctrines which, while there is no warrant for them in the past, may be in contradiction with the existing and received conclusions of ecclesiastical, or even profane, science."[32]

THE DEVELOPMENT OF DOCTRINE

We previously mentioned the theological acumen of Lord Acton. Given the temper of the time he manifested his own intellectual daring in mentioning at the very beginning of the essay the development of doctrine. He was a most courageous man. The theory was untenable and heretical among ultramontanist theologians and philosophers. In their mind it smacked of Darwinism, which they conceived as a threat to biblical exegesis. John Henry Newman's work, *An Essay on the Development of Christian Doctrine*, published in 1845, had already placed the future cardinal under a cloud, where he remained in Roman circles until after the election of Pope Leo XIII to the papal throne in 1878.

The theory of the development of doctrine was not new to Acton. He had learned it in his youth from such men as Drey, Mohler and Dollinger at the University of Munich. It seems that Newman arrived at the theory and wrote his essay without knowing that the same teaching was being propounded among the Bavarian theologians. Acton explained his concept of the development of doctrine in these words:

"For the full exposition of truth is the great object for which the existence of mankind is prolonged on earth. It may be that individual goodness is not greater, or the proportion of the saved larger, than in earlier times; but Almighty God is more fully known, the articles of faith are multiplied, and the certainty of knowledge is increased. This growth in knowledge is not by new revelations or by a continuance of inspiration, but it is a conquest of the Christian mind in its conflict with the phases of untruth. It is earned by exertion; it is not simply given by faith itself. The development of doctrine is essential to the preservation of its purity; hence its preservation implies its development; and the intellectual act which accompanies belief is the agent of the progress of the Church in religious knowledge. In the course of this process she lays under contribution all human learning, which she exacts and sanctifies by using it. As she does not possess at once the fullness of all knowledge, and as her authority leaves many things uncertain, she must rely on other resources for that which is not hers by inheritance, and her demand must necessarily promote the supply of that on which she so much depends."[33]

In the final pages of the essay Acton returned to the theme of the development of doctrine, making a practical application of its implications:

"The Church must always put herself in harmony with existing ideas, and speak to each age and nation in its own language. A kind of amalgam between the eternal faith and temporal opinion is thus in constant process of generation, and by it Christians explain to themselves the bearings of their religion, so far as their knowledge allows.... From time to time a very extensive revision is required, hateful to conservative habits and feelings; a crisis occurs, and a new alliance has to be formed between religion and knowledge, between the Church and society. Every

victory thus gained, though in its personal aspect it is a victory of inno-
vators over those who seem to stand in the old paths, and to defend the
interest of the unchangeable, is in reality a victory of truth over error, of
science over opinion."[34]

John Courtney Murray, the most prominent theologian the
Catholic Church in the United States has produced, declared that the
theory of the development of doctrine was perhaps the most singular
theological concept produced in the English-speaking world of the nineteenth century. Newman and Acton were give short shrift at the First
Vatican Council. Ninety-three years later followed the Second Vatican
Council; this was, many said, Newman's and Acton's council.

The fathers of the Second Vatican Council were electrified on
the morning of October 22, 1964, when Lawrence Cardinal Shehan of
Baltimore rose to speak. He said: "More than one hundred years ago,
John Henry Newman, who afterwards was named a cardinal of the holy
Roman Church, wrote a great work, the *Essay on the Development of
Christian Doctrine*, in which is found the sentence, repeated in various
ways: 'A power of development is a proof of life.' This same truth, which
is of great importance for our *schema*, is sketched, I believe, in various
places and in diverse ways, if not openly expressed, in the encyclical
Ecclesiam Suam of Pope Paul VI...where it states: 'The Church...advances
more and more in the awareness of its duty, of the nature of its mysteries, of its doctrines....'"[35]

FELLOW STUDENTS

The three pieces of Lord Acton's writing that we have briefly
examined are no more than a poor widow's mite compared to the
overflowing treasury of his published works. Taken together, these three
do represent, I believe, the core of Acton's principal preoccupation in his
life and thought.[36] In these, as in all his published works, he was pre-
eminently the church historian. This discipline he employed to a
remarkable degree in his writings and researches, enabling him to examine the most diverse and differing issues of his own time within the
framework of historical scholarship. He developed this ability in
Munich, refined it during his controversial years in England as editor of

The Rambler, exercised it in Rome during the First Vatican Council and, as Regius professor of history at Cambridge University, he was able to pass it on to his students in the twilight of his life. McNeill pointed out the even broader and long-term influence of the scholar of Aldenham when he wrote:

"Acton's influence, nevertheless, was far greater than might be expected. More than any other single man, he transplanted German thoroughness and historical method across the Channel. As a result, in the English universities writing history from anything but primary sources became unprofessional after Acton's time, as it had been in German academic circles from Ranke's days. In addition, so far as I can discover, Lord Acton was the first Englishman to view British, American, and Continental European history as a common whole, and to imprint upon this synthesis what Herbert Butterfield has aptly termed the Whig interpretation of history, that is, the notion that all mankind has been toiling onward and upward through time toward the pinnacles of English (and/or American) constitutional liberty."[37]

In our time, as every educator knows, the study of ecclesiastical history has fallen upon bad times in the curricula offered by our Catholic seminaries, universities and high schools. No one in recent years has deplored this neglect and warned of its dire consequences in the areas of Catholic scholarship and action more than the eminent dean of American Catholic church historians, Monsignor John Tracy Ellis. The preceding pages have been an exercise in sketching how Acton employed history in commenting on current events. By way of conclusion it is well to consider briefly Acton's own understanding of history and its use as he discussed it in his *Inaugural Lecture on the Study of History*. His address was given in June, 1895, shortly after his appointment as Regius professor of modern history. With appropriate modesty, Acton saluted his audience with the words, "Fellow Students."

Several facets of this lecture cast Acton in an altogether different role. He is now the university don addressing his remarks to youthful minds. He is in academe for the first time in his life and thus employs the literary style and language of his surroundings. He is not the polemicist, not the theologian, not even *per se* the historian. The lecture is more in the manner of an admonition of a father (he was then sixty-one years old) to his sons. The writing of history is not what matters in this lecture; rather, the love and pursuit of truth, instilled in his students, is its principal concern. He is not another Ranke in the sense that the latter was the "father of the seminar," for that was not Acton's gift. He was, however, similar to Ranke and Ferdinand Braudel, who came after him, in being a diligent devotee of the footnote. It is of more than passing interest to note that in the essay on "Ultramontanism" (an essay that was at least three times the length of this one) he employed only fifty-one footnotes, and in the two lectures on the "History of Freedom" he used not a single footnote. In this lecture he made 105 citations. Footnote 35 consisted of 136 lines and over 1,600 words; footnote 43 of 82 lines and over 1,000 words; footnote 74 of 84 lines and over 1,200 words. Perhaps Acton was trying to teach his pupils something by the proliferation of "fly specks" on the bottom of the page! The length of the footnotes far exceeded the length of the text.

In recent years someone remarked, "He would fit in well at the University of Chicago!"

Lord Acton took the occasion to express his fundamental attitude toward history when he stated: "We can found no philosophy on the observation of four hundred years, excluding three thousand. It would be an imperfect and a fallacious induction. But I hope that even this narrow and disedifying section of history will aid you to see that the action of Christ who is risen on mankind whom he redeemed fails not, but increases; that the wisdom of divine rule appears not in the perfection but in the improvement of the world; and that achieved liberty is the one ethical result that rests on the converging and combined conditions of advancing civilization."[38]

He filled his students with hope when he said, "...in the second quarter of this century, a new era began for historians."[38] This era he elaborated upon, citing three advances in the science of history, namely, the opening of more and more archives, the advancement of a truly critical spirit, and the increasing practice of impartiality, or objectivity. "The main thing to learn," he said, "is not the art of accumulating material, but the sublimer art of investigating it, of discerning truth from falsehood and certainty from doubt." He further indicated the advances made in related sciences of law, economics, philosophy, and religion, returning to his favorite theme: "Towards 1820 divines began to recast their doctrines on the lines of development, of which Newman said, long after, that evolution had come to confirm it."

For the most part, however, the lecture was more in the nature of a homily than an essay. He set before them several maxims to follow in their research and writings:

"No political dogma is as serviceable to my purpose here as the *true historian's maxim* to do the best he can for the other side, and to avoid pertinacity, or emphasis on his own."[39]

"...there is virtue in the saying that a historian is seen at his best when he does not appear."[40]

"Whatever a man's notions of these later centuries are, such, in the main, the man himself will be. Under the name of History, they cover the articles of his philosophic, his religious, and his political creed. They give him his measure; they denote his character; and, as praise is the shipwreck of historians, his preferences betray him more than his aversions."[41]

He Is of This Age

Lord Acton's place in history was, perhaps, best described by Dr. G.P. Gooch, one of his younger colleagues at Trinity College, Cambridge, who wrote: "It was Acton's lifelong opposition to totalitarianism in every form which accounts for the spectacular revival of interest in the man and his writings in the middle decades of the twentieth century. Fifty years after his death the lonely scholar has come into his own."[42]

Robert Schuettinger, in his study of Lord Acton's works, offered this admonition:

"The remaining years of the twentieth century will be more bearable if more people put into practice some of the truths Acton tried to teach: that there is more to humankind than material nature; that every person is important; that every person's conscience must be respected; that the state was made for people, not people for the state; that the test of a free society is the treatment of its minorities; that duties are as important as rights and that liberty is necessary so that people may fulfill their duties; that ordered liberty is the most delicate fruit of a high civilization; that all persons need an area they can call their own so they can make the fullest use of their talents; and that since all power tends to corrupt, the best way to prevent its misuse is to 'cut it up into little bits.'"[43]

Miss Himmelfarb, Lord Acton's most sensitive biographer, deserves the last word: "He is of this age more than of his." ✂

REFERENCES

1. Himmelfarb, Gertrude, ed., *Essays on Freedom and Power*, World Publishing Co., Cleveland, 1964, p. 23.
2. Schuettinger, Robert L., *Lord Acton: Historian of Liberty*, Open Court, LaSalle, Ill., 1976, pp. 180-81.
3. This biographical sketch is based chiefly on the article by H.A. MacDougall, "John Emerich Edward Dalberg Acton," *Catholic Encyclopedia*, vol. 1, McGraw-Hill Book Co., New York, 1966, pp. 101-02.
4. Chadwick, Owen, *Acton and Gladstone*, The Athlone Press, London, 1976, pp. 49-50.
5. Himmelfarb, p. 17.
6. Dalberg, John Emerich Edward, Lord Acton, *Essays in the Liberal Interpretation of History*, ed. by William H. McNeill, University of Chicago Press, Chicago, 1967, p. xii. Most of the quotations from Lord Acton's writings will be taken from this work. It will be referred to hereafter simply as McNeill.
7. McNeill, p. xiii.
8. McNeill, p. xv.
9. McNeill, p. 243-44.
10. McNeill, p. 245.
11. McNeill, p. 252.
12. McNeill, p. 257.
13. McNeill, p. 264.
14. McNeill, p. 268.
15. McNeill, p. 272.
16. McNeill, p. 273.

17. McNeill, p. 276.
18. McNeill, p. 277.
19. McNeill, p. 288.
20. McNeill, p. 292.
21. McNeill, p. 299.
22. McNeill, p. 160.
23. McNeill, p. 163.
24. McNeill, p. 166.
25. McNeill, p. 171.
26. McNeill, p. 188.
27. McNeill, p. 197.
28. McNeill, p. 210.
29. McNeill, p. 206.
30. Himmelfarb, p. 23.
31. McNeill, p. 161-62.
32. McNeill, p. 211.
33. Schuettinger, p. 145.
34. Schuettinger, p. 237-39.
35. Yzermans, Vincent A., *American Participation in the Second Vatican Council*, Sheed & Ward, New York, 1967, p. 197.
36. The best bibliography of the works of Lord Acton I have found is in Schuettinger, *op. cit.*, pp. 201-35; the best bibliography of books and articles about Lord Acton that I have seen appears in the same work, pp. 191-200.
37. McNeill, p. xviii.
38. McNeill, p. 320-21.
39. McNeill, p. 329.
40. McNeill, p. 330.
41. McNeill, p. 343.
42. McNeill, p. 320.
43. Gooch, G.P., *Under Six Reigns*, Longmans, Green & Co., London, 1958, p. 187.
44. Schuettinger, p. 187-88.

1979

 LASKA'S FIRST PASTOR

The author wrote a brief history of the beginnings of the Catholic Church in Alaska in 1979, entitled St. Rose of Wrangell. *At that time the editorial decision was made to omit this biographical sketch from that work for reasons of space. This is the first time this biographical sketch appears in print.*

John Althoff and his companion, Louis Eussen, stood on the dock at Victoria, Vancouver Island, on a crisp, chilly November 25, 1878. Both had been fellow-students at the American College of the Catholic University of Louvain, Belgium; both had been ordained to the priesthood only a few months previously; both had volunteered to labor in the Catholic missions of the Pacific Northwest. They had been encouraged by the rector of the college, Monsignor John deNeve, to become priests of the four-year-old Diocese of Victoria and serve under a fellow alumnus of the college, Bishop Charles John Seghers.

A coach met them at the dock and immediately drove them to the bishop's residence. There Althoff, the son of a wealthy merchant family in Haarlem, The Netherlands, met a short, sturdy man with deep-set blue eyes who appeared to be even younger than his thirty-nine years. Althoff removed his kid gloves and, taking the man to be a servant, asked him to carry his baggage into the bishop's house. A few moments later, to his embarrassment and consternation, the twenty-four year old priest discovered that the "servant" was Charles Seghers, the second Bishop of Vancouver Island.[1]

In such a way both newly-ordained priests were welcomed to the Diocese of Victoria, an area comprising all of present-day British

Columbia, Yukon Territory and Alaska. The young priests from the small countries of Belgium and Holland could not possibly comprehend the vastness and immensity of this missionary diocese, at that time, *the* largest territorial diocese in the Catholic world.

For the next five months Althoff remained at the bishop's house, studying Russian and various Indian dialects. Seghers, who made his first missionary journey to Alaska in 1877, was resolved to establish the Catholic Church in "the great land," for such is the meaning of the native word, "Alaska." Even though he had already been appointed Coadjutor-Archbishop of Oregon City, he would not depart until that goal was accomplished. For five months Seghers took measure of this man and decided that Althoff would be the first permanent Catholic priest in Alaska.

On one of the closing days in April, 1879, Seghers and Althoff were boarding the sailing ship, "Olympia." Their destination was Fort Wrangell and Sitka, the most populous centers in the recently purchased territory of the United States which many called "Seward's folly." Strangely, neither was an American: one a Canadian by adoption and the other a Hollander. The ship stopped at ports of call along the way and Seghers bade farewell to the Catholic communities in these places. At the same time he introduced the newly-ordained priest who would in time serve many of these people.

Wrangell on the Stikine River

Several reasons prompted Seghers' choice of Wrangell as the beachhead of Catholicism in Alaska. Although Sitka was the territorial capital and former capital of the Russian colony, its citizens and the Indians in the neighboring villages were a lawless, riotous refuse of humanity and what little religion remained still bore the stamp of Russian Orthodoxy. Sitka would be named a mission parish, dependent on Wrangell, the mother parish of Alaska. The native people in the Wrangell area had not as yet received the good news of Christianity to any considerable extent and thus afforded a more fertile field for evangelization.[2]

Apart from the two citizens whom Seghers already knew – Alexander "Buck" Choquette and James King Lear – there were an unknown number of Latin Americans in the area who were at least nominally Catholic. These *Latinos* had been imported earlier to work in the neighboring gold mines. The Presbyterian Church was already present in Wrangell in the person of Mrs. Amanda MacFarland and the Reverend S. Hall Young. That Church was established in Alaska two months after the Catholic parish of St. Rose of Lima was organized.[3] Ecumenical cooperation was non-existent; religious rivalry was, unfortunately, a sign of Christian conviction.

Seghers and Altoff entered the lovely Wrangell harbor and disembarked on May 2, 1879. Choquette had left instructions that the two clerics be warmly welcomed. No doubt one of the members of the welcoming committee was Lear, for his dance hall (the old barracks he purchased from the United States Army which had departed from the area in 1877) was the site of the first Mass on the following morning. The archbishop offered Mass in the presence of a handful of whites and 120 Indians. Seghers' motive for choosing Wrangell was prompted by the insistence of the Irish miners who worked in the fields. They would be the backbone of the first parish in Alaska.

On this occasion, the archbishop announced that Father Althoff would be their pastor and the parish was to be named in honor of St. Rose of Lima. He expressed his confidence "that this great and holy virgin, the first saint of America, would take this new mission under her special care and protection."[4] The prelate was not unaware of the number of Latin Americans present at the Mass; nor was he ignorant of the fact that one of the first three Spanish-speaking priests in Alaskan waters a century before, Cristobal Diaz, was a native of Lima, Peru.

That same day Seghers presented Althoff with a parish record book in which he inscribed in his own hand the proceedings of that historic day. For the next 17 years Althoff duly recorded the vital statistics of the parish and its environs in the same book, which is still used at the present time for the same purpose.

Five days later the two missionaries disembarked from the "California" at Sitka, the farthest outpost of American disorder and lawlessness. On May 9, the feast of St. Gregory Nazianzen, the archbishop again gathered about the altar the small community of whites and Indians and established the mission parish named in honor of St.

Gregory, one of the three Cappadocian Fathers of the Church. It was appropriate, indeed, that the second Catholic parish in Alaska, located in the former seat of Russian territorial government, should be named in honor of a saint revered by both Roman and Orthodox Christians.

Seghers announced that Althoff would visit the settlement regularly from Wrangell as well as make visits to many villages as far away as Haines, many miles distant. Thus the archbishop fulfilled his dream and returned to Victoria for his farewell sermon and blessing on June 29. He immediately departed for Oregon City where he was installed as coadjutor archbishop two days later. He left behind at Sitka the young priest who would serve in Alaska for the next five years as "Rome's solitary sentinel."⁵ One pauses to marvel at the daring of Seghers and the courage of Althoff, wondering which of the two manifested the greater folly of the Cross.

Seldom in the history of the Church has one man been given so monumental a challenge and, seldom again, had any single individual accomplished so much with so little as Althoff did in the following 17 years. He had no vast organization behind him, such as the Benedictine monks in the Middle Ages or the Jesuits who came after his time to Alaska. He had only an "obedience" from his superior who at that very moment was paradoxically no longer his religious superior. He was utterly alone, dependent solely on Providence and the generosity of his wealthy family in Holland.

From Wrangell he spread the fire of faith in countless Indian villages and settlements along the coast and on the islands of southeastern Alaska. He visited these villages – now more populous and prosperous – for a day or two, traveling along the Inside Passage before there was any such thing as a marine highway and regularly scheduled ships. Among his stations were Sitka, Kasan, Telegraph Creek, Juneau, Douglas, Yakutat, Haines, Craig, and Petersburg, all duly noted in his parish record-book. During these years he returned from time to time to Victoria to seek spiritual solace and material supplies. For a time it seemed during these early years that his parish was wherever he laid his head rather than the crude log cabin that his "loyal Irish Catholics" built for him along the shore of Wrangell harbor.

On May 15, after Seghers had departed, Altoff returned to Wrangell and there composed a letter to the *Northwest Catholic Sentinel* of Victoria recounting the events of the previous two weeks. The letter is the first document of the Catholic Church in Alaska and reveals the keen perception of the young cleric. Therein he mentioned that Seghers had accepted a donation of a parcel of land and the Catholic men of Wrangell agreed to build a church and priest's residence on the site of the present parish buildings. (Clear title to this land continued to be a legal contest for the following 17 years because of the difficulty of possessing land in the Territory of Alaska.)

Althoff's hopes were high at this time, only to be tempered in the following months and years by many disappointments. He wrote: "Military power having failed to tame the children of the Forest, let the Catholic Church show that she can subdue their hearts." He noted the generosity of the Irish among his little flock: "When there is a question of taking an *active* part in the foundation of a mission then the Irish Catholic steps forward, volunteers, promises his mite and shows himself here as everywhere the pioneer of Catholicity." He also paid tribute to the Stikine Indians whose chiefs, Hootchenoo, Takoo, Sundum and others promised to embrace Catholicism: "The Stickeen Indians in general dress well, and appear rather clean. Their houses are substantial, good buildings; the most remarkable feature is that they blacken their faces and would surely frighten a stranger."[6]

Althoff made Wrangell his base of operations for three years. According to reports, he was immensely popular and well- liked by most whites and natives throughout southeastern Alaska. He was generous to a fault, begging from his wealthy family and friends in Holland money and supplies to be used in his apostolic work. He was extremely careful – fussy, one might say – about the vestments and sacred vessels he used in religious ceremonies. He himself was willing to sleep on the floor of a shed, which he did frequently, but nothing was too good or expensive for the worship of God. He did, however, indulge in one personal pleasure. Each shipment that arrived from Holland carried several boxes of fine smoking tobacco for one of his many pipes. His popularity was attested in an anecdote recorded by Sister Margaret Cantell:

"On New Year's Day, 1880, five visitors called on him so that, on the holiday, he would not be lonely. The visitors came one after the other. Each was dressed up in an appropriate way for the holiday. But after a while, Father noticed that each man was dressed the same. The camp had contributed the best of what each man had. Each visitor to Father had dressed in the same fashionable clothes and come to call in succession all through the afternoon of that New Year's Day!"[7]

However, Altoff was not without a rival during these early years in Wrangell. Religious bigotry frequently and regrettably appeared during these years of sectarian rivalry. One individual in particular, Mrs. Amanda MacFarland, director of the Presbyterian School for Girls, watched him like a hawk. Shortly after his arrival MacFarland wrote her superior, the Reverend Sheldon Jackson, "The Catholics are invading our territory. Among the passengers on the 'Olympia' was a Romanish bishop and priest. They at once established a mission."[8] In her subsequent reports to Jackson she dutifully recorded Althoff's activities and did not disguise her glee in what she considered his failure in attracting new adherents to the Catholic fold. On one occasion she jubilantly reported, although incorrectly, that Althoff had abandoned the mission and returned to Nanaimo, Victoria Island.

On the other hand, relations between Althoff and the Rev. S. Hall Young, the Presbyterian minister who arrived in Wrangell less than a year before Althoff, were cordial. Young invited the bishop and priest to his home for dinner shortly after their arrival. Young offered his advice freely, urging both men to establish their mission not in Wrangell but in the Indian village of Kotzlitzaqn, twelve miles away. Seghers did not follow the advice. In subsequent years, Young recorded in his autobiography that the Catholic Church was completed before the Presbyterian one, standing side by side on the hillside overlooking the harbor on a street that was later called Church Street. Young wrote: "Their little church was completed before ours, and services were held in it for a couple of years, when Father Althoff was removed to the new town of Juneau...."[9]

Unfortunately, Althoff left no record of his own feelings over the apparent lack of success in his Wrangell parish. Although he was respected and loved as an amiable gentleman and friend, that in itself did not insure an overflowing crowd in his small church. As a matter of fact, he recorded in his parish record book only thirty-eight baptisms in the first five years of his labors. This number included all the settlements and villages he visited. He was, however, present on that historic day, May 13,

1880, when Bishop Jean Baptiste Brondel, Seghers' successor in Victoria, arrived in Sitka and performed the first Confirmation in Alaska territory aboard the "U.S.S. Jamestown." Such significant events, however, were few and far between. Gerard Steckler, in his unpublished biography of Seghers, stated the matter directly: "Notwithstanding his great personal popularity, John Althoff led an extremely lonely life in southeastern Alaska for many years."[10]

GOLD IN JUNEAU

When Richard Harris and Joseph Juneau discovered gold at Silver Bow Basin along the Gastineau Channel in 1880 another boom was on. Thousands of prospectors, camp followers and entrepreneurs poured into what was first called Harrisburg and later Juneau. Althoff followed the crowd. On July 17, 1882, he offered the first Mass in Juneau in the log cabin church which stood for many years as an historic site. The small church he built, largely with his own hands, was dedicated in 1885 under the patronage of the Nativity of the Blessed Virgin Mary. This was the nucleus of the "Catholic block" in Juneau. The same church, rebuilt in 1910, incorporated parts of Althoff's original building. In time it became the cathedral church of the Diocese of Juneau, created on June 23, 1951.

Once again Althoff found himself among his loyal "Irish Catholics," who proved to be his strong right arm. Juneau was a far richer field for his apostolate than Wrangell. He found many Catholics, nominal at least, among the thousands who poured into the area. Again he was popular among the rough and ragged citizens of the booming townsite and was known for many years after his departure as the "friend of the miners." He foresaw a greater future for the Church in Juneau than in Wrangell. Nothing, perhaps, gave greater evidence to that development than the citizens of the town demanding an organized government and other prerequisites of civilization.

From Juneau as his base, Althoff continued to care for the spiritual needs of the Catholic people throughout southeastern Alaska. For some time during this period he was recalled to Vancouver Island because of the shortage of priests. There he served as pastor of Nanaimo and, presumably on an irregular basis, made pastoral visits to Alaska.[11]

After serving five years as Archbishop of Oregon City, Seghers requested Pope Leo XIII to re-appoint him to the Diocese of Victoria. Once again he concentrated his attention on the Alaskan missions. He had secured new recruits from the American College of Louvain. Thus he was able to send Althoff back to Juneau and a newly-ordained priest, William Lambert Heynen, to Sitka. Althoff was no longer the sole Catholic priest in the Territory of Alaska. He now had a brother-priest nearby in the United States' vast unknown and unappreciated territory. A year later two additional priests came to Alaska with Seghers on his fifth and fateful voyage of 1886 when he was murdered. These were the two Jesuits, Fathers Paschal Tose and Aloysius Rabout, the nucleus of the Jesuit missions which continue to the present time.

Seghers described the Juneau that Althoff returned to in 1886 as he saw it the same year: "The houses seem to have tumbled pellmell from the skies. One faces west, another looks to the rising sun, a third turns its back to the sea; again, another seems suspended from the side of the mountain."[12] After the archbishop's departure Althoff set in motion the process that culminated on Sept. 11 in the arrival of three Sisters of St. Anne to staff a hospital. Their superior, Sister Mary Zeno, S.S.A., is recognized as the pioneer sister of Alaska.

Althoff offered the Sisters his own humble residence and he moved into the neighboring shed. That same year the Sisters opened the first hospital and the first Catholic school in Alaska. In later years Althoff repeatedly gave credit to the coming of the Sisters of St. Anne as a major cause in the establishment of the Catholic Church in Alaska. With the Sisters in Juneau and Heynen in neighboring Sitka, Althoff enjoyed the companionship and consolation of his brother and sisters in religion. He was no longer "Rome's solitary sentinel."

A FEW INCIDENTS

Although his family was wealthy, Althoff himself lived a frugal life. The money he received he lavished on others. A common sight along the paths of Juneau was Althoff, like the Pied Piper, leading a little band of ragamuffin children to the general store. He outfitted them in new clothing and, knowing their tastes, never failed to supply them with candies. He regularly planned picnics for the children, especially those of extremely poor families. With food and goodies neatly packed, he would lead them out to the woods and spend the day with them, leaving them dreaming of "sugar plum fairies" throughout the night.

On one occasion a destitute black man died. Althoff dressed him in his own best suit, laid him in a coffin he made himself, and gave him a decent Christian burial.

One of Althoff's more daring adventures occurred when he received word in Juneau that John Speckbacker of Sitka, a lapsed Catholic, was dying. The word in Juneau that day was that the Inside Passage was besieged by one of its many terrible and treacherous storms. Weather did not daunt his courage. He found a Catholic native who was willing to go with him in his canoe across the 20 miles of turbulent, storm-tossed waters. On the first day, the fury of the storm threw the two men up against a sheltering shore. The next day the two set out again and, in spite of the continuous storm, the weary and worn-out voyageurs arrived at the door of the dying man's cabin. Too late. The widow, also a lapsed Catholic, told how John had asked for an old prayerbook hidden in a valise and the two together, in their native German tongue, recited over and over the centurion's prayer, "O Lord, I am not worthy that Thou should come under my roof, say only the word and my soul shall be healed."

Althoff prepared the man's body for burial, announced the hour of the funeral Mass and, with all stores and shops in Sitka closed, performed the final rites of the Church before an over-flowing crowd. More than that. He took up a collection among the townspeople for the destitute widow and her two children. From his own pocket he purchased a sewing machine so that she was able to make a livelihood. In time, he received the woman back into the Church and baptized her two children. Later, he provided her with passage for her and the children to return to her family in continental United States.

When some of the Sisters of St. Anne departed from Juneau to open a mission school at Holy Cross on the Lower Yukon River, he not only bade them farewell with a blessing but from his own resources gave them two complete sets of Mass vestments and one hundred dollars – no mean sum in those days. Sister Mary Zenan, S.S.A., who had worked closely with the pioneer priest in Juneau, penned this tribute to his memory three years after his death: "Never man rendered service with more Christ-like willingness and joy, not to the Sisters only or to the Catholics, but to everyone whose need came within reach of his knowledge."[13]

DEPARTURE AND DEATH

Father Althoff's labors in Alaska came to an end in 1895, 17 years after he first landed in Wrangell. On July 24, 1884, Pope Leo XIII separated the entire Territory of Alaska from the jurisdiction of the Bishop of Victoria and placed it under the care of the Jesuit Fathers. The following year Althoff left "the great land" to return to serve in his home Diocese of Victoria. He had recorded only 93 baptisms for these 17 years. Only the recording angel knows all his other acts of goodness.

Shortly after returning to Victoria he was assigned as pastor of the mission church in Nelson, British Columbia. While there he built the imposing edifice, mostly from his own inheritance, which today is the cathedral church of the Diocese of Nelson. There he is remembered as a gentle, kindly, holy man.

One who especially remembers him is Sister M. Carmen Pisacreto, S.S.A. When she was orphaned, together with her two brothers, Althoff undertook the role of their guardian and supervised their upbringing and education. In Nelson, Sister Carmen as a child was affectionately known as "Father Althoff's Mary." She recalled his friendliness to everyone as he walked the streets of Nelson; she was also amazed by the rack with twelve different pipes in his study.[14]

When the Archdiocese of Vancouver was created in 1908, Althoff became affiliated with that see. He served for many years as its vicar general while continuing as pastor in Nelson. As far as can be learned, he never returned to the scenes of his early labors in southeastern Alaska. He died on Dec. 30, 1925, in the forty-seventh year of his priesthood, beloved by clergy and people. He is recognized as one of the fathers of the Catholic Church in the Pacific Northwest. His grave is located on a knoll overlooking the other graves in the cemetery in Nelson. ❧

References

1. The only English-language biography in print is *The Apostle of Alaska: Life of the Most Reverend Charles John Seghers*, by Sister Mary Mildred, S.S.A., St. Anthony Guild Press, Paterson, NJ, 1943.
2. Worthy of mention is the visit of Father Veniaminof to the area in 1843. The incident is recounted in Clarence L. Andres' *Wrangell and the Gold of the Cassiar*, Luke Tinker, Commercial Printer, Seattle, WA, 1937, pp. 18-9.
3. Young, S. Hall, *Young of Alaska*, Revell Press, New York, NY, 1927, p. 179. Young writes: "But the third of August, 1879, is one of my unforgettable dates. After all the expeditions, sightseeing, planning for the church and the new MacFarland Home, feasts and counsels with the Indians, this was the day when we gathered up the riper fruits of two years' seed-growing and organized the first Protestant church of Alaska."
4. *The Catholic Sentinel*, June, 1879, no page number given. A letter sent by the Rev. John Althoff to the Rev. J. J. Jonckau, Victoria, V. I.
5. The expression was coined by John Ireland, Archbishop of St. Paul, when he referred to Monsignor Augustine Ravoux, pioneer missionary priest in the Upper Midwest. From 1844 to 1851 Ravoux was the only Catholic priest located in the present States of Minnesota, North Dakota and South Dakota. The author has taken the liberty of applying the same apt phrase to Father Althoff in Alaska.
6. Althoff, *op. cit.*
7. Cantwell, Margaret, Sr., "The Best That We Had," (unpublished manuscript), Archives of the Archdiocese of Anchorage, I, 1-54.
8. Jackson, Sheldon, *Alaska, and Missions on the North Pacific Coast*, Dodd, Mead & Co., New York, NY, 1880, p. 163.
9. Young, *op. cit.*, p. 181.
10. Steckler, *op. cit.*, p. 153.
11. *Ibid.*
12. DeBaets, Maurice, *Vie de Monseigneur Seghers*, p. 154, Quoted in Sister Marie Ann Eva, s.S.A., *A History of the Sisters of Saint Anne*, Vantage Press, New York, NY, 1961, p. 328.

13. Zenon, Mary, Sr., "The Life of Father John Althoff", *Ave Maria*, (Apr. 10, 1928), p. 452.
14. Letter from Sister Carmen, S.S.A. to the author. Feb. 24, 1979.

1981

 HANGING CHURCH AND
WARFARE

Dr. John Summerville, a peace advocate in California, invited the author to deliver a major address concerning the role of religion in peacemaking. I was to deliver this address before an International Conference on the Holocaust and Genocide, scheduled for June 20-24, 1981, in Tel Aviv, Israel. The conference was cancelled because of diplomatic pressure from the government of Turkey. This speech has never before been published.

As we gather here in this land made holy by so many manifestations of God's presence among men we are forced by the very air we breathe to recall the saving history that has made all of us children of God. In our discussions and deliberations we are being guided by the word of God spoken to Moses on a mountain not too far from here: "I have set before you life and death, the blessing and the curse. Choose life, then, that you and your descendants may live."[1]

This passage from sacred scripture, as you know, comes from the end of the book of Deuteronomy, the last book of the Torah. Many of you know better than I that the parchment scroll of the Torah is copied lovingly and reverently by hand. According to ancient tradition the scribe must use a quill for his pen so that the ink will tenderly and gently touch the paper of the parchment. No metal instrument is permitted in executing so important and sacred a work. Biblical scholars tell us that the prohibition of using metal stems from the Hebrews' ancient fear of using metal to mold false gods. If I may be permitted a modern *midrash*, I like to think that the prohibition of using metal also stems from the innate longing for peace of the Jewish people. Metals are symbols of violence, war and greed, and these are the false gods among us today at whose altars too many of our fellowmen pay homage.[2]

I am honored to be a part of this conference, for as a Roman Catholic priest I am committed to the preservation of religious values in a confused and confusing world. As I thought of preparing this paper, a quotation from a man who was not a religious leader but a professional soldier came frequently to mind. At the signing of the instrument terminating hostility between Japan and the Allied forces aboard the battleship "Missouri" on 2 September, 1945, General Douglas MacArthur made these remarks:

"Men since the beginning of time have sought peace.... Military alliances, balances of power, leagues of nations, all in turn failed, leaving the only path to be by way of the crucible of war. We have had our last chance. If we do not now devise some greater and more equitable system, Armageddon will be at our door. The problem basically is theological and involves a spiritual recrudescence and improvement of human character that will synchronize with our almost matchless advances in science, art, literature and all material and cultural developments of the past two thousand years. It must be of the spirit if we are to save the flesh."[3]

I am convinced that you agree with me in the proposition that MacArthur enunciated on that occasion: "*It must be of the spirit if we are to save the flesh.*"

In my own thinking I have even gone one step further in my reflections on peace. I believe that peace is not just one among many societal needs and goals: it is at the very core of all the problems that afflict mankind today. Civil and human rights, poverty, hunger and starvation, racial and ethnic prejudice and hatred, immigration and housing – the entire litany of woes – are with us precisely because mankind lacks the spiritual foundation for peace. One of the most powerful civil and human rights leaders of our generation, Martin Luther King, Jr., stated this conviction in these words:

"We must transform the dynamics of the world power struggle from the nuclear arms race, which no one can win, to a creative contest to harness genius for the purpose of making peace and prosperity a reality for all the nations of the world. In short, we must shift the arms race into a 'peace race.' If we have the will and determination to mount such a peace offensive, we will unlock hitherto tightly sealed doors of hope and bring new light into the dark chambers of pessimism."

That, as I see it, is the purpose of such a conference as this. When enough people throughout the world on the grassroots level have the "determination" – which I interpret as spiritual power – then we will "shift the arms race into a peace race." The will for peace is of the spirit and for that reason religious values must be given primary consideration and practical priority in the hearts and minds of all true peacemakers. This, then, is the premise on which I base the following observations.

∿   ∿   ∿   ∿   ∿

The first and fundamental principle is that peace is a precious gift of God. This point is essential for two reasons. First, peace is an attribute of the spirit; it is internal, radically rooted in the very beginning of the person and independent of external conditions and conventions. Peace considered simply as a "cessation of hostility" or as a treaty signed by warring nations or as a state of law and order (such as the Pax Romana imposed by an imperial army) may well be "the tranquillity of order," but it is not authentic peace.

Secondly, peace cannot be externally imposed by any individual, government or international body. Helpful and necessary as these institutions may be in maintaining a state of tranquility, they cannot create peace. They may be peace-keepers, but can never be peacemakers. Ultimately, only a Supreme Being can create peace and that Being whom I call God does so within the deepest recesses of the individual spirit. For this reason young people are so absolutely correct when they sing in one of their peace songs: "Let there be peace on earth, and let it begin with me."

All this, I know, implies a great deal of faith in the goodness and power of God. Faith in what God reveals is not just wisdom, not just some helpful suggestion, but a mind-set and a lifestyle. Faith transcends reason, drawing its motivating force from the penetrating brilliance and power of God's revealed word and work and not from the shifting shadows of human intellect. In that light, I submit for your consideration this proposition: Pacifism is the greatest folly to those who have no faith. For the peacemaker, however, faith is the only valid weapon that makes "peace on earth among men of goodwill" a reality.

One further point about the relation between faith and peace is essential. I firmly believe that the vast majority of people throughout the world possess faith in a Supreme Being, no matter by what name that Being is known. For that reason, faith is the universal foundation on which we can build a world of peace.

Having made these statements I must add a definition and a distinction. For a definition of peace I turned to the sacred scriptures of Christians and Jews and find therein 362 references to peace.[4] Herein we also find the various kinds of peace that we refer to in any discussion concerning peace. Peace can be personal, fraternal, national and international; there are also negotiated peace settlements, armistices, cease-fires and other forms of political and military interventions. Here, for the present, I have been speaking about personal peace. One biblical scholar defined it as "synonymous with (the individual's) good life, for it involves his healthful sleep, length of life, posterity, and a tranquil death after a full life." This is the concept of peace that has formed the fabric of what we call our Judaic-Christian culture.

In a penetrating article entitled, "The Jewish Tradition of Peace," Rabbi Asher Block builds a case for the pacifism of the Jewish people. He writes: "...there is within the general flow of biblical thought a distinct anti-war current that surges to the surface time and again. Aside from well-known and oft-quoted passages, such as the vision of Isaiah and Micah (of swords beaten into plowshares) and Zachariah's affirmation (not by might of power, but by the Lord's spirit), there are a lot of other biblical texts that come clearly within the purview of a non-violent orientation to life."[5]

The same author also points out the present stance concerning peace within the Jewish community. He continues: "World Jewry is now at a crucial crossroad in its long career. On one side, the mood of nationalism and the surge of militarism are at their highest peak in nineteen hundred years. On the other, the zeal for the "Torah" is far from vanquished in Jewish life."[6]

In the light of that ancient Jewish tradition the theme of this Conference on the Holocaust and Genocide makes all serious-minded people concerned with peace raise fundamental questions concerning peace, at which, unfortunately, the cynic scoffs and the pious is too often content to do no more than pray. The following words, uttered by Robert H. Jackson, U.S. Chief Prosecutor at the Nuremberg trials, need to be repeated many times and especially at this moment:

"These two-score years in this twentieth century will be recorded in the book of years as some of the most bloody in all annals. Two world wars have left a legacy of dead which number more than all the armies engaged in any war that made ancient or medieval history. No half-century ever witnessed slaughter on such a scale, such cruelties and inhumanities, such wholesale deportations of peoples into slavery, such annihilations of minorities....

"These deeds are the overshadowing historical facts by which generations to come will remember this decade. If we cannot eliminate the causes and prevent the repetition of these barbaric events, it is not an irresponsible prophecy to say that this twentieth century may yet succeed in bringing the doom of civilization."[7]

As solemn as Jackson's words are it is obvious that they have not been taken seriously by many of the world's religious and political leaders in the past thirty years. They simply fail to see that by ignoring the Holocaust they are daily opening wider the door for genocide on a global scale, which I call omnicide. Rabbi Irving Greenberg in his penetrating essay, "Cloud of Smoke, Pillar of Fire: Judaism, Christianity, and Modernity after the Holocaust," makes this dire prediction:

"For both Judaism and Christianity (and other religions of salvation – both secular and sacred) there is no choice but to confront the Holocaust, because it happened, and because the first Holocaust is the hardest. The fact of the Holocaust makes a repetition more likely – a limit was broken, a control or awe is gone – and the murder procedure is now better laid out and understood. Failure to confront it makes repetition all the more likely. So evil is the Holocaust, and so powerful a challenge to all other norms, that it forces a response, willy-nilly; not to respond is to collaborate in its repetition."[8]

The first step all religious people must take is our accepting our responsibility as a people who profess to be the children of God in a common brotherhood with all men and women. Confession is a cleansing process. I would like to be optimistic and say that all Christians readily admit their complicity in this crime against humanity, and so I would hope and pray. Realistically, however, you know as I know, that the Christian church still has a long way to go in learning lessons from the Holocaust.

But the very reason for my being here today is to offer at least a sign of hope. I believe that the Church is radically changing in its approach to modern warfare. This change – or rather as I prefer to see it, return to primitive Christian teaching and practice – might well be the most significant development in the Christian church in our lifetime.[9] On this theme I welcome the occasion to share a few further observations with you.

Ꮗ Ꮗ Ꮗ Ꮗ Ꮗ

Jesus proclaimed peace by his life and teachings. But Jesus was a man of his times. He knew the Hebrew scriptures and drew his own teachings on non-violence from those sacred books. He was a non-violent man and asked that his followers be the same. He reaffirmed for Christians the traditional Jewish abhorrence at the shedding of human blood, which the Bible sees as a heinous crime in the eyes of God.[10] While Jesus taught what can only be described as pacifism, he did not come to the position *de novo*, but rather out of the Jewish tradition of which he was a part. This teaching of Jesus has been adequately and admirably summarized by Jean Lassurre in these words:

"It is surely disturbing to find that this idea of defense, self-defense, which is the basis of the traditional militarist doctrine has no Biblical support, and that the expression itself does not appear a single time in the New Testament. No single text can be invoked that would explicitly justify 'self-defense'; on the contrary, Jesus seems to have excluded it (Luke 9:24; 17:33). In fact there is not even a passage positively justifying or recommending the legitimacy of active and violent 'resistance' to injustice. In the New Testament, if there is a question of resisting, it is only resisting the devil, or God, never of resisting men."[11]

In the scriptures, peace is always considered as a gift of God and the presence of God is the singular condition for peace. So priceless a gift was peace that it came to be used as a greeting, and that ancient Hebrew greeting Jesus frequently used when he said, "Peace be with you!" or "Go in peace." A casual "hello" is a poor relation of the solemn "shalom!" C.L. Mitton writes, "With the word of peace went the actual bestowal of peace, and if this proffered gift was spurned, the peace returned to him who had offered it."

The Christian church readily adopted this teaching concerning peace. It prized peace as a superior good and readily understood the greetings of interior and exterior peace when the Apostle Paul addressed them in his letters with such words as, "May God our Father and the Lord Jesus Christ give you grace and peace."[12] It accepted the teaching of non-violence that Jesus proclaimed[13] and carried it out in their private and public lives. It considered dissension, disunity, strife and war not only a serious wound within its own body but also in the civil body. It was, in a word, made up of pacifists, and pacifism was considered the only way of life for a Christian.

Hence, war was proscribed and military service was forbidden. Thus St. Martin of Tours resigned his military commission when be became a Christian; St. Sebastian was shot through with arrows by Caesar's soldiers when he refused to bear arms. This was the practical application of the Lord's command: "Thou shalt not kill," and their Savior's words: "Put away the sword, all who take up the sword shall perish by the sword."[14] Their refusal to carry arms in Caesar's legions was precisely one of the reasons others considered them enemies of the state. Their external pacifism was motivated not only by the prohibition to kill but also the first and fundamental divine command: "Thou shalt not have false gods before me." Just as the Jewish prohibition of using a metal instrument in writing the scrolls of the Torah was prompted by an abhorrence of metal by which false gods could be fashioned, so the Christian's refusal to carry weapons was motivated by a dread of idolatry in which Caesar's person and power were divinized in the military.

After a careful study of the first three centuries of Christianity, church historian Roland H. Bainton came to this conclusion: "The age of persecution down to the time of Constantine was the age of pacifism to the degree that during this period no Christian author to our knowledge approved of Christian participation in battle."[15] It is of more than passing significance, I believe, that this same period is called by church historians the age of martyrs.

I have mentioned this fundamental teaching of Jesus and the practice of the early Christian church because, as I see the signs of the times, we are gradually returning to that position. It is a purifying experience for all Christians, and as you read the daily papers you see that it is also a painful and wrenching one. I am going to pass over the centuries since the Emperor Constantine (313 A.D.) when the "just war" theory popularized by Saint Augustine (d. 430 A.D.) was accepted by the Christian church. It is a sad history, and tragic, prompting one authority to declare that religion has caused more wars than it has prevented. The history of the Christian church as peacemaker since Constantine is not one of pride and edification to the world today.

❧   ❧   ❧   ❧   ❧

But now I want to share with you my hope for the future, for I believe, as our scriptures tell us, "there is a future for the man of peace."[16]

Last November I wrote an article for the *New York Times* in which I said that the issue of peace is causing a revolution within the churches in the United States that has never been witnessed before in our history. I was pleased several months ago to read an article by a prominent educational consultant stating a similar thought. Dr. Lloyd J. Averill wrote: "One of the most promising developments in the moral awareness of the Christian community, and of the nation at large, is the abandonment by members of the Roman Catholic hierarchy of a traditional 'just war' doctrine, at least as it applies to the use of nuclear weapons."[17] It is of more than passing significance that over half of the American Catholic hierarchy has already publicly endorsed a nuclear weapon freeze and over three score of them have become active members of Pax Christi - USA, the largest Catholic peace organization in my country.

For many years I had thought that the Society of Friends, or Quakers, had taken a page from the Christian gospels, and made a fetish out of it. (In recent years I realize how terribly wrong I have been.) As early as 1660 the Quakers issued a declaration to which they have been admirably faithful ever since. They declared: "We do testify to the world that the Spirit of Christ which leads us into all truth, will never move us to fight any war against any man with outward weapons, neither for the Kingdom of Christ nor for the kingdoms of this world."[18] It is impossible to estimate the influence that the pacifism of the Quakers has had upon the Christian body. My guess would be that it has been greatly respected and widely imitated in recent years.

Within the last two generations, peace has become a growing concern among all bodies of Christianity. No doubt the ecumenical movement has played a key role in this development, for many Christians have come to the awareness that a "divided" Christianity is a contradiction. The bearers of the gospel of love and peace must have hearts open in love and hands extended in peace to all men. True ecumenism is more than an intramural affair; it must embrace all people everywhere.

Nor can we fail to recall the encyclical letter of Pope John XXIII entitled *Peace on Earth* which has, in my estimation, a greater influence throughout the world than any other single document of a religious leader in our century. This "peasant pope," christened Angelo Giuseppe Roncalli, practiced what he preached. Who does not recall the day he met with a group of Jewish leaders, walked up to them, extended his hand, and said, "I am Joseph, your brother." The words Pope John penned 19 years ago merit even today serious consideration and reflection. In one passage he wrote:

"All must realize that there is no hope of putting an end to the building up of armaments, nor of reducing the present stocks, nor, still less – and this is the main point – of abolishing them altogether, unless the process is complete and thorough and unless it proceeds from inner conviction: unless, that is, everyone sincerely cooperates to banish the fear and anxious expectation of war with which men are oppressed. If this is to come about, the fundamental principle on which our present peace depends must be replaced by another, which declares that the true and solid peace of nations consists not in equality of arms but in mutual trust alone."[19]

Within the past year Christian bodies throughout the world have mounted an unprecedented peace offensive. Permit me to cite only a few of these developments:

- The heads of the Anglican provinces throughout the world pledged to work for multilateral disarmament.
- The World Council of Churches and the Lutheran World Federation held major international conferences on the urgency of nuclear disarmament.
- The Russian Orthodox Church hosted a conference attended by most of the Christian churches to promote the cause of peace and disarmament in the world.
- Anti-nuclear demonstrations swept across Europe in opposition to the placing of nuclear missiles on European soil. Many of these demonstrations were either promoted or sponsored by religious groups.
- The superiors of the four major Franciscan families, representing thousands of Franciscan religious men and women, issued a statement committing the followers of Francis of Assisi to "assume a leadership role in the work for peace."
- All religious peace organizations throughout the United States have reported an unprecedented phenomenal growth in membership during the past year.[20]
- Peace communities, groups of men and women who live together or come together frequently to promote peace, are mushrooming throughout the world. It is impossible to add the number of advertisements that appear in peace publications that are similar to this one: "We are interested in forming a World Peacemakers-type group in the Greensboro, North Carolina area. Please contact...."[21]
- The American Catholic Bishops are presently drafting a pastoral letter on the morality of war that promises to be a major statement of conscience. It seems at this stage three issues are clear: (1) It will condemn the use of nuclear weapons as immoral. (2) It will state that conventional war is not necessarily moral just because it is nonnuclear. (3) The unresolved moral issue at this stage remains the morality of stockpiling nuclear weapons as deterrents.[22]
- Eloy Ramos of Amarillo, Texas, took an irrevocable step of conscience by resigning from his job at the USA's final assembly point for nuclear

weapons. He said, "I guess on my last day (at work) I will put up a sign saying I have gone on a journey in search of God." Ramos, I believe, is in the vanguard of countless workers who will be resigning their jobs because of their companies involvement in the arms race and their commitment to peace.[23]

These and numerous other examples sustain and support me with a hope that I pray you share. They represent the "groundswell" that Archbishop John Roach, president of the U.S. National Conference for Catholic Bishops, observed when he said, "There is close to a groundswell of people who are terribly concerned with the possibility of nuclear warfare. They see it as an impossible solution to tensions, are very frightened and are prepared to rally around any anti-nuclear cause."

As a Christian my life and faith has become more meaningful because I am a part of that "groundswell." I find personal strength in the awareness that millions of othes, such as you, have made peace the object of your lives. My own peace prayer is expressed in these words Pope John Paul II uttered on February 25, 1981, near the site where the first atomic bomb fell in Hiroshima:

"Let us pledge ourselves to peace through justice. Let us take a solemn decision, now, that war will never be tolerated or sought as a means of resolving differences; let us promise our fellow human beings that we will work untiringly for disarmament and the banishing of all nuclear weapons."[24]

Above and beyond the confidence such prayer inspires, more than the encouragement derived from the current religious activities for peace, and infinitely more trustworthy than all the negotiations and treaties drafted by statesmen are the words that God speaks each day to every member of his family on earth: "Watch for the whole-hearted man, and mark the upright; for there is a future for the man of peace."[25]

This day, in this land made holy by the presence of God among men, my prayer for each of you is also that of the royal psalmist:

"For the peace of Jerusalem pray:

'Peace be to your homes!

May peace reign in your walls, in your palaces, peace!'"[26] ❧

References

1. Deut. 30:19.
2. Cf. Beerman, Leonard I., "The Blessing and the Curse," *Choose Life*, Fellowship of Reconciliation, Nyack, NY, 1982.
3. MacArthur, Douglas A., *Reminiscences*, McGraw-Hill Book Co., New York, 1964, p. 276.
4. Cr. *Nelson's Complete Concordance of the New American Bible*, ed. by Stephen Hartdegen, Liturgical Press, Collegevill, MN, 1977.
5. Block, Asher, "The Jewish Tradition of Peace," *Fellowship*, Feb., 1953, Nyack, NY.
6. *Idem*.
7. Quoted in Schoenberger, Gerhard, *The Yellow Star*, Bantam Books, New York, 1979, p. 211.
8. Greenberg, Irving, "Cloud of Smoke, Pillar of Fire: Judaism, Christianity, and Modernity after the Holocaust," *Auschwitz: Beginning of a New Era?*, ed. by Eva Fleischner, KTAV Publishing House, Inc., New York, 1977, p. 20.
9. By far the one book that influenced me most in my re-thinking of the issue of peace is: Douglass, James W., *The Non-Violent Cross*, The MacMillan Co., New York, 1966.
10. Cf. Gn. 4:8-10; 9:5-6; Deut. 5:17; Prov. 24:17-18; Mt 5.
11. Lasserre, Jean, *War and the Gospel*, Herald Press, Scottdale, PA, 1962, p. 31.
12. Gal. 1:3.
13. Cf. Mt 5:38-48.
14. Mt 26:52.
15. Bainton, Roland H., *Christian Attitudes toward War and Peace*, Abdingon, Nashville, TN, 1960, p. 71.
16. Ps. 37:37.
17. Averill, Lloyd J., "Nuclear War," *Christian Century*, Apr. 14, 1982, p. 437.
18. Brinton, Howard H., *The Peace Testimony of the Society of Friends*, American Friends Service Committee, Philadelphia, PA, 1981, p.666.

19. John XXIII, Pope, "Encyclical Letter 'Peace on Earth,'" *Renewing the Earth: Catholic Documents on Peace, Justice, and Liberation*, ed. by David J. O'Brien and Thomas A. Shannon, Image Books, Garden City, NY, 1977, p. 151.

20. Cf. Turner, Darrell, "The Mainstream of World Religious Leadership Jointed in Urgent Efforts to Stop the Nuclear Arms Race in 1981," *Religious News Service*, Year-end, 1981, New York. This and the above items have been taken from this article.

21. *Sojourners*, 11 (April, 1982), no. 4, Washington, DC, p. 42.

22. Cf. Kaufman, Ben, "Nuclear deterrence's morality 'central issue' for bishops," *National Catholic Reporter*, 18, no. 28, May 14, 1982.

23. Cf. Goodman, Terri, "Pantex worker quits," *National Catholic Reporter*, 18, no. 19, May 21, 1982.

24. John Paul II, Pope, quoted in *National Catholic Reporter*, 18, March 5, 1982.

25. Ps. 37:37.

26. Ps. 122:6-7.

1981

 CATHOLIC REVOLUTION

While the American Catholic bishops were deliberating over the drafts of their war and peace pastoral, the New York Times *published this brief article on its Op-Ed page in the issue of Nov. 18, 1981. The article is based upon the testimony of Cardinal John Krol of Philadelphia before the U.S. Senate Foreign Relations Committee.*

Something is stirring in the Roman Catholic Church in the United States that portends an explosion between church and state that will make the abortion issue, the school-aid controversy, and the tax-exempt status of churches look like a child's sparkler on the Fourth of July.

It is, in my judgment, the most significant revolution within the American Catholic Church since Lord Baltimore's contingent of Catholics disembarked on Maryland's shores in 1634.

Stated simply, the Church in the United States is becoming a "peace" church. That is to say, in recent years it has moved dramatically and swiftly from the company of mainline Protestant and Evangelical churches into the quiet meeting place of the Society of Friends.

This revolution is being waged painfully in the hearts and minds of Catholic thinkers and leaders. Thank God, the American bishops are shouldering their responsibility of leading this revolution, at times to the chagrin and vocal opposition of their flocks. They are emerging more and more as worthy successors of Thomas à Becket. Their words and actions are not in any sense pious rhetoric.

One might date the revolution from Sept. 9, 1979, when John Cardinal Krol of Philadelphia, in the name of the majority of the bishops, before the Senate Foreign Relations Committee stated the clear, unequivocal position of the Catholic Church in the United States concerning disarmament and nuclear war. His testimony can be summarized briefly.

1. Our obligation to control the threat of nuclear destructiveness is more fundamental than the requirement to limit the possession of certain weapons.

2. The use of any strategic nuclear weapons whatsoever against any targets even in response to prior Soviet use of them is morally unacceptable.

3. Any threat to use the strategic nuclear arsenal is condemned. Even deterring the Soviet Union by threat of nuclear retaliation for aggression is out of bounds morally because it is immoral even to intend to do what is intrinsically immoral.

4. The Church lends its moral authority to the quest for bilateral and legally sanctioned limits on weapons.

5. The Church goes one step further and requires at least of its own members unilateral renunciation of the right to use, or the threat to use, those strategic nuclear weapons still allowed under the arms-control agreement.

The implication – perhaps a better word is "application" – of this teaching undoubtedly will set the teaching Church and some of its members on a collision course in the area of this Catholic moral imperative. Moreover, it will put the Catholic Church's teaching and practice in direct conflict with a Government that says and acts to the contrary.

Since Cardinal Krol's testimony, dozens of Amerian Catholic bishops have enunciated these same principles in their speeches, pastoral letters, and in interviews and articles in diocesan newspapers. The reactions in their flocks have been mixed: some vehemently oppose their stand, others just as ardently support it.

At least two bishops have spoken out boldly and courageously, emphasizing that unilateral disarmament is the only Catholic position to take. There may be more, but the two whose statements I have read are Archbishop Raymond T. Hunthausen of Seattle (who was supported by the suffragan bishops of the Pacific Northwest) and Bishop LeRoy Matthiesen of Amarillo, Texas (who was supported by the other nine Catholic bishops of Texas). Archbishop John R. Quinn of San Francisco on Oct. 4 issued a pastoral letter that said the "just war theory" no longer applies because of the essential difference between nuclear and conventional war.

A prominent Catholic who is a justice on the supreme court of one of our states said to me recently: "I am persuaded unilateral disarmament must begin. I hope the Church can change the climate of opinion to make this possible."

The Catholic bishops will hold their annual meeting in Washington next week. It remains to be seen what action they will take. Will they issue a statement on unilateral disarmament or wait until 1982 when they already plan to publish a lengthy pastoral letter on war and peace?

What will be the reaction of Catholic leaders, military officers, and Government officials if and when the bishops say formally and officially that unilateral disarmament is "the primary imperative," which they already have done individually and unofficially?

That's what I mean when I say there is a Catholic revolution. ∞

1984

 ANTUARIO DE CHIMAYO

This unique pilgrimage shrine in the American Southwest is located in New Mexico, "the Land of Enchantment." The beauty of the surrounding land and mountains and the serenity of this sacred spot attracted the author to it several times. He wrote this article in 1984 for The People of God, *newspaper of the Archdiocese of Santa Fe.*

"We expect about 30,000 pilgrims this Holy Week," said Father Casimiro Roca as he sat in the tiny office of Holy Family rectory, Chimayo, in 1984. No one would know better than Father Roca, for he has given his time and talent, heart and soul, to the Santuario de Chimayo day and night for the past 30 years.

The Santuario de Chimayo is one of the most popular shrines in the United States, attracting hundreds of thousands of pilgrims and visitors each year from every corner of the United States, Mexico, Canada and distant countries in Asia and Europe. Father Roca estimates that even on the coldest days in winter at least 50 pilgrims will stop by to pray; on weekends in summer as many as 3,000 people will find their way to the Santuario.

Few places in the United States have been as richly endowed with a wealth of natural beauty as the Santuario. The small adobe church with its twin bell towers is quietly tucked away in a little corner of God's majestic creation. The peaks of the Sangre de Cristo mountains stand in the background as silent sentinels. The swiftly flowing waters of the Santa Cruz River behind the shrine reminds the pilgrim of the timelessness of God's goodness and beauty.

Long before the appearance of written records and the coming of the Europeans, native Americans came to this spot in quest of the sacred soil which they believed had curative powers. Archaeologists believe that the Indians lived in this area as early as 1100 A.D. The sheltering walls of the mountain range served as protection against the cold winds from the north and the river provided the water necessary for an agricultural society.

By the time of the Spanish Reconquest in 1693 the Indians had moved from the valley. The natural beauty and resources beckoned the colonizers. The area of Chimayo became one of the earliest Spanish settlements in New Mexico. The original site is still inhabited and is located about a mile from the Santuario.

In its almost 300 years of recorded history two words describe the lifestyle of the inhabitants of Chimayo valley. The millions of pilgrims who have found their way to pray at the Santuario have also captured their spirit. The words are *simplicity* and *silence*.

The orchards in bloom on a crisp spring morning, the smell of newly-mown alfalfa in plots of land bordering the river, the cattle slowly moving in the pastures along the river bank, are only a few indications of the simplicity and silence of the fertile valley sheltered by the craggy red-rock walls of the mountains.

The two principal industries in the Chimayo valley are agriculture and weaving. The excellent craftsmanship of Chimayo hand-woven rugs is known throughout the world. The Ortega Weaving Company employs over 200 people in a type of cottage industry that modern industrial entrepreneurs are striving to imitate.

A tiny chapel, such as St. Rita's perched on a mountaintop, or a mysterious *maroda*, such as the one located on an obscure winding dirt road near the original site of Chimayo, are only two small indications that God guards this sacred valley and His people with a special, loving care.

The "high road to Taos," now known as New Mexico state highway number 76, was used in times past by Indians to visit neighboring tribes, officials to carry out orders from government officials in Santa Fe, and by trappers with packs of furs to trade in Taos. It also witnessed throughout the centuries countless pilgrims who come and pray – and ask for miracles – at the Santuario.

Pilgrims to the Santuario will walk from places as far distant as

Gallop and Albuquerque; a few will be carrying hand-hewn wooden crosses in loving memory of their Savior. Some will come praying and singing in small groups; others will come individually in silent meditation. A few will drop on their knees in front of the Santuario and make the last few hundred feet of their pilgrimage shuffling along on their knees.

Rich and poor, young and old, strong or weak, healthy or sick – all will be struck by silence and simplicity; all will find in their own hearts a miracle of faith. The silence and simplicity strikes sparks of hope and love. That "miracle" sinks its roots in the Catholic history of New Mexico and Chimayo and continues today through the labors of a single priest, Father Roca. The history of the Santuario explains its sacredness; the priest reveals the love of God among His people.

FACTS AND LEGENDS

The building of the Santuario, a fascinating story in itself, is a matter of history and easily documented. The reason for building the distinctively New Mexican adobe church, however, is shrouded in a mystery that has given rise to many popular legends. These legends are considered by some as fanciful and by others as devotional.

First, the facts.

In the far eastern section of the Central American nation of Guatemala, near the borders of El Salvador and Honduras, is the city of Esquipulas. Thousands of pilgrims each year visit the magnificent basilica in the heart of this city of 11,000 people to visit and pray before "the miraculous image of the "Black Christ." The "Black Christ" is a crucifix carved from dark balsam wood in 1594 by the famous Guatemalan artist, Quirio Catano. The crucifix came to be venerated under the title of "Our Lord of Esquipulas."

Fray Pedro de Figuera, the Archbishop of Guatemala during the years 1735-1751, had a great devotion to Our Lord of Esquipulas and claimed he was miraculously cured from an incurable illness by his prayers to Jesus under that title. He made a pious vow to build a basilica to house the crucifix. The building was completed in 1759, eight years after his death. To this day devotion to Our Lord of Esquipulas, or the "Black Christ," is popular in Central America.

Devotion to Our Lord of Esquipulas came to New Mexico with the early settlers of the Chimayo valley. Among these settlers who arrived in the area of El Potrero (now a part of Chimayo), about 1696, were the Ortega, Trujillo, and Mascarenos families, many of whose descendants still live in the area. In the early years they were served by the priests from San Juan, but from 1751 until 1961, the people of Chimayo received the services of the priests of Santa Cruz parish, or, as the ancient documents called it, *"Ville de Santa Cruz de la Canada de los Españoles Mexicanos."*

At the beginning of the eighteenth century the name of Abeyta (Veitia, Beitia, Veithia, Abeitia, Abiytia) begins its close connection with devotion to "the miraculous image of Our Lord of Esquipulas." According to Fray Angelico Chavez's *Origins of New Mexico Families*, a certain Diego de Vectia came with the colonists from Zacatecas, Mexico, in 1695 and settled in Santa Fe.

One of his children, Antonio de Beytia, is mentioned as a member of the militia at Santa Cruz in 1735. His one son, Miguel Manuel, married Maria Francisca Chavez in Santa Fe on Sept. 12, 1744. In the course of the years the family name took the form of Abeyta.

The Abeyta family continued to live in the Santa Cruz and La Puebla areas throughout the eighteenth century. In 1797 Bernardo Abeyta married Rita Valerio in Chimayo and then moved into that community. After his wife's death, in 1806, he married again, this time Maria Manuela Trujillo, a descendant of one of the original settlers of Chimayo.

The baptismal records of Santa Cruz parish give an indication that devotion of Our Lord of Esquipulas was present as early as 1805. In that year the parish priest, Father Sebastian Alvarez, baptized a child with the name of Juan de Esquipulas, son of Mariano Abeyta and Juana de Herrerra. Subsequently many children were christened with the name of "Esquipulas" or "Jesús de Esquipulas." Usually devotion to Our Lord or a saint exists for some time before a child in the family is given the name.

The existence of devotion to Jesús de Esquipulas, or the Black Christ, probably came to New Mexico, and the area of Chimayo, through some person or some families who had firsthand knowledge of the shrine of Esquipulas, Guatemala. One of the early missionary priests cultivated the devotion among the people of the area. What can easily be understood is the popular association of the healing mud from the springs in Esquipulas with the ancient Indian use of the soil in Chimayo as a curative remedy. This can further be attested to by the similarity of the carved image of Christ Crucified in Chimayo and the Black Christ in Esquipulas.

On March 14, 1813, Bernardo Abeyta had his son christened with the name of Tomás de Esquipulas. Eight months later, on Nov. 15, he formally petitioned the pastor of Santa Cruz, Father Alvarez, in the name of the 19 families residing in El Potrero, to build a chapel "to honor and venerate, with worthy worship, Our Lord and Redeemer, in his Advocation of Esquipulas."

The following day, Nov. 16, the pastor wrote the Vicar General of the Diocese of Durango, Mexico, that "the miraculous image of Our Lord of Esquipulas had already been honored for three years in the *Hermita*." This was a small chapel built in the home of Bernardo Abeyta at his own expense. In the same letter the pastor wrote that Bernardo Abeyta had already chosen the site for the chapel, "the most decent and appropriate spot at the said plaza of Rancho del Potrero, which is called El Santuario de Esquipulas, where they can worship Our Lord." Permission was granted by the Vicar General, Francisco Fernandez Valentin, on Feb. 8, 1814, and transmitted through the Franciscan Superior, Francisco de Otocio, to Bernardo Abeyta in April, 1815.

The room that still stands with the hole filled with blessed earth and its adjoining room filled with *santos*, crutches and other memorabilia of pilgrims, most probably was the original chapel in the home of Bernardo Abeyta. The present adobe church, with its massive walls and bell towers was built in 1816 through the donated labor of the devout people of Chimayo. The four feet thick adobe walls were fashioned from the very earth surrounding the Santuario and the huge timbers, called *vigas*, were hewn and transported from the forests on the surrounding mountains.

The interior of the Santuario today, with the exception of the wooden floor, is not too different in appearance from when it was completed in 1816 or shortly thereafter. The crucifix of the Lord of Esquipulas is six feet in height, painted dark green and decorated with golden leaves. It is not blackened and seems to be the work of an unknown *santero*. The five magnificent *reredos* (a series of sacred paintings) were the work of artists in the area at the time of the building of the Santuario. One of these was José Aragon and the other was Molleno, called the "chile painter." Possibly José's son, Miguel Aragon, was the painter of one of the *reredos*.

The images on the *reredos* reflect the devotion of Catholic Spain transported centuries ago to New Mexico. The saints depicted on the *reredos* in striking, rustic simplicity reflect not only the religious history that was so integral a part of the lives of these pioneers, but also the creative imagination of the builders and artists of this period.

The simplicity of the adobe church and its artistic furnishings blend exquisitely into the simplicity of the natural surroundings, making a perfect marriage between art and nature. The Santuario today is, perhaps, maintained better today than ever before in its long history of over 170 years. Undoubtedly, this is due to the zeal and industry of Father Roca and the present-day people of El Potrero.

The pilgrim today could spend a week studying the *reredos, bultos,* and other artistic works, such as *El Señor Santiago* (the image of St. James on horseback), and possibly learn there more about Spanish art and history than in a year's course at a university. Culture is a by-product of prayer; the more one prays at the Santuario the more one is imbued with a deeply religious and human culture.

Bernardo Abeyta lived to see the completion of his dream in the Santuario and witnessed the coming and going of thousands of pilgrims from hundreds of miles to pray before the image of Our Lord of Esquipulas and take blessed earth from the hole called *el pozito*. He died on Nov. 21, 1856, and was buried within the walls of his beloved chapel.

The Santuario remained in the hands of his family and its members guarded, preserved and cared for it with a loving and lively devotion for over 100 years. His daughter, Carmen, married into the local Chavez family.

In 1928 a group of people in Santa Fe purchased the chapel from the Chavez family and deeded it to the Archdiocese of Santa Fe. Archbishop Albert T. Daeger, O.F.M., accepted the deed and turned the Santuario over to the care of the parish of Santa Cruz, which was staffed by priests of the Congregation of the Sons of the Holy Family. In 1959 Father Casimiro Roca came to Santa Cruz and took charge of the Santuario. And that is another story....

Popular Legends of Santuario

The devotion of Bernardo Abeyta to the Crucified Lord of Esquipulas is an enduring monument in the Santuario of Chimayo. As a devout member of the Penitentes, Bernardo undoubtedly possessed a great devotion to the passion and death of the Savior. Unfortunately, Bernardo left no known written record of the motives that prompted him to request the building of the Santuario in 1815.

As often is the case, when history fails popular imagination is more than ready to supply details. These, in time, become folk legends and as they are told and re-told, more often than not, fancy supplies what fact beggars. This is the case in the story of the Santuario. A person would be foolhardy, however, to disregard legends completely. Although flourishes may be added in the course of time, underlying most legends is an important kernel of truth.

More than that. Even the elaborations of a bold and bare legend bear witness to values that are often more enduring and more important than the cold, hard facts. In the case of the Santuario the legends reveal a faith and a culture that is more valuable than any monument of brick or stone – or adobe.

Two of the legends concerning the origin of the Santuario offer a reason for its building and at the same time reflect the faith and culture of a marvelously sturdy people living in an area which was then the northern frontier of Mexico and beyond the greedy arms of the western expansionists of Texas and the United States. Even then these people were New Mexicans, endowed with a rich heritage that neither nature's adversities nor man's oppression could destroy. These two legends reveal that heritage, perhaps, more than any encyclopedia of facts.

One of the legends is recorded by Mr. Stephen F. de Borhegyi in his article published by The Spanish Colonial Arts Society, Inc., in 1956. There he writes the following account:

"It was during a Holy Week when Bernardo Abeyta, a good member of the fraternity of Jesus Nzrareno of Penitentes, was perform- ing the customary penances of the society around the hills of Potrero that he suddenly saw a bright light shining from a hole in the ground near the Santa Cruz River. He rushed to the spot and with his bare hands dug out the miraculous crucifix of Our Lord of Esquipulas. He called all the people of El Potrero to see and venerate the precious finding. He soon notified Father Sebastian Alvarez, and a procession was organized to take the crucifix to Santa Cruz. It was placed in the niche of the main altar. Next morning the crucifix disappeared from its niche and was found again in the same hole where it was first discovered. Another procession was formed to carry it back to Santa Cruz, but the same thing happened this time and once more after it had been taken to Santa Cruz for the third time. By this everyone understood that the crucifix wished to remain in El Potrero, and, to venerate it properly, a chapel was built above the hole."

The other legend is based on a fact. According to the archives of the Diocese of Durango, Mexico, a Guatemalan priest accompanied the first settlers to the Chimayo valley. This unknown priest served as a missionary to the surrounding Indians and ministered to the early settlers. He was killed by the Indians and buried by the settlers in El Potrero.

Now the legend, as recorded in a booklet published by the Sons of the Holy Family in 1982 elaborates this fact as follows:

"In 1810 the Santa Cruz River flooded and both the crucifix and the body of the martyred priest were uncovered by the water. Some older people who had known the priest while alive shouted: *'Miren, el Padre de Esquipulas'* ('Look, the Father from Esquipulas'), and so the crucifix came to be called Our Lord of Esquipulas, named after the village where the priest came from. This same spot where the crucifix and the body of the priest were found was considered a sacred place by the Tewa Indians long before the Guatemalans and the Spanish came to Chimayo."

Many other legends concerning the origin of the Santuario sprang up in the course of time. One originated among the Indians of the Isleta pueblo, another among the Martinez family in Santa Cruz, still another among the people of the Picuris pueblo. One originated in more recent times with a story told by Maria Martinez, the famous potter of San Ildefonso pueblo.

In the course of time and the telling of the story from one generation to the next, *Santo Niño de Atoéha* came to be associated with the Santuario. In more recent times this gradually included devotion to the Infant Jesus of Prague, whose statue is prominently displayed in the chapel.

In his attempt to unravel history from legend, fact from fancy, after his study and research of many months, Mr. Borhegyi offers what this writer believes to be the best explanation for the existence of the Santuario. Borhegyi writes:

"During the lifetime of Bernardo Abeyta, who was presently the only one who clearly understood the connection between the healing power of the earth and 'Our Lord and Redeemer, in His Advocation of Esquipulas,' there was little confusion as to the miraculous discovery or its true meaning. In all likelihood, Bernardo Abeyta, having some form of firsthand knowledge of the healing properties of the earth near the shrine of Esquipulas in Guatemala, associated it with the similar health-giving properties of the mud in Chimayo to worship and venerate Our Lord of Esquipulas above the pit of mud believed also by the Indians to have special healing powers. He probably gave directions to the *santero* how to carve and paint the Crucifix of Our Lord of Esquipulas to resemble its Guatemalan counterpart."

MODERN CRUCIFIX OF CHIMAYO

Behind the main altar of the modern church of the Holy Family in Chimayo, about two miles from the Santuario, hangs a truly remarkable crucifix. Few pilgrims who pass through Chimayo on their journey to the Santuario fail to 0stop to admire and offer their prayers before this marvelous piece of modern art.

The crucifix that hangs in Holy Family Church is an admirable counterpart of the crucifix that adorns the main altar in the nearby Santuario. The crucifix in the Santuario is a testimony to the faith and devotion of Bernardo Abeyta over 170 years ago. The crucifix in Holy Family church is a witness of the faith and devotion of one of America's well-known and loved artists today.

The story of the Crucified Lord of Esquipulas that hangs in the Santuario finds its echo and re-presentation in the same faith and devotion found in contemporary man through the story of the crucifix that hangs in the church of the Holy Family. Bernardo Abeyta did not leave a record of the crucifix in the Santuario; fortunately, the story of the crucifix in Holy Family church has been told by Father Roca.

In the summer of 1964 the people of Chimayo had completed the building of the new Holy Family church. The interior, however, had not been completely furnished and decorated. One afternoon a group of visitors stopped by to visit the new church and examine its interior. Father Roca greeted them and conducted an impromptu tour.

The group said they were actors and making a film in the area. This did not impress Father Roca too much because he knew many actors and artists visited the area of Santa Fe. Before leaving, however, one of the members of the group invited Father Roca to dine with them at the nearby Ranchero de Chimayo.

"I met them there at five o'clock," said Father Roca. "We had a very good dinner and a very lively conversation. By the time we rose to leave it was eight o'clock. I explained to the group that I had to be back at the church because the young people will be there practicing a guitar Mass."

One of the group offered to take the priest back to the church. When the two arrived Father's companion said he would like to go in and see the young people practicing their guitar Mass.

"You should have seen it!" exclaimed Father Roca, recalling the incident. "As soon as we entered the church the youngsters came running to greet us, shouting 'Burl Ives! Burl Ives!' I must admit that at that time I didn't even know who Burl Ives was. I was embarrassed."

The popular folk singer picked up a guitar and began to sing with the young people. He listened to their requests and played and sang the musical numbers they requested. He was completely relaxed and the youngsters were thrilled by the experience. After several hours of singing and harmonizing Burl Ives bade the group farewell.

Father Roca escorted the musician to his car. As he was leaving, Burl Ives told the priest that he wanted to give something for the church and he would send it along in a few months.

"I thought no more about it," said Father Roca. "For several weeks the young people could talk about nothing else than their session with Burl Ives. It was, as they say, 'the big event' of the town. Three or four months passed and then one day a transfer company delivered a huge crate addressed to me. I opened it excitedly and there was this beautiful crucifix. You can see it yourself when you go to the church."

The crucifix was carved by Burl Ives himself. It follows carefully the traditional features of the crucifixes carved 200 or 300 hundred years ago by the native *santeros*. One distinctive feature of this crucifix is the hair on the head of the carved body of Christ is real human hair. The expression on the face is one of intense suffering with a marked beauty of quiet acceptance.

"Many of the youngsters," said Father Roca, "who sang with Burl Ives that night have left Chimayo. When they do come back, though, they often visit the church to pray before the crucifix carved by Burl Ives and given as a gift to the people of Chimayo."

Priest Marked Anniversaries

When the people of Holy Family parish celebrated their annual fiesta in honor of *El Señor Santiago* in July, 1984, they had an added reason for their festivities. On that occasion they marked the fortieth anniversary of ordination and the thirtieth year of the coming of Father Casimiro Roca to the area of the Santa Cruz valley. He was appointed to another parish in Colorado. His departure was tinged with sadness because he left behind more than 30 years of dedicated material and spiritual work at his beloved Santuario de Chimayo. Those who know the short, smiling priest who speaks with a pronounced Spanish accent also know that the Santuario is a famous pilgrimage shrine of the Southwest today chiefly because of Father Roca.

In 1984 Father Roca looked back over the past 30 years and his labors in the Santa Cruz valley, and especially at the Santuario de Chimayo. I sat with him in the tiny office of Holy Family rectory one evening shortly after he returned from the eight hours each day he spent at the Santuario.

That day, like almost every other day of the year's 365 days, he offered Holy Mass in the Santuario at seven o'clock after the *mayordomo*, George Chavez, and his wife had opened the doors and lighted the candles. He now enjoyed the "luxury" of his small office beside the main entrance, since the gift shop has recently been moved to a building across the creek that runs in front of the Santuario.

Throughout the day he greets a constant stream of pilgrims,

visiting with them, asking where they are from, assuring them he will pray for them and their needs, sometimes hearing their confessions, other times giving them a brief history of the Santuario. With George Chavez at his side they survey the property of the Santuario, noting what needs to be repaired, what improvements should be made and what details must be attended to in preparation for one or another pilgrimage group that will come next week or next month. The heroism of his day lies in the dedication he shows as a good administrator and the pastoral concern and affection he shares with all who come to the Santuario.

"I was born in Barcelona, Spain," he said, twirling a pencil in his hand. "I spent part of my seminary training in the underground because it was during the time of the Spanish Civil War. The crimes and killings I witnessed were terrible, just terrible." He paused a moment in recollection and the pain on his face registered the sadness in his heart as he recalled the martyrdom of his two brothers and other seminarians and priest friends.

"After my ordination my superiors said they wanted to send me to work in Italy. I was so eager to escape the fury and destruction in Spain I said I would be willing to walk all the way to Italy if I could get there." He smiled at the thought and the exuberance of youth.

"They finally sent me to the United States," he continued, "and I arrived at Santa Cruz in 1954. At that time I was put in charge of the missions at Truchas, Cordova, Rio Cito, Chimayo, Trampas, and the Santuario at El Potrero."

He preached a mission in Truchas five months after he came to Santa Cruz. Following that the people of the Truchas asked to build a church there, which they did during the following year. Father Roca was then given charge of the missions as his sole responsibility the next few years.

In 1959 the people in Chimayo asked to have a parish established. Father Roca proceeded to purchase the property on which the present church stands. Archbishop James Davis of Santa Fe appointed him pastor and told him he could select the title of the new parish. In honor of his own religious congregation, Father Roca named the parish Holy Family. During this time he was also pastor of the Santuario

"When I came in 1954," he recalled, "the Santuario was almost falling down. The walls were cracking, there was no plaster on the walls.

Only the four walls were standing."

He continued, "I noticed that even animals were inside the building. Pigeons and bats flew in and out of the cracks in the walls. The doors were dilapidated and the steep steps made the entryway dangerous. In 1960 I decided to dedicate myself to the restoration of the Santuario."

Erosion over the decades had almost completely wiped away the bank on the east side of the building to such an extent that the east wall of the church was in danger of tumbling down. Father Roca enlisted the aid of the men in the area and they filled in the embankment with over 15,000 tons of dirt. They then poured cement for the retaining wall to stop further erosion and thus saved the structure."

Over the following years priest and people worked together in restoring the exterior of the venerable building. Throughout the years they continued to apply paint, stucco, and plaster to the outside of the building. "We even added a foot of dirt to each of the four walls for support," the priest said smilingly as he recalled those years.

As time passed Father Roca and the dedicated people of Chimayo turned their attention to the interior of the building. "Everything inside is one hundred percent original," Father Roca said. "Nothing has been touched inside. The paintings and carvings date back to the years it was built. Of course, we had to clean the walls and floors, fix the doors and apply new coats of paint. We do this now about every three years."

In 1960 Father Roca enlisted the help of the men in Chimayo to build a small rectory. This was constructed in 30 days during the month of December and Father Roca moved into it after the open house on the Feast of the Holy Family, 1961. The following years the people built the parish hall and used it as a church for several years. Father Roca began calling together the people from the three existing small chapels within the area of Chimayo and molded them into a single community. In 1964 construction began on the present church and rectory of the Holy Family in Chimayo.

Through the priest's efforts the Santuario was designated a "registered national historic landmark" in 1970. Under this designation "this site possesses exceptional value in commemorating or illustrating the history of the united States."

"I called this the year of the great discovery for outsiders and tourists," Father Roca recalled. "At first, I was fearful that the visitors would destroy the peacefulness and prayerful atmosphere of the spot. But that was not the case at all. Never have I seen an individual or a group disrupt the harmony of the place or show any kind of disrespect."

One of the tasks that Father Roca carried on week after week was answering the hundreds of letters he received from people all over the United States and the world who have made a pilgrimage to the Santuario. "This is a pleasant task," he said, "and one that I enjoy. But, you know, it does take time."

Invariably people ask the priest if the hole with the blessed soil is miraculously refilled as one of the legends states. "I fill the hole and I bless the soil," he said. "When people ask me if this dirt cures I tell them it is not the dirt, but your faith, that cures. I believe that the cures and the 'miracles' are caused by faith. I tell them to take some dirt as a memory of your visit to the Santuario."

After a visit with Father Roca one is struck by the joyfulness and the placid simplicity of this little man. He had given 30 years of his life to the Santuario. The spirit of simplicity and silence that envelopes the Santuario has, without a doubt, cast its spell in the heart and soul of this little man who is a giant in the faith. ∾

1987

ATICAN II LIVES ON

October 11, 1987, marked the twenty-fifth anniversary of the opening of the Second Vatican Council. Mr. Robert P. Lockwood, editor of Our Sunday Visitor, *invited this author to write a commemorative article to mark the occasion since he served as the newspaper's correspondent during the four sessions of the Council. This article appeared in the Nov. 8, 1987, issue of that publication.*

C hange! Change was the buzz word of the first generation of the post-conciliar Church. We indulged in a sometimes wild spree of moving furniture around in our houses of worship. We created with little preparation and less understanding new structures and organizations. We scourged ourselves with endless meetings, which sometimes appeared as meetings just for the sake of holding meetings. We inflicted ourselves with a terrible soul-searching, administered too often by pop-psychologists and amateur sociologists, which brought many of us to the brink of desperation and despair. We were overcome, and sometimes over-awed, by "instant" theologians and religious educators who, after a few summer sessions or workshops, proclaimed themselves "authorities" on the teachings of Vatican II.

This was also a time of deep sadness. Confusion spread like a virus among the People of God. Millions took a walk – and never came back. Priests and religious men and women abandoned their traditional posts in favor of other occupations in which many of them sincerely believed they could better serve God's people. Schools closed. Seminaries and novitiates were sold. Morale was at its lowest in the history of the Catholic Church in the United States.

In all this anguish and turmoil many failed to see that a renewal was also taking place. Lay people were taking on new ministries, from eucharistic ministers to hospital administrators. A blooming charismatic apostolate bore witness to the presence of the Holy Spirit at work in His Church. More and more people sought deeper understanding of the faith through scripture courses and adult education programs. There were, beneath the surface, other signs of life!

Yet, as I witnessed and experienced these high and low tides in the Church, both sad and glad, good and bad, I continually asked myself, "What's missing?" If we did get sidetracked, as I believe we did for a while, if we failed to understand fully the teaching of Vatican II, if there have been aberrations, disappointments and failures – "Where did we go wrong?"

Many times I re-read Pope John XXIII's opening address and more and more little phrases like these jumped out at me: "spiritual riches," "medicine of mercy," and "goods of divine grace." Then it struck me like a thunderbolt: *We missed the profound spiritual dimension of the Second Vatican Council.* Its success lay not in the externals of the organization but in the internal spiritual life of the organism. Pope John and Vatican II sought to make us saints, not social activists.

In order to flourish the spiritual life demands two prerequisites which are in short supply today. These are *simplicity* and *silence*. Neither as individuals nor as Church will we begin to see the fulfillment of Vatican II without these two virtues.

Simplicity implies that we do not need – in fact, we can be enslaved by – the multiplicity of organizations, meetings and a constant bombardment of words, words, words. Simplicity means we can easily "do without" most of the gadgets and devices of an ever-expanding technology. Simplicity forces us, sooner or later, to come to the awe-filled truth that only in the emptiness of our own being can we truly find our God.

Silence reminds us that God is not found in a whirlwind of activity in a world more threatened by noise than air pollution. Silence leads us into the desert (even in our own kitchens and backyards) where we can discover God – and ourselves.

After 30 years of writing and speaking I am working on this hidden agenda of Vatican II. *It is not too late to find it.*

Postscript. While serving as a working journalist during these years I felt at times that I was receiving the best post-graduate education that a Catholic priest could receive anywhere. I was interviewing men who gave me a cross-section of the Catholic Church in the world. Among some of these that I particularly recall were Cardinal Franciscus Koenig of Austria, Archbishop Denis Hurley, O.M.I. of South Africa, Archbishop Harold Henry, C.S.C. of Korea, Bishop John Taylor, O.M.I of Sweden, Auxiliary Bishop (later Archbishop) Marcos McGrath, C.S.C. of Panama, Canon Francis Houtart of Belgium, Father Hans Küng of Switzerland and Father Placid Jordon, O.M.I. of Germany.

The interview which I considered to be my greatest coup was with the four theologians banned in 1964 from speaking at The Catholic University of America. They were Fathers John Courtney Murray, S.J.. Godfrey Diekmann, O.S.B., Gustave Weigel, S.J. and Hans Küng. I gathered them together one evening for dinner at the Pensione Sitea and taped an interview. This was published in the *American Benedictine Review* and appears elsewhere in these pages. ❧

1989

NATOMY OF A PRESBYTERY

The publication of a photo directory of the priests of the Church of St. Cloud was one of the projects undertaken during the centennial year of the local church in 1989. Father Robert Rolfes, assistant diocesan chancellor, asked me to write an historical essay for this publication. The work was distributed only among the members of the local presbytery, This is the first time it has been published for the general public.

In the years gone by it was customary among many priests in Canada to place the letters "P.P." behind their names. When I asked what the letters represented one priest told me they stood for "Parish Priest." In recent years I learned that Father Andrew Nolan also signed "P.P." behind his name. Years ago I thought that was, indeed, a strange custom. It took me more than a few years and many experiences to come to realize that for an ordained minister of Christ "Parish Priest" was, indeed, a fine title.

Priests, we know, are public figures, whether they like it or not. The public has always had a fascination for priests, whether they be the youngest associate pastor or the bishop of Rome. Writers are both intrigued and puzzled by priests, hence they are often the principal characters in novels and plays. Perhaps Chaucer inaugurated the procession of priests of English letters with his tale of the priest in *The Canterbury Tales*. Henry Morton Robinson may have inaugurated the contemporary deluge of literary works about priests with his 1950 novel, *The Cardinal*. Bing Crosby and Barry Fitzgerald created two proto-types of pre-conciliar priests in the motion pictures, "Going My Way," and "The Bells of St. Mary's." Collen McCollough's *The Thornbirds* introduced the English-speaking reading and viewing public a sometimes shocking image of the priest. From Graham Greene's masterful *The Power and the Glory* to Andrew Greeley's best-selling *The Cardinal Sins*, the priest continually holds the interest of the American reading public. Perhaps two local novelists, J. F. Powers and Jon Hassler, have used members of our presbytery as images of priests that figure in their works.

THE PARISH PRIEST

The chief characteristic of the presbytery of St. Cloud is that throughout its one hundred years its members were predominantly parish priests. This is not unusual, for almost without exception they were ordained with the conviction in their own minds to serve people in parishes. I learned that very young in my own life.

I recall a rainy day when I was standing at the side door of Crosier Preparatory Seminary with Father John Van den Bosch, O.S.C. At the time he was dean of discipline and, most probably, it was one of those rare occasions when he and I visited on matters other than disciplinary.

He asked me, "Why do you want to be a priest?"

Assuming a pious stance wholly unbecoming to me, which now I realize he readily saw through, I answered, "To become holy."

"Then you'll never make a good priest."

Startled, I asked, "Why not?"

Letting the smoke from his cigarette form a halo over his head, he slowly replied, "Because a priest is ordained not for himself but for people."

It took me more than a few years to realize fully the depth of wisdom and reams of theology in that simple statement.

Parish priests have been the mortar which held the bricks of this local church together. Bishops could accomplish almost nothing without their loyalty and support. For the most part, and by overwhelming numbers, the parish priests cooperated fully with their chief shepherds. The strongest bonds of cooperation and affection were those forged during the brick and mortar years of Bishop James Trobec (1897-1915). His relations with his priests were the most fraternal and amicable of any bishop before or after him.

There were, however, two periods when the bonds between bishops and priests were severely tested. The first was during the first decade of the administration of Bishop Joseph F. Busch (1915-1953). The fault, as in most cases where there is something to be desired, was on both sides. The young bishop was impetuous in imposing the social teachings of the Church upon a body of priests who know little about that teaching as embodied in papal directives. On the other side, most priests preferred to maintain the status quo.

The second was in the first decade of the administration of Bishop George H. Speltz (1968-1987). In this case, however, it was not so much the bonds between bishop and priests as bonds between priests and priests that were strained. This was the era of the late sixties and early seventies following the Second Vatican Council. It was a time of conflict throughout the modern Church, amply evidenced locally by the twenty-six members of the presbytery who left the active ministry. At this time we are still too close to that era to evaluate it completely, but the scars and the pain will last into the next century.

Fortunately, the many blessings we enjoy today in the Church of St. Cloud have been the results of a wholesome cooperation by priests with their bishops. Little wonder, then, that the Fathers of the Second Vatican Council called priests "cooperators in our order."

Throughout these one hundred years priests also served as diocesan officials in such positions as vicars general, chancellors, editors and directors of various offices. In such capacities they were called to serve as auxiliaries to the parish priests. Their success or failure in these offices was determined by how well or how badly they performed their services to parish priests. Fortunately, for the good of these "official" priests themselves as well as the Church of St. Cloud, most of these also served at the same time in the parochial ministry. One immediately thinks of Monsignor T. S. Ziolkowski who, during his term as chancellor, also served as chaplain of the Poor Clare Sisters and pastor of Immaculate Conception Parish in Becker. From 1968-1990 Father David Rieder has served as director of the diocesan Bureau of Education and throughout that same period as pastor of St. Patrick's Parish in Minden Township, Benton County.

Priests and People

A truism stated many times in many ways expresses the relation of a parish priest to his people: A priest is formed by his people as much as – and perhaps more than – people are fashioned by their priest. The bonds between parish priest and people in the Church of St. Cloud have generally been close. Several factors attest to that happy relationship.

By comparison with parishes in many other dioceses, parishes in this local church were generally small in area and the number of parishioners, relatively few. This enabled the parish priest to know his people individually, not infrequently on a first name basis. This also enabled the people of the parish to know their pastor "warts and all." Secondly, for the most part in these one hundred years at least fifty percent of the members of the presbytery were sons of the Church of St. Cloud and their numerous relatives were scattered throughout many parishes. Bonds of blood thus strengthened the ties between priests and people. Thirdly, the pioneer Catholic families brought with them either from the old country or from the eastern states a profound reverence and love of priests (this was especially true of the Polish and Irish immigrants). Catholic people were both honored and flattered when they could "help the good Father" or when the parish priest was present at family gatherings marking first communions, weddings or funerals.

These strong bonds between parish priest and people, however, were not universal and at times were stretched to the breaking point on both sides. A few examples suffice:

When Father Charles Pfeiffer as pastor in Duelm clobbered one of his parishioners over the head with a board from the picket fence or when Father Frank First as pastor in St. Rosa greeted a trustee at the door with a loaded revolver pointed at the latter's heart, relations between pastor and people left something to be desired. On the other hand, when a group of men in Pierz set off dynamite at the rectory or when two ladies in St. Anna rose in the pew one Sunday and jeered the pastor during his sermon, again, relations between people and pastor left something to be desired. Perhaps the saddest confrontation took place in the rural parish of St. Anthony in 1916 when three men of the parish physically abused the pastor, Father Ignatius Tomazin. They literally drove the golden jubilarian to such a depth of depression that a few days later he committed suicide by jumping out of a sixth floor window of the Sherman Hotel in Chicago.

Some priests were, unfortunately, obstreperous, autocratic and authoritarian, and this cannot be denied. In most of these cases they were unloved by their people. Stories are still told in Melrose how people crossed the street in order to avoid greeting a pastor. Monsignor Francis Gilligan of the St. Paul Seminary put it succinctly when he used to say, "Every pound of clericalism produces an ounce of anti-clericalism."

KINDS OF PRIESTS

Priests usually come in all shapes and sizes and are all manner of men. There are the young, usually associate pastors, in the vigor of the green years. These are always popular, especially among the young, and often endowed with boundless zeal (perhaps energy would be a better word). They are determined to convert the world.

There are the middle-aged priests who have learned from experience – sometimes happy and other times sad – that this is not the best of all worlds, that there must be a heaven because there is no absolute justice here, that even with the oil of ordination on their hands and the best of intentions in their hearts they must accept the fact that they can only accomplish so much in one day. They have learned to recognize the presence of sin and evil in the world around them and within themselves. They find their satisfaction at the end of each day by breathing a prayer, "Well, Lord, at least I tried to do my best."

The older priests are the senators, those men bent from the burden and heat of the day. Their eyes are dimmed but their minds contain a storehouse of wisdom. Their hands are shaky but their hearts are brimming over with a silent, content love of God and His people. They find satisfaction when they meet an older couple with four bright-eyed grandchildren who say to him, "Father, you married us at the cathedral in 1944." They find reassurance for their own lives when they attend a first communion Mass and watch eighty-three children approach the altar for the first time and are filled with hope when they assist at the Mass of the Chrism and are surrounded by many younger and more talented priests.

One has to be a parish priest to know what this is like and lived long enough to know a variety of priests. An Irish bishop tried to explain the life of the parish priest when he wrote in the pages of *The Furrow*: "God is in the bits and pieces of every day."

Parish priests do not generally make headlines; as a matter of fact, most shun them more than being caught in Minnesota blizzard. They are the foot soldiers on the front line of battle against the world, the flesh and sometimes unruly members of their own parish. Their greatest challenge is the routine of daily living, such as the appointments in the office, work with children and youth in the classroom, the meeting of the parish council, the leaky faucet in the church basement, listening to the trials and tribulations of the parish's custodial engineer, the pettiness and rivalries among the members of his own flock. They are "the bits and pieces" God uses to make of them the saints He wants them to become.

These priests of the Church of St. Cloud have lived for one hundred years a life so routine that those who do not understand the priesthood would call it boring. Such observers, however, fail to understand the marvels of God's grace which shine forth even in the "bits and pieces of every day." These parish priests, for the most part, came to understand the mysteries of divine grace and saw the splendor of life, human and divine, in the ordinary events of their own and their people's lives. In doing this they learned the nature of holiness which St. Therese, the Little Flower, said consisted in "doing the ordinary things extraordinarily well." Their commitment made fidelity their predominant virtue.

VIRTUES AND VICES

If fidelity was their most conscious external virtue, charity was even greater as the interior motivating force. I recall several years ago when one of my nephews was down and out without a job. His pastor, one of the older members of this presbytery, approached him and gave him four hundred dollars. "This might help you," said the pastor, "to make a little Christmas for your wife and five children." I have never let that pastor know that I knew this because, I am sure, he would be embarrassed by others knowing his good deeds. But his act was only one of the hundreds of thousands of similar deeds performed by the members of this presbytery who strive to let their light shine on a candlestick but want their good deeds hidden under a bushel basket.

Priests like to think they are worldly-wise when it comes to dealing with a knight of the open road, but every panhandler from St. Paul to Seattle knows that most priests are pushovers when it comes to giving a handout. There are few, if any, men, women or children in the Church of God who could not recount at least one good, kind word or deed a priest had given them. Gruff as some of them were in many external ways, they never refused to aid a person in need.

Stating that fidelity and charity were their conspicuous virtues does not imply that they had no faults. They are of common clay and their feet were sometimes stuck in the mud of this earth while their eyes gazed upon the heavens. They might on occasion be faulted, with some justification, of teetering on the dangerous side of mediocrity.

Their local church was not conspicuous; their parishes were generally small; their people's concerns were relatively limited. There existed from the beginning the danger of being parochial, in the pejorative sense of that word. While this parochialism, paradoxically, enabled them to serve as good pastors, at the same time it led some of them all too easily into the area of smugness and complacency. The range of their reading was much too narrow. The cultivation of the arts was too often neglected. The difficulty many experienced in accepting the teachings of the Second Vatican Council indicated that they were babes in the woods in understanding the philosophical and theological explosion going on well before the Second World War. Such scholars as Scheeben, Rahner, Suhard and Congar were not their fellow travelers on their intellectual journey.

In later years most of these good men staunchly defended the papal encyclical, *Humanae Vitae* in a most admirable manner. Unfortunately, through some inexplicable mental block, they completely ignored the teachings of the same Pope Paul VI in his other encyclical, *Populorum Progressio.* Generally speaking, they did not feel it imperative to disturb the comfortable either in their own ranks or among their people. In other words, all too often they failed to fulfill a prophetic role.

Closely associated with this ever-present danger of surrendering to mediocrity was the all too common vice found among most professionals, namely, jealousy. Generally, if any member of the fraternity raised his head above the crowd he became the target of criticism, whether deserved or undeserved. Too often uniformity was confused with unity, conformity with loyalty. From the beginning there had been among some of the members of this presbytery this enfeebling fault which tried to level all priests down to the same common denominator. Jealousy is the stepchild of mediocrity.

This was the first problem Bishop Trobec faced even before his consecration as he tried to solve the conflict between Monsignor Joseph Bauer and Father Edward Jones. In more recent years the same vice appeared under the guise of egalitarianism which strives to erase all distinctiveness among priests, regardless of age, experience, position or merit. There is, whether some like to acknowledge it or not, a vast difference between a priest ordained forty years and one ordained five years – and in ways which have little to do with age.

If clerical jealousy was endemic to the priestly calling that other bane on the spiritual life – ambition – was dealt a deadly blow in the late 1960's. For many decades many priests strove to arrive at a "good parish," which, in some minds, was considered to be one with a large church, a parochial school and one or more assistant priest. A dash of the purple was also part of that ambition. In the post-conciliar years that temptation was removed by two notable factors. The first was the discontinuance of personal stole fees and the standardization of salaries; the other was the increasing difficulties in financially maintaining a parochial school.

Another form of clerical ambition was removed when the presbyteral council voted, and Bishop George Speltz approved, that parish priests have a term of office consisting of six years, renewable for another six years. Thus the death blow was dealt to any future possibility of such long-term pastorates as Monsignor Peter Kroll's fifty years at St. John Cantius in St. Cloud and Father Joseph Linz's thirty-eight years at St. Margaret's in Lake Henry. The irremovable pastor faded into the sunset.

In spite of these faults, or vices if you will, an admirable fraternity existed and was cultivated among the members of the presbytery. In earlier years it was manifested by an avid interest in cards. Priests gathered around the table for a friendly game of skat, bridge or poker. These gatherings were not structured; they just happened at the drop of a hat. Priests gathered regularly also as neighbors for Forty Hours devotions, patronal feasts and parish missions. These were occasions not only for liturgical services but also the time when priests leisurely enjoyed each other's company and conversation.

In later years more structured activities were introduced to develop priestly fraternity. Thus such events as the annual clergy golf tournament and, for some years, the bowling tournament, deanery days and Emmaus groups were created. One laudable means was the introduction of a weekly day set aside by several groups throughout the diocese to prepare the Sunday homily. At no time did the bond of fraternity manifest itself more clearly than at the time of a priest's funeral and, to a lesser degree, the funeral of a priest's parent. As the pace of life quickened priests found they had to make room in their schedules for clerical gatherings lest their fraternity be destroyed.

Clearly associated with, and in some ways a part of, the presbytery of the Church of St. Cloud were those members of religious communities who also labored within the diocese. One would not be a wide-awake observer if he did not recognize that a certain rivalry existed between the diocesan and religious clergy. But this contest may have been more marked between superiors than among the general body of priests. Diocesan priests in the field worked shoulder to shoulder and hand in hand with Benedictine, Crosier, Franciscan and Precious Blood priests with little, if any, distinction or animosity. The conflict between "seculars" and "regulars" was a myth perpetuated throughout the years by a very small group. As a matter of fact, the vast majority of diocesan priests were educated by and grateful to religious priests for their training during seminary years.

Gifts of Parish Priests

Priests also brought many gifts to the Church of St. Cloud. This is not saying, however, that they were all extremely gifted men. Nonetheless, each had particular gifts of nature and grace and thus in various ways each in his own life fulfilled the words of St. Paul: "*There are different gifts but the same Spirit; there are different ministries but the same Lord; there are different works by the same God who accomplished all of them in everyone*" (1 Cor 12: 4-5).

The people they served recognized these gifts in their priests and understood well that not every priest was endowed with all the gifts that they might wish to see in their pastors. On the other hand, if left to the wishes of some parishioners, the priest would have a job description that even the Cure of Ars would be unable to fill. Nonetheless, their comments about their priests reflected what they considered to be the virtues of a good parish priest.

In their estimation a good pastor must be kind to all his people, especially old people; he must be prompt in visiting the sick and patient with a loving concern for children and youth. He should be a good organizer and shrewd administrator, but in more recent years these qualities were not reckoned too highly because these ministries could easily, and in many cases more effectively, be filled by competent lay people. The priest, however, must conduct a good liturgy, or as some would say, be an effective presider of the assembly. Most of all, the people want a good homilist who would unfold to them through his own study and prayer the relevance of the Word of God in their lives.

CAUSES OF TENSION

In recent years a marked anxiety exists in the presbytery. It is not simply the usual tension engendered by the generation gap nor the old way in contrast to the new way. The tension is much deeper and thus has the potential of being more damaging. One middle-aged priest expressed that stress in the following words:

"The malaise is really profound among my age group. We have the feeling that the last one out will have to turn out the lights. We often feel unsupported and distrusted by those above us and those below us in the Church. Neither people nor bishops nor pope seem to have any hesitation about making demands, using insults and coercion to achieve their will and expecting conversion of persons without conversion of institutions. Rebellion came after our day in the seminary. In our day – out of obedience – we emptied our heads and hearts and spirits of the old. We gave up the faith of our youth which had moved us to the seminary in the first place. Out of obedience to the Council and pope we put ourselves on the line for reformed liturgy, reformed ecclesiology, reformed catechetics and reformed social justice teaching. Perhaps our expectations were too high or too immature. But we do not feel that we were terribly successful at the reforms. Now to make matters worse, we are again blamed for the destruction of the faith, the destruction of the church. It seems that we can be neither conservative enough to please hierarchical types nor liberal enough to please liberationists. All of this is exacerbated by living in a society in the western world in which community is degraded and the individual is exulted. We end up, in the final analysis, feeling that we belong to no one."

The present malaise among the clergy is manifested by a pervasive sense of sadness and stress. The bishops of the United States took note of this phenomenon and in 1982 addressed a statement concerning the damaging effects of stress in the ranks of the clergy.

This sadness and stress among the priests of the Church of St. Cloud arises from their inner pastoral concern about two major phenomena that have appeared very recently, no further removed than the present generation. These are the obvious lack of loyalty to the Church and the decreasing credibility of the members of the Church which many of the disaffected call "the institutional church."

The declining attendance at weekly Mass even in the most solidly Catholic communities is but the most obvious manifestation of this lack of loyalty. One priest in our ranks put it this way: "In the past most Catholics stayed with the church even through conflicts, today many Catholics just walk away to another church or to no church." The Church has not been spared this lack of loyalty which also manifests itself in most of its institutions.

The credibility gap has manifested itself in two disparate ways. As the Catholic body becomes more and more educated it rejects the simplistic answers and sometimes atrocious catechesis which, unfortunately, are still being offered by not a few members of the presbytery. On the other hand, the faults and scandals of a few leaders of the Church have been given wide publicity by the mass media. This is grist for the mill of those who want to find fault and afford them the opportunity to discredit even more their sometimes cynical ridicule of the Church.

In recent years, too, society from the family to the workplace has begun to notice stress and burn-out and frustration as never before so that a whole new vocabulary and science have developed around these topics. The priest today finds himself in this same society. The simplicity and very structured faith and life of the past are no more; they have been replaced by a complexity which sometimes causes not a few priests to feel that the whole world is unraveling around them. Nor can it be denied that many more demands are placed upon the priest today than in previous generations.

FILLED WITH HOPE

This lack of loyalty and credibility has been a heavy burden for most priests to carry. Every time they come up against these phenomena the more acute their stress and the deeper their sorrow. Nonetheless, with an "ain't-down-yet" resiliency they strive to live by hope.

Their hope is not for pie in the sky. They look to the beginnings of this presbytery in 1889 and see that from fifteen priests and 30,000 Catholic people this local church has flourished and continues to flourish throughout these one hundred years. The hope of this presbytery rests on the firm conviction that God guides this Church of St. Cloud with His own loving providence. Fortunately, that hope burns brightly in most members of this presbytery today.

They much prefer to live their lives in the shadow of a holy hope founded upon the one who sits on the Throne and says, "*See, I make all things new*" (Rev. 21:5). ∾

1990

ACREDNESS OF THE WORD

The author frequently discussed the sacredness of the written and spoken word with Alfred G. Muellerleile, Father Godfrey Diekmann, O.S.B. and others. In 1991 the writer wrote this essay in memory of the distinguished St. Paul typographer and printer. It was published by the National Catholic Reporter.

My mother could never leave bread on the table without covering it with a napkin. As a boy I asked her once why she did that. "The bread we eat at the table," she replied, " is sort of a symbol of the sacred bread we receive in holy Communion." I never forgot that.

As I grew older and began writing I came to realize, little by little, that words also had a profoundly symbolic, quasi-sacramental character, like my mother's bread had for her. I often wished that I were a theologian in order to be able to present the mystical character of the written and spoken word. At times I reflected on God's creating word and the Incarnate Word of God. Both of these profound mysteries I saw – was I alone? – reflected in the human word. Always, however, I felt inadequate to express these thoughts because of my lack of theological training.

Nonetheless,I reflected many times on that thought, started a file on the subject and I once wrote Father Gustave Weigel, S.J., to see if he might be able to direct me to some references. I knew, too, that my friend, Alfred Muellerleile, the printer, shared with me this profound respect for the word and we frequently discussed this subject. I recall also asking Dr. Franz Mueller at the University of St. Thomas if he was aware of any work on the subject. He dropped me a note citing Romano

Guardini's statement concerning "the primacy of the Logos over the chaos" and referring me to volume four of the *Theological Dictionary of the New Testament*. For the most part, however, I was running into stone walls and, time after time, bemoaned my lack of theological training.

I did come, at least tentatively, to two conclusions, but even these I had difficulty formulating. I even felt at times that people would laugh at me if I tried to express them. Now that I am older, I say to myself, "Let them laugh." Here goes.

First, the written and spoken word is creative, just as the first recorded words God spoke were creative. So we read in the third verse of the Book of Genesis: "God said, 'Let there be light,' and there was light." Again and again "God said" and the universe burst forth as His creation because of His word. God continued to speak His word, revealing Himself to His creatures. That creative word of God continues to be spoken:

Isaiah recalls the on-going creation of the universe: "Lift up your eyes on high and see who has created these (Is 40:26)."

The author of the Letter to the Hebrews put it well in the first words of his letter: "In times past, God spoke in partial and various ways to our ancestors through the prophets; in these last days, he spoke to us through a son, whom he made heir of all things and through whom he created the universe... (He 1:1-2)."

Such reflections brought me to the great, central mystery of our Christian faith: God became man. How magnificent that the God-Man should be proclaimed in the prologue of St. John's Gospel in words echoing the opening words of God's creation: "In the beginning was the Word, and the Word was with God, and the Word was God (Jn 1:1)." How inexplicable, at least to me, that the other name of Jesus would be "the Word." I cannot recall how often I reflected that this world-shattering mystery of our faith was dependent upon words: "Mary said, 'Behold, I am the handmaid of the Lord. May it be done to me according to your word' (Lk 1:38)."

One scrap I found in my files contained a sentence I jotted down which I liked and whose author's name I failed to note: "The human response to the Word of God constitutes a complex interior attitude which bears all the marks of theological life: faith, since the Word is revelation; hope, since it is a promise; love, since it is a rule of life." And is it not significant that we refer to Word and Sacrament in our sacred liturgy? Is it not also significant that it is by *words* read from a book or spoken from memory that we bring the Eternal Word of God to be the Bread of Life for His brothers and sisters? How often I wished I were a theologian!

OUR FEEBLE ATTEMPTS

When the first man or woman took a primitive tool in hand and scratched on the wall of a cave, the skin of a goat, a clay tablet or a bundle of weeds stitched together and called papyrus, something marvelous and mysterious happened. He or she created a word. In the flow of time words were formed from letters called an alphabet. The word was drawn by artists, set in type by printers, painted on signs by officials and garbled by a child on the mother's knee. Throughout the early Middle Ages monks elegantly copied the word in now priceless manuscripts and in the fifteenth century Johann Gutenberg started a revolution by inventing moveable type. In time the word became everybody's property and especially those essayists, humanists, historians, journalists, philosophers and poets who came to be called merchants of words.

The word became the preserve of saints, such as St. Francis of Assisi's *Canticle of the Sun*, the tool of statesmen, such as Niccolo Machievelli's *The Prince* which elevated political duplicity to the status of a diplomacy, and Tom Paine's *Common Sense* which fostered an American revolution. The word was enshrined in a book called *The Bible*, the all-time best-seller. Unfortunately, the word was also profaned by unworthy scribes who produced, promulgated, prostituted and proliferated it to appeal to the lower instincts of human nature.

The word, written and spoken, has a life of its own. Well might it survive at least five thousand years. It is the creator of culture and civilization; the word becomes the building blocks of wisdom.

So I wondered often, "How dare Lerner and Lowe, in that stunning musical, *My Fair Lady*, put into Eliza Doolittle's mouth, 'Words, words, words, I'm so sick of them.'" Millions of people might agree with her, but not me. True, indeed, that millions of words are spewn out each day by the electronic media, so much so that the press, radio and television become our masters instead of what Pope Pius XII called them, "the marvelous inventions of God." The word makes possible such a master-piece as Leo Tolstoy's *War and Peace*; Lawrence Olivier's majestic *Hamlet*; and Neil Diamond's "Song Sung Blue." We live by the word – even braille – and cannot live without words.

Those examples alone indicate the sacredness of the word. We reach a higher plane when we consider that the word on earth reflects the Word in heaven. The mystery of the word on earth is, admittedly, dim and dull in the light of the Eternal Word. In His shadow everyone can make his own Jeremiah's words, "Ah, Lord God, I know not how to speak; I am too young (Jer 1:6)."

I spent many years seeking some confirmation of these thoughts. I found it only on Feb. 16, 1993, when I read these words of St. Athanasius: "As the word we speak is an image of the Word who is God's Son, so also is the wisdom implanted in us an image of the Wisdom who is God's Son." ᕙ

1991

MA'S VERY GOOD BISCUITS

This essay I wrote in 1991 as a tribute to the faith of my mother and father. Although the incident happened in 1931, I only learned of it some years after I was ordained from my mother and Father Adrian Van Zuphten, O.S.C. It was published in the September, 1993, issue of Pastoral Life.

One of the teachings of the Catholic Church is what theologians call the *sensus fidelium*. In my own thumbnail knowledge of theology I interpret that Latin expression, which literally means "the sense of the faithful," to mean this: God's Providence directs the members of the Church in such a way that as a body they will "sense" or "feel" generally the rightness or wrongness of actions and the truthfulness or falsehood of religious doctrine.

I do believe that my parents had a firm grasp of this teaching. They not only lived by it but in at least one clear and dramatic case they practiced it. Although the event happened in the mid-1930's I only learned about this unusual incident several years after I was ordained a priest from my mother. When I asked her why she did not tell me about it earlier she simply replied, "I didn't think you were old enough."

Sometime after my mother told me this story I asked Father John Vander Hulst, O.S.C. about it and he confirmed what my mother told me. At the time this incident happened he was the prior of Crosier Monastery in Onamia. A jolly man who reminded one of Friar Tuck, he was one of earlier pioneering Dutch priests who came to the United States. The second part of the story happened about 20 years later, in the early-1950's.

One weekend in the 1930's our family drove to Onamia to visit my grandparents. As usually happened when we visited, Father Vander Hulst came for Sunday dinner to visit with my father. This particular Sunday he brought with him a man whom he introduced as Bishop Cornelius van Lerde. to give the person a name. My parents were highly honored and we children were somewhat dumbfounded to meet a real bishop. Before departing Father Vander Hulst asked my father if when our family departed later in the afternoon he would drive the bishop back to St. Paul. Both mother and father were deeply honored by the request.

As we approached St. Paul that evening the bishop asked if my parents would mind his staying at our home a few days before continuing on his travels because he had some business to do in Minneapolis. And so he did.

During the first day of his stay my mother asked if he would like to meet our pastor, Father Alois Ziskovsky. The bishop replied negatively, saying that he just wanted a few days of rest. At dinner that evening he asked if my father would drive him to the Andrews Hotel in Minneapolis because he had some business to do. He suggested that my father need not wait but should return at 12:30 in the morning and pick him up there.

Of course, my father said yes. That evening he also gave my mother a bundle of clothing to wash and among them she noted many pieces of civilian clothing.

Each day the bishop slept until late in the morning and coming downstairs he expected the comparatively lavish breakfast my mother prepared for him. I call this "lavish" because this was at the height of the Depression and my parents were far from well-to-do. He conversed little with my mother, taking a walk about the neighborhood in the afternoon and remaining in his bedroom most of the time. Mother thought this a bit strange but felt his reluctance to carry on a conversation was due to the broken English he spoke. Each evening my father drove him to Minneapolis and picked him up again at the Andrews Hotel at 12:30 in the morning. Each evening the bishop carried a small briefcase.

After about five days my mother said to father, "I don't trust this man."

"Why? He's a bishop. Father Vander Hulst recommended him."

"I know, but I just can't figure out what kind of business he would have in Minneapolis so late at night. I'm going with you tonight. After we leave him off we will drive around the block and park opposite the hotel and just watch for a while."

So they did. After sitting in the car for about fifteen minutes they noticed the bishop coming out of the hotel, dressed in civilian clothes with a woman whose arm was wrapped in his. (The Alvin burlesque theatre was only a few blocks from the hotel.)

"That's it!" said mother. "I'm going to call Father Ziskovsky as soon as we get home."

She told the pastor about the bishop who was staying at our home and what she noted and thought about him. "Now, now," the pastor counseled, "you and Alfons just go on the way you have been. Have Alfons pick him up tonight and act just as if nothing happened and you have no suspicions. I will get back to you tomorrow."

The bishop was, indeed, a priest of the Crosier Order who spent many years as a missionary in Brazil in that area where the Crosiers had many missions. A Crosier traditionally served as a bishop in that area and had spiritual jurisdiction over the priests and people. Upon the death of the bishop, van Lerde expected to be appointed his successor. He was not. No doubt deeply angry and frustrated, he left the missions, purchased the robes of a bishop and went traveling throughout the United States soliciting funds for what he called "my poor missions in Brazil." As a matter of fact, he was the poor one, indeed.

After my mother told me this story I asked her why she became so suspicious of the so-called bishop.

"There were several things," she replied. "First, it seemed strange that he didn't want to meet Father Ziskovsky. And I never saw him with his prayerbook and I knew priests had to say certain prayers every day. Perhaps what bothered me most of all was that he never went to church to offer Mass." *Sensus fidelium!*

❧   ❧   ❧   ❧   ❧

The morrow dawned, a cold, stormy March day. My Dad went

to work and we children hurried off to school. Mother began baking bread. She heard the front doorbell ring and went to answer it. She noticed two big black cars parked in front of the house.

"You can't imagine my surprise," she said to me, "when I opened the door and there stood Father Ziskovsky, another priest and Archbishop John Gregory Murray." The other priest was a Father Gregory who was chancellor of the archdiocese at that time. Although flustered, she ushered them into the living room and said she was baking bread.

"Would you like to have a cup of coffee and a biscuit?"

"Where is that man?" asked the archbishop.

"In the first room on your right at the top of the stairs."

The archbishop marched up the stairs. The pastor said he and Father Gregory would enjoy a cup of coffee. The two of them and my mother sat around the dining room table.

"I couldn't make out what he was saying," my mother recalled, "but I could sure hear the archbishop talking a mile a minute. He sounded angry."

After some time the archbishop descended the stairs, walked into the dining room and sat down.

"Father Gregory," he said, "that man is packing. You take him to the union depot and don't leave him until you have him placed on the next train to Chicago. Go back to the office and call the chancellor there and tell him about this man's coming. Father Ziskovsky will drive me back to our office."

My mother was more than a little shaken by all this ecclesiastical talk and no doubt showed her confusion. Kindly the archbishop thanked her for her help, explained that the man was a fraud and church officials throughout the United States were looking for him. And he thanked her again.

"Now, Mrs. Yzermans," he said, "I will have that cup of coffee and one of your fresh biscuits." My mother thought he said that to help put her at ease.

I had also learned later that this man had been traveling around the United States taking up collections in parishes for the "Crosier poor missions in Brazil." Of course, he was a fraud and pocketed the money. The Catholic bishops were aware of his presence in the country but had no way of locating him until this day.

❧   ❧   ❧   ❧   ❧

Those who knew Archbishop Murray were aware of the fact that he possessed a phenomenal memory. Some 20 years later I became involved in this incident in a rather unusual manner. That involvement underscores the touching humanness of the little Archbishop of St. Paul.

When serving as an assistant pastor of St. Mary's Cathedral, St. Cloud, I was told by my pastor to go to the chancery in St. Cloud. Bishop Bartholome had called and asked for one of the assistants to drive Archbishop Murray and him to St. John's Abbey because the archbishop wanted to visit with the abbot. The only contacts I ever had with the archbishop were the day he confirmed me in 1936 and listening to him as he preached in the chapel of St. Paul Seminary. I, too, was a bit nervous.

As I drove out to the abbey the archbishop sat next to me and Bishop Bartholome in the backseat. The archbishop asked me my name.

"Father Yzermans, Your Excellency."

He paused a moment. "Do you have relatives in St. Matthew's parish in St. Paul?"

"Yes, they are my parents."

"How, then, did you become a priest of the Diocese of St. Cloud?"

I reminded him of the archdiocesan regulation that stated anyone who spent time as a member of a religious community would not be accepted as a candidate for the priesthood by the archdiocese. I told him that I spent more than a year as a novice in the Crosier Order.

He thought for a moment. "How are your parents?"

"In very good health, Archbishop."

"Does your mother still make those very good biscuits?"

"People say so."

"You know, I once had coffee and biscuits with your mother in your home?"

"I do. My mother told me about it only a couple of years ago."

"When you see your mother please give her my warmest greet-ings. Tell her I still remember her biscuits."

"I will."

And the subject changed to other matters.... ∽

1991

 HURCH'S MILLENIUM IN
AMERICA

*Former Governor of Minnesota Elmer L. Anderson and Father
Joseph Linn, Knights of Columbus Council of Big Lake,
underwrote the costs of publishing a booklet in 1991 entitled* First
Evangelizer of the First Diocese. *It was mailed to every
Catholic and Lutheran pastor in Minnesota at that time.
Subsequently it was published in the Winter, 1993, issue of* U.S.
Catholic Historian.

The Catholic Church's *Statistical Yearbook for 1989,* the latest available year, contains an especially interesting item. For the first time, it listed statistics for Greenland. There are one parish, one priest and fifty-four Catholics among the 80,000 inhabitants of the largest island in the world.[1] Greenland is an autonomous yet integral part of the Kingdom of Denmark and its few Catholic people are members of the Diocese of Copenhagen.

These statistics call to mind a heroic episode in American Catholic history little known even among professional historians. That history includes the first evangelization of the western hemisphere; the baptism and burial of the first Europeans on the North American continent; the creation of the first diocese in the western hemisphere; the restoration of Christianity in the northern reaches of the western hemisphere almost three centuries after it disappeared. The quincentenary of the landing of Columbus affords "a teaching moment" for recalling a phase of American Catholic history almost forgotten and frequently ignored.[2] These events are the subject of this essay.

The astonishing voyages of the Norsemen throughout the early Middle Ages are well known. Their raids along the coasts of Europe, and all the way into the Mediterranean as far as to Constantinople, brought fame to the Norsemen and fear to others as they spread death and destruction along their way, even causing parents to instill discipline in their children with the threat, "The Vikings will get you." Yet these intrepid seamen with their long boats established a kingdom in Ireland, gave England one of its great rulers, King Canute, and left their name in that part of France which we call Normandy today. William the Conqueror who changed the course of world history in 1066 was a descendant of a Viking king. They colonized Iceland, a massive undertaking, 600 nautical miles from Norway; it was a renegade in Iceland who discovered and colonized Greenland 200 miles from Iceland. These were relatively brief journeys for adventurous sailors who traveled as far as Constantinople. However, these voyages in the northern ocean were treacherous and resulted in the loss of many lives because of the Arctic storms and the presence of icebergs. Sailing in these regions was limited chiefly to the late summer months. Nonetheless, as Winston Churchill wrote, "The soul of the Vikings lay in the long-ship," and G. J. Marcus, in his article in *The Irish Ecclesiastical Record*, made this pertinent observation:

"The oak-keels of the Viking longships had furrowed the seas of Europe from the Baltic to the Aegean; the terror inspired by their visitations had caused a new petition to be added to the litany.... For generation after generation Norsemen, Swedes and Danes, ranging ever further afield, had fought, burnt, looted and conquered on almost every coast in Europe. There never was a people for whom the sea has meant so much as these Scandinavians. The immense, loosely-knit confederation of the North was linked together, not, as in the case of the Roman Empire, with roads, but with river and searoutes."[3]

THE CONVERSION OF THE NORSEMEN

Throughout the eighth and ninth centuries the Christians of England and the surrounding isles prayed, "From the fury of the Norsemen, O Lord, deliver us." However, the deathknell of the raiding and plundering by the Vikings was sounded at the birth of Olav Trygvesson. The zeal of this most remarkable king was ultimately the cause of the establishment of the Norse Church in North America.

Olav Trygvesson was born in Norway in 968 and spent his youth at the home of his uncle, Sigrud Ericson, in Russia, where the Vikings had established settlements along the long rivers and ruled over the local Slavic peoples. When nineteen years old, he resolved to return to his native land to claim the crown which had been denied him. However, storms in the Baltic Sea drove him and his companions ashore where they wintered near the mouth of the Vistula River. There he married Geyra, the daughter of Mieczyslaw (964-992), father of Boleslaw I of Poland. After three years Geyra died and Olav entered upon a four-year career as a full-fledged Viking. He and his crew ravaged parts of modern-day Germany, Holland, Belgium, France, Ireland, England and Scotland until they arrived in the Scilly Islands in 994. A Christian hermit subdued the Viking, instructing him in the Christian faith and baptising him and his companions. Olav sailed to England as a man of peace, there meeting and marrying Gyda, the daughter of Olav Kvaran, the deceased Norse King of Dublin. Civil war in Norway brought Olav back to his native land where he was recognized as the legitimate king by the Thing (Parliament) in 994. For three years he traveled throughout the land, subduing rebellious factions and introducing Christianity, sometimes by persuasion and at other times – as was common in those times – by the sword. In 997 Olav dispatched a Saxon priest, Thangbrand, to introduce Christianity to Iceland, six hundred miles west of Norway. Olav brought bishops, priests and clerics from England to serve the needs of the nascent Christian Church in Norway and Iceland.[4] This action on the part of King Olav set in motion a religious rivalry that would continue throughout the early Middle Ages. (King Olav Trygvesson should not be confused with St. Olav Haroldson who became king of Norway in 1016.)

The German Archdiocese of Bremen struggled for many years to exert its jurisdiction over the Church in Norway as it had done in Denmark and Sweden. Earlier, St. Ansgar, the Benedictine monk named Archbishop of Hamburg, was appointed by Pope Gregory IV as papal legate to Scandinavia. In 847 he was transferred to the see of Bremen and continued to supervise the missionary work in Sweden and Denmark. He also held jurisdiction over Norway inasmuch as he was the metropolitan of the dioceses in Scandinavia. Such was the ecclesiastical situation until the Archdiocese of Lund was created in 1104 to which the dioceses in Norway were attached. During this period the archbishops of Bremen attempted to introduce the customs and traditions of the German Church into Norway but met with staunch resistance from the Anglo-Saxon clergy. Not until the establishment of the Archdiocese of Trondheim in 1152 was the Church in Norway freed of foreign jurisdiction. Even after that time, however, it bore the stamp of the Anglo-Saxon Church from which its early bishops and priests had come.[5]

Eric the Red

One of Olav's subjects was Eric Thorvaldson, known as Eric the Red in the Icelandic sagas, a powerful man with great wealth who succeeded in acquiring as many enemies as friends. After committing the crime of manslaughter, he was exiled from Iceland. Unable to return to Norway for the same reason, and having heard of a new land to the west sighted by his friend, Gunnibjorn, Eric set the sails of his ships westward. He discovered what he thought was a large peninsula lying 200 miles from Iceland. The year was 985. He named his discovery Greenland, thinking the name would attract settlers to come to his new land. He received permission to return to Ireland to seek settlers for his new colony. The following year he sailed from Iceland with a flotilla of twenty-five ships loaded with colonists; thirteen (some chronicles say fourteen) were lost at sea but twelve arrived safely in Greenland. The settlers established two colonies, 180 miles apart, on the shores of Greenland facing the present Baffin Island. They named one the Eastern Settlement, or Brattahild, near the present Julianhaab, and the other the Western Settlement, near the present Gothab. Eric claimed his land along the shore of a fjord near Brattahild, and named it Ericsfjord. He and his wife, Thorhild, had three sons, Leif, Thorvald, Thorstein, and one daughter, Freydis. The Flatey Book mentions Eric's status in Greenland: "Eric the Red took up his abode at Brattahild, and was in great consideration, and honored by all."[6]

The Norsemen held personal freedom as one of their greatest values. They were fiercely attached to that freedom and thus fought against any effort to curtail it, for example, by paying either taxes to the state or tithes to the Church. This devotion to freedom made them a race of rugged individualists and this left its mark on how they lived and how they established colonies. Thomas Willson emphasizes this fact in his book, *History of the Church and State in Norway:*

"The settlers did not live in towns or villages, but each man had his own farm or *gaard,* though, for protection's sake in earlier times, they were usually not very far off from one another. This absence of towns, and division of the land into freeholds, was a characteristic of the Norwegians, and exercised a very remarkable influence over their subsequent history; for it was always the country parts, and not the towns, where the preponderating political power lay, and the free landowners, unfettered by feudalism, and practically without an aristocracy (the chiefs were only the larger landowners), controlled and directed the policy of the nation, meeting in the assemblies, or *Things,* where all free men had an equal voice."[7]

In 999 at the age of nineteen, Leif Ericson, oldest son of Eric the Red, and his companions sailed for Norway on a trading mission. Leif was described as "a large and powerful man, and of a most imposing bearing, a man of sagacity, and a very just man in all things." They arrived at Trondheim and wintered there as guests of King Olav Trygvesson. During the winter months the king persuaded Leif and his companions to accept Christianity and they were baptized. The account of Leif's conversion is recorded in two sagas, each with slight variations. Both deserve to be quoted at length to show the style of the writers of the two different sagas. The central character in *The Saga of Olav Trygvesson* is, of course, the king himself and thus in this narrative Leif enters as only a minor character. Briefly Leif's conversion is recorded:

"The same spring King Olav also sent Leif Ericsson to Greenland to proclaim Christianity there, and Leif went there that summer. In the ocean he took up the crew of a ship which had been lost, and who were clinging to the wreck. He also found Vinland the Good; arrived about harvest in Greenland; and had with him for it a priest and other teachers, with whom he went to Brattahild to lodge with his father Eric. People called him afterwards Leif the Lucky; but his father Eric said that his luck and ill luck balanced each other; for if Leif had saved a wreck in the ocean, he had brought a hurtful person with him to Greenland, and that was the priest."[8] (Eric looked upon Christianity as an evil influence, threatening the existence of his pagan gods. It is doubtful whether he ever was baptized.)

In *The Saga of Eric the Red*, Eric and his children are the central characters. In this saga the exploits of Leif, his brothers and sister are given a more extensive treatment. This document, as well as others, records the introduction of Christianity into the western hemisphere. At the same time it gives an account of Leif's commission as the first Christian evangelizer of the new world. Snorre Sturlason, Iceland's greatest writer in the Middle Ages, gives this account of Leif's commission:

"Leif and his companions... arrived in Norway in the autumn. Leif went to the court of King Olav Trygvesson. He was well received by the king, who felt that he could see that Leif was a man of great accomplishments. Upon one occasion the king came to speak with Leif, and asked him, 'Is it thy purpose to sail to Greenland in the summer?' 'It is my purpose,' said Leif, 'if it be your will.' 'I believe it will be well,' answered the king, 'and thither thou shalt go upon my errand, to proclaim Christianity there.' Leif replied that the king should decide, but gave it as his belief that it would be difficult to carry this mission to a successful issue in Greenland. The king replied that he knew of no man who would be better fitted for this undertaking, 'and in thy hands the cause will surely prosper.' 'This can only be,' said Leif, 'if I enjoy the grace of your protection.' Leif put to sea when his ship was ready for the voyage.... Leif landed in Ericsfjord, and then went home to Brattahild; he was well received by everyone. He soon proclaimed Christianity throughout the land, and the Catholic faith, and announced King Olav Trygvesson's messages to the people, telling them how much excellence and how great glory accompanied this faith. Eric was slow in forming the determination to forsake his old belief, but Thonhild embraced the faith promptly, and caused a church to be built at some distance from the house. This building was called Thonhild's Church, and there she and those persons who had accepted Christianity, and they were many, were wont to offer their prayers."[9]

This quotation is remarkable inasmuch as it reveals a strain of anti-clericalism present throughout Norwegian Christian history. Priests were always relatively few and far between in Norway and Norwegian

Christianity was always dominated by the laity. Thus, when the Reformation came, many Norwegians welcomed freedom from "priest-craft." Norwegian Lutherans even in the United States continue this traditon. For many years Norwegian Lutherans in this country feuded and fought over the relation of the ordained ministry and the priesthood of all believers. This continues at the present time as the Evangelical Lutheran Church of America struggles in drafting a document on ministry.

VOYAGES TO VINLAND

After returning to Greenland in 1000, Leif set his mind to explore the lands further west which Bjarni Herjulson had sighted earlier when his ship was thrown off course on his journey from Iceland to Greenland. Leif had heard that Bjarni and his crew had sighted trees in that land. Since no trees grew in Greenland, Leif knew that lumber was a most valuable commodity. He purchased Bjarni's ship and with a crew of thirty-five men sailed for this unknown land, unwittingly tracing Bjarni's course in reverse. Traveling along the western Greenland coastline he crossed Davis Strait to Baffin Island – a relatively short distance of eighty miles – where he and his crew went ashore. He noted the land was rocky and called it Helluland. They set their sails in a southerly direction along a land with a long beach of white sand (near Cape Porcupine, Labrador) and again went ashore, noting with satisfaction that the land had many forests. *The Saga of the Greenlanders* noted that Leif said, " This land shall have a name according to its appearance, and we shall call it Markland."[10] Boarding their ship again, Leif and his crew sailed in a southerly direction two more days and came to a land where one of the crew discovered grapes ripe for the picking from their vines. Leif named this new land, the land of the vine – Vinland the Good; there they built a traditional Norse long house and spent the winter. Thus in the year 1000 Leif and his men became the first Europeans to live on the continental land mass of the western hemisphere.

The following spring Leif and his crew returned to Greenland with many marvels to tell about the new lands they discovered. Thorvald,

Leif's brother, felt that the new land should be explored more thoroughly so he set out with thirty men the following year on a more extensive exploratory voyage. They came to Leif's long house and wintered there. The following year they continued their explorations, sailing in a south-easterly direction. The expedition ran into foul weather and while they headed for the shore, the keel of their long ship broke. Thorvald called the site Keelness. On this journey Europeans met for the first time the Native Americans and, shortly thereafter, a battle ensued between the residents and the intruders, the first recorded battle between European and Native Americans.

Thorvald's reaction to the Native Americans, however, was in marked contrast to the policy of later European explorers. He commanded his crew: "We shall put up our war-screens along the gunwales, and defend ourselves as well as we can; but not use our weapons much against them." Thorvald was mortally wounded in the battle and instructed his crew to bury him in this new land and place a cross over his grave. Thus in 1002 Thorvald became the first European and Christian buried in the new world.

The following year Eric's other brother, Thorstein, resolved to go to Vinland in order to bring back Thorvold's body and bury it at Ericsfjord. He outfitted Thorvold's vessel, chose a crew of twenty-five men, and with his wife, Gudrid, unfurled his sail. His journey, however, was not auspicious. Thorvald and his crew spent the summer sailing in unknown waters and "in the first week of winter they landed at Lysefjord in Greenland, in the western settlement." (The Norsemen reckoned the first Saturday after October 14 as the beginning of winter.) While wintering in the western settlement Thorstein died. His host prepared Thorstein's body for burial and, as soon as sailing was possible in the spring he took the body and Gudrid, the widow, back to Ericsfjord.

The voyage of Eric's sister, Freydis, to Vinland was the bloodiest and brought dishonor to the name of Eric the Red. The same summer that Thorstein had sailed for Vinland, a ship from Norway commanded by the two merchant-brothers, Heige and Finboge, arrived at Ericsfjord. They wintered there as guests of Leif and became acquainted with Freydis who successfully persuaded them to sail with her on a commercial voyage to Vinland promising that they would equally share the profits when they returned to Greenland. The two contracting parties agreed to sail the following spring, stating that each group would consist of thirty men, not counting the women who accompanied both groups. From the outset Freydis broke the contract, smuggling aboard her ship six extra men.

The enterprise became a disaster. Freydis used every ploy to make life miserable for the brothers and the members of their crew, ensnaring in her deceitful and treacherous plot her own husband, Thorvald. In the still of the night Freydis led her husband and their men to the brothers' camp and there slew the brothers and their men. Her crew would not, however, kill the women so Freydis herself took the axe and killed the five women. She threatened the members of her crew with death if they revealed the crime when they returned to Greenland with their expensive cargo of furs, skins and lumber. Rumors soon spread abroad, and Leif learned of the crime after torturing three of Freydis's men to discover the truth. Leif was saddened by the report and said, "I do not care to treat my sister Freydis as she deserves; but this I will foretell of them, that their posterity will never thrive." The descendants of Freydis and Thorvald were held in contempt for many years in Greenland.

In the summer of 1008, Thorfinn Karlsefne, a wealthy Norwegian merchant, sailed his ship into Ericsfjord. He, too, was a guest in Leif's house and there met Gudrid, Thorstein's widow. As they passed the long, dark winter nights Thorfinn learned of the voyages to Vinland and all the while his glances at Gudrid became more and more frequent. He asked Leif for Gudrid's hand and the two were married. Gudrid and others urged Thorfinn to undertake a journey to Vinland and by winter's end he resolved to do so. He gathered together a crew of sixty men and five women and asked of Leif to buy his long house there. Leif refused, thus indicating his own intention of some day returning to Vinland. He did, however, give Thorfinn permission to use it. The following summer Thorfinn and his crew sailed for Vinland.

They found Leif's long house and around it constructed their settlement. Thorfinn ordered that a sturdy fence be built around the settlement, for as the saga relates, "After that first winter, and when summer came, they were aware of Skraelingers being there; and a great troop of men came out of the woods." *Skraelinger* was the Norse word for "puny" or "small" and, most probably, the Norsemen used the term derisively for the new people they encountered.

The native people came to barter with the newcomers, exchanging furs and skins for milk and cheese. The following winter the natives returned again with furs and skins to barter but this time they wanted weapons. Thorfinn refused their request. One of the natives, however, tried to take an axe and one of Thorfinn's men killed him. The other natives immediately fled but Thorfinn feared they would return again, this time not to barter but to wage war. Thorfinn set forth a battle plan for his men and the saga continues: "The Skraelingers came to the place where Karlsefne proposed to fight; and there was a battle there, and many of the Skraelingers fell.... They then fled to the forest as fast as they could, and so closed the battle."

The colonists remained throughout the winter, but by summer Thorfinn felt prudence was better served than valor so the expedition returned to Greenland. Thorfinn's colony, which survived three years, was the first such attempt by Europeans in the new world. Thorfinn and his wife, Gudrid, brought back from Vinland a treasure more precious in their eyes than all the furs and skins and lumber in their ship. Gudrid gave birth to a son, Snorre, the first child to be baptised on the American Continent.

Thorfinn did not remain in Greenland long. He loaded his ship with merchandise and sailed for Norway the following summer. After disposing of his cargo in Norway, he turned the prow of his ship to Iceland and there purchased an estate called Glambairland where he lived until his death. Gudrid, his wife, continued to manage the estate until their son, Snorre, reached adulthood. After Snorre's marriage Gudrid had a church built at Glambae and then entered the convent, leading a hermit's life until her death. Snorre had a son, Thorgeir, whose daughter, Ingveld, was the mother of Bishop Brand. Snorre's daughter, Halfrid, was the mother of Runold, the father of Bishop Thorlak. Snorre, the child of the new world, strengthened the faith of the old world in the persons of his two great-grandsons.[10] Bishop Brand Saemundarson served as the Bishop of Holar in the north of Iceland from 1168 to 1201. Bishop Thorlak Runolfsson served as Bishop of Skalholt in the south of Iceland from 1118 to 1188.[11]

THE DIOCESE OF GARDAR

After one hundred years of colonization the Greenlanders had achieved political independence and were well-established and prosperous enough to think in terms of their own local church. They desired to have their own bishop and diocesan curia.

By a strange quirk of history, the first diocese in the western hemisphere is associated with the name of the treacherous Freydis. In an interpolation in *The Olaf Sagas,* a passage taken from the Flatey Book which was written between 1387 and 1395, is the following reference: "These were Eric's children – Leif, Thorvald, and Thorstein; and his daughter was called Freydis. She was married to a man called Thorvald; and they dwelt at Gardar, which is now a Bishop's seat."[12]

One of the earliest references in the Icelandic manuscripts to a bishop in the new world, however, is found in the *Icelandic Annals* written by the priest Einar Haflidason about 1280. Under the events taking place in 1121, Haflidason notes, "Bishop Eric Uppsi sought Vineland." In another series of annals, written by another priest, Magnus Thorhallsson, and completed before 1305, is found this passage under 1121, "Eric, the Bishop of Greenland, went in search of Vineland." Another collection written by Arni Magnusson no later than 1419, makes the same statement for the year 1121. Adam of Bremen also makes mention of Bishop Eric's voyage.

No historian doubts the existence of Bishop Eric, although the circumstances of both his voyage and his disappearance will probably always remain a mystery. In another Icelandic scientific work, *Rimbegla,* which is distinct from the sagas, Eric is listed as the first Bishop of Gardar, Greenland. This is obviously in error, as we shall see. Most probably, Eric was a missionary bishop, sent from Norway or Iceland to Greenland to ordain and confirm in the Church established there at the time Leif brought Christisnity to the island. Bishop Eric heard of Vinland and people living there so he resolved to go there.[13]

The disappearance of Bishop Eric set in motion a series of events that definitely gave Greenland its own first resident bishop who created the first diocese in the western hemisphere at Gardar. These events are recorded in the *Saga of Einar Sokkesson*. The Christian people in Greenland, after having the experience of Bishop Eric living among them for some time, desired to have their own permanent bishop. A layman, Sokke Thorerson, addressed the people at the 1125 *Althing* (Parliament) urging that a country so flourishing as Greenland (at that time it was an independent republic, similar to Iceland) deserved to have its own resident bishop and a diocese created by duly constituted authority. He asked the assembly to make contributions for the establishment and maintenence of this diocese in Greenland.

Judging from the next action, Sokke's appeal met with a generous response from the Christian people of Greenland. Einar Sokkesson was named the leader of a delegation to present this request to the Norwegian King Sigrud the Crusader (1090-1130). The king was pleased with the petition and appointed Arnold, a priest in service at the royal court, to fill the position as first Bishop of Gardar. Arnold protested his unworthiness but bowed to the royal will after Einar took an oath "to defend with all his power and authority the ecclesiastical rights, to preserve all moveable and real estate given and consecrated to God, to protect it against violence, and punish assailers; finally, to be the protector of all diocesan property." Arnold traveled to Lund to receive episcopal ordination from the Archbishop of Lund who had received from Rome the privilege of naming and ordaining the suffragan bishops of that metropolitan see. All the dioceses of Sweden, Denmark, Norway, Iceland, the Shetland and Orkney islands, and now, Greenland, fell under his ecclesiastical jurisdiction. In fact, however, for many centuries the kings of Sweden, Norway and Denmark retained the right of filling the chief ecclesiastical offices.

GROWTH OF THE DIOCESE OF GARDAR

Bishop Arnold arrived in Greenland in 1126, after a year's delay in Iceland. He established his episcopal see at Gardar and chose the church dedicated to St. Nicholas, patron of seafarers, as his cathedral. According to one historian, "Bishop Arnold seems to have been a typical medieval prelate, humble and devout in private life, but zealous and unbending in all matters touching what he regarded as rights of his office and his diocese."[14] He must have been a man with a constitution of iron and a zeal that knew no bounds to have set the nascent local church on a solid foundation during the twenty-six years he spent in Greenland. So well did he labor that the diocese he founded survived for more than three hundred years.

The population of the Diocese of Gardar, which included the entire island of Greenland and Vinland, was estimated to be between 2,000 and 10,000. The former rather than the latter seems to be closer to the truth. The chief reason for the establishment of a diocese in Greenland was its great distance from the rest of the known world. One modern writer called it "the diocese at the world's end." A contemporary author who described the situation in Greenland at the time of Arnold's appointment wrote: "The people in this country are all Christians and have churches and priests. If the land lay near some other country it might be reckoned the third of a bishopric; but the Greenlanders now have their own bishop, as no other arrangement is possible on account of the great distance from other people."[15]

The census of Greenland at the time of Bishop Arnold's arrival reveals the existence of a Church already in a flourishing condition. The Eastern Settlement had 190 and the Western Settlement 90 homesteads. These homesteads would be more comparable to a shire in England than to a one-family unit. There were twelve churches in the Eastern Settlement and four in the Western Settlement. The relatively high number of churches was due to the severity of the weather which prevented traveling a long distance during the winter months. The churches generally measured forty-eight to sixty feet long and twenty-four feet wide. According to recent archaeological excavations, the cathedral at Gardar was larger, being cruciform in shape, with a nave measured eighty-eight feet and fifty-two feet at its widest breadth. Most of the churches were constructed of local red sandstone. At the present time the sites of some of these churches have been excavated.[16]

Two religious communities existed in Greenland. The Sisters of St. Benedict had a monastery of Rafnsfjord and owned a considerable amount of land in the surrounding area. A group of Canons Regular, most probably following the Rule of St. Augustine, also had a monastery in the Eastern Settlement. Both monasteries were centers of learning for the

Christian people of Greenland.[17] The Canons Regular conducted a seminary to educate local young men for the priesthood. In the early years, however, Adam of Bremen, writing in the middle of the eleventh century, states that emissaries from Greenland came to his archdiocese seeking priests to serve in Greenland.[18]

CHANGES IN THE CHURCH IN NORWAY

Bishop Arnold returned to Norway in 1150, after serving twenty-six years in Greenland. Two years later a significant development of the Church in Norway took place. Cardinal Nicholas Breakspeare (who in 1154 succeeded to the Chair of Peter as Pope Adrian IV, the only Englishman to serve in that position) arrived as papal legate to Norway. More than any other individual, he is credited with giving a firm organization to the Church in Norway. In July, 1152, he convoked and presided over a representative assembly of the entire country at Trondheim. At that time Trondheim was established as an archdiocese, thus freeing the Church in Norway from its ties with the Archdiocese of Lund which at that time was in the territory of Denmark. The new ecclesiastical jurisdiction was, without a doubt, the vastest in the world at that time. The suffragans of the Archbishop of Trondheim were the Bishops of Bergen, Stavanger, Oslo and Hamar in Norway; Skaalhot and Hole in Iceland; Gardar in Greenland; Kirkebo in the Faeroe Islands; Kirkevaag in the Orkney Islands and Sodor in the Isle of Man.

The right of naming and ordaining bishops for the suffragan sees was given to the Archbishop of Trondheim at this assembly, strengthening the power of the Church by removing this right from the Norwegian kings who had previously named bishops. The assembly and its legislation succeeded in binding the Church in Norway firmly to the Holy See and the discipline of the universal Church. For centuries the Norwegian people held Cardinal Breakspeare in the highest esteem, in many places revering him as a saint.

A point of interest at the present time is the manner in which the papal legate dealt with the issue of celibacy. Willson in his authoritative history of the Norwegian Church describes the issue which became a non-issue in the Cardinal's mind:

"There was one point, however, in which he failed. The papal power at this time tried everywhere to enforce the new doctrine of celibacy of the clergy, and it was only to be expected that the cardinal would attempt to do the same in Norway. We have no clear information as to what was done by him in this direction, but later on, when the bishops sought to enforce it on the Parish priests, as part of the discipline of the Church, it was resisted by the clergy, on the ground that Nicholas had attempted it, and finding the oppostion too great, he had then given them permission to marry. It is hardly likely that the cardinal had given any formal permission, for what was entirely contrary to the designs of the papacy at the time; but it is probable that, perceiving the clergy were very determined on the point, and being a very far-seeing and prudent man, he did not wish to risk the success of the other great results which he had achieved by insisting on the celibacy of the priests, and his acquiescence in this was taken by them as a formal permission. The cardinal doubtless saw, and rightly, that celibacy of the clergy would follow, when the authority of the bishops, who were directly under the papal power, began to make itself felt."[19]

It is interesting to note in this regard that in the Icelandic sagas the wives and children of the priests are frequently mentioned. The papal mandate of clerical celibacy did not easily take root in either Norway or the western Norse settlements; its practice, it would seem, was more the exception than the rule. More than a century later, in a letter to Archbishop Sigurd of Trondheim dated May 16, 1287, Pope Gregory IX issued this directive: "It was laid before us in your name that both in the diocese and in the Province of Trondheim, there has increased a detestable abuse – namely, that priests living there contract marriages and behave as married lay people.... Preferring rather to perish than to obey, they pretend to be justified by long-lasting custom. We order that...you endeavor to extirpate this abuse and apply the ecclesiastical censures to the rebellious, if there be any."[20]

After this assembly of 1152 Bishop Arnold was assigned to the new diocese of Hamar. He died sometime before 1164, the year that Orm succeeded him as Bishop of Hamar. John I Khul was appointed bishop of Gardar when Arnold resigned in 1150 and held that position until his death in 1187. John II, called the hawk, was an official in the Archdiocese of Trondheim when appointed Bishop of Gardar in 1188. He governed that see until his death in 1209. It is generally believed that during the excavations of the cemetery in Gardar the remains of this bishop were uncovered. From his skeleton, he appeared to be a powerfully-built man of middle age and in his right hand was a carved walrus-ivory crozier and on his finger a gold ring.

THE BISHOPS OF GARDAR

The list of the Bishops of Gardar who lived in Greenland continues until 1377. After that date, when the right of appointment to suffragan sees was transferred from the Archbishop of Trondheim to the Roman Curia, the list of appointments continues until 1537. It is doubtful, however, if many, if any, of the bishops appointed after that date ever lived in Greenland, although some may have visited there. Thomas O'Gorman in his history observed that Eric Walkendorf, the last Roman Catholic Archbishop of Trondheim, was seeking information about the Church in Greenland with the intention of restoring communications with his suffragan see. Then, O'Gorman observed, "the Reformation swept over Norway, ended the hierarchy there, and then silence and oblivion fell upon Greenland."[21]

For the most part there are lengthy intervals between the death of one bishop and the appointment of a successor for Gardar. The reason is, of course, the lack of communication caused by the long periods of time in which no ships from Greenland arrived in Norway. The same reason accounts for the discrepancy in the number of years each bishop governed the see. For example, the ship *Olafssud* that arrived in Bergen in 1383 brought the news that Bishop Alf had died five years earlier. Two more years passed before his successor, Bishop Henry, was consecrated. The list of the Bishops of Gardar who succeeded Bishop John II and lived in Gardar follows.

Bishop Helgo (1212-1280) collected funds to help finance the Crusade mandated by the Fourth Lateran Council in 1215. It is probable that some Greenlanders took part in this crusade.

Bishop Nicholas (1234- c. 1240) only arrived in Greenland five years after his consecration.

Bishop Olav (1246-1280) was ordered to use his office in bringing independent Greenland to submit to the Crown of Norway. Bishop Olav sailed for Norway in 1264; he was shipwrecked off the coast of Iceland where he remained for two years; he assisted at the ceremony investing the pallium on Archbishop Haakon of Trondheim in 1267; he returned to Greenland in 1271 and died there in 1280.

Bishop Theodore (1288-1314) waited eight years between his nomination and consecration before the conflict between the archbishop and the cathedral chapter over who had the right to choose suffragan bishops was resolved. Theodore returned to Norway about 1309 and died there five years later.

Bishop Arne (1314-1349) proceeded to Greenland immediately after his consecration, arriving there less than a year after that date. A false report reached Norway in 1343 that Arne had died and the archbishop consecrated John Skalli as Bishop of Gardar. The mistake in the report was discovered in time so that John Skalli was sent as the Bishop of Holar, Iceland. The Black Death swept through the Scandinavian countries, no doubt including Greenland, during Bishop Arne's rule and this disaster almost completely broke all communications between Norway and Greenland. One chronicler wrote, "All but one Norwegian bishop and one canon of the metropolitan chapter of Thronheim fell victim to the epidemic." The Church was as debilitated as civil society.

Bishop Alf (1365-1377) was a priest of the Diocese of Bergen. The Diocese of Gardar was without a bishop for seventeen years between the death of Bishop Arne and the consecration of Bishop Alf because of the chaotic conditions of society following the Black Death. It would seem that the plague's effect in Greenland was most severe, for Bishop Alf seems to be the last bishop who resided in Gardar.

The Bishop of Gardar throughout these centuries was the most wealthy and important person on the island. From time to time the bishop's residence was enlarged, with the dining hall – the largest in the settlement – measuring fifty-two by twenty-three feet and capable of seating a hundred people. Here the bishop entertained merchants from Norway and, on the great feasts of the Church, hosted the leading members of the settlements. As time passed the land holdings of the bishopric increased, so that by the fourteenth century the diocese owned the entire Einarsfjord district, large islands at the entrance to Ericsfjord and hunting grounds on the east coast. Upon his death in 1347 King Magnus Ericson left a substantial legacy to the cathedral church of Gardar.

The bishops who were consecrated for the Diocese of Gardar following Bishop Alf were: Henry (1385-1394), George (1385-1394), Peter Staras (1394-1401), Eskil (1401-1411), Jacob Petersson Treppe (1411-1424), Robert Ryngman (1425-1431), Gobelinius Bolant (1431), John Erler de Moys (1432-1433), Bartholomew (1433-1440), Gregory, (1440-1462?), Andrew Mus (1462-1476), Jacob Blaa (1481-1492), Matthias Knutsson (1492-1518?) and Vincent Petersson Kampa (1519-1537).

It would seem that some of these bishops visited Gardar for brief periods of time. This can be deduced from the letter of Pope Nicholas V that will be treated later. The period of "thirty years" Pope Nicholas mentions most probably occured either during or after the time of Bishop Gregory. The lack of precision in letters indicates the poor communications that existed between the Bishop of Rome and the far-flung Province of Trondheim during this period. It is noteworthy that Bishop Vincent, the |ast named to Gardar, was appointed by Pope Leo X at the request of King Christian II of Denmark who had the intention of restoring the Greenland colony.

The last recorded testimony of the existence of the Church in Greenland is a marriage certificate dated April 19, 1409. This document states that two priests, Indrid Andresson and Paul Hallvardsson witnessed the marriage of Thorstein Olafsson and Sigrid Bjarnadottir. It further states that the ceremony took place in the Hvalsey church and both Icelanders and Greenlanders were present. The last recorded voyage from Bergen to Greenland was registered the following year. These facts indicate the decline in the Church but not the eradication of the settlers.

Several factors converged to bring about the ultimate disappearance of the Norse Church in Greenland. The Black Death that swept across Europe in 1349 devastated the shipping center of Bergen, cutting off Greenland's life-line. The rise of the Hanseatic league fifty years later continued to destroy the prominence of Bergen as a shipping center. Weather conditions added to the Greenlanders' plight. Arctic snow and ice descended lower and lower in the northern seas, causing many ports in Greenland to freeze over; many of the fjords were closed by ice most of the year, and some of them permanently. Eskimo people arrived in Greenland and descended upon the Norse settlements. Some historians speculate that the weakened Greenlanders who survived these material deprivations and attacks from the Eskimos ultimately inter-married with them and adopted their ways.[22]

Greenland waited more than a century to hear another Christian voice. On July 3, 1721, Hans Egede, a Lutheran pastor from Denmark, sailed to Greenland, looking for the old Norse colony. Finding no Norsemen he devoted himself to the conversion of the Eskimo people. He established a colony at Godthab and inaugurated regular commerce with Denmark. Ill health forced him to return to Denmark where he became superintendent of a seminary dedicated to supplying pastors for the Greenland mission.[23] Egede has been called by some historians "the Apostle of Greenland." He was, without a doubt, the apostle to the Eskimos in Greenland.

The Catholic Church returned to Greenland in 1960 with the arrival of Father Michael Wolf, an Oblate of Mary Immaculate, who established a parish in Godthab. With the installation of Thule Air Force Base a Catholic chaplain, Father John McDonough, was assigned to that post in 1965. Recently McDonough recalled some of his experiences in Greenland:

"During my stay I had the opportunity to meet two of the Lutheran pastors who worked in the area. I don't remember their names but they were very kind and devoted to the Greenlandic natives. Greenland is considered a county of Denmark and was fully supported by the Danish church. The state religion was Lutheranism and almost all the natives belonged to this church. The presence of the Lutheran church was strong in the villages surrounding the Air Base, much stronger among the Greenland natives than among the Danish native people. I must say that I considered the work of the government of Denmark as very kind towards the natives; encouraging them to develop the tools needed to live in the twentieth century while remaining loyal to their native traditions. Life is very severe in that part of the world."[24]

Father Franz Hoyos, O.M.I., serves as pastor of the Catholic church in Godthaab at the present time. Catholic chaplains continue to serve at Thule Air Force Base.

LETTERS OF THE POPES

The fact remains that the Diocese of Gardar was established in 1124, administered for more than 250 years by resident bishops, and for another 150 years men were appointed to the see of Gardar, even though most of them never set foot in Greenland. Those who have difficulty accepting the witness of the Icelandic sagas, the chronicles kept by monks in English and German monasteries and the brief references of Adam of Bremen as trustworthy cannot reject the authenticity of the witness found in the Vatican archives.

The world's fair in Chicago in 1893, held to commemorate the fourth centenary of Columbus's landing in the new world, was, ironically, the occasion for the opening of American minds to that body of knowledge which came to be called the pre-Columbian discovery of America. The Vatican display at that fair consisted of papal letters preserved in the Vatican archives concerning the Norse church in medieval America. J.C. Heywood published in that same year *Documenta Selecta,* a photographic fascimile of these papal letters with a limited edition of twenty-five copies.[24] It is also interesting to note that Thomas O'Gorman, professor of church history at The Catholic University of America and later Bishop of Sioux Falls, South Dakota, published an article in the *Catholic University Bulletin* in 1895 entitled "The Medieval American Church," based on the contents of these papal letters.

Rasmus Anderson, a noted American Norse scholar, went to Rome in 1900. He probably had heard of Heywood's volume and went in search of the documents in the Vatican archives. These he felt would be even greater substantiation than that given by Adam of Bremen and the English and German chroniclers to the testimony of the Icelandic sagas. The letter Pope Gregory IX addressed to Archbishop Sigrud of Trondheim on May 5, 1237, was known from other sources. Seven popes had written letters concerning the Church in Greenland. The names of the other popes and the dates of their |etters are:

Pope Innocent III	February 13, 1206
Pope John XXI (three letters)	December 4, 1276
Pope Nicholas III	January 31, 1279

Pope Nicholas III   June 9, 1279
Pope Martin IV   March 4, 1281
Pope Nicholas V   September 25, 1448
Pope Alexander VI   (No date), 1492

The first seven letters were addressed to the Archbishop of Trondheim in whose province was the Diocese of Gardar. The letter of Pope Nicholas V was addressed to the Bishops of Skaalholt and Hole, Iceland, and the letter of Pope Alexander VI was addressed directly to Mathias Knutsson, the Bishop-elect of Gardar. Each of these letters give insights into the condition of the Church in Greenland.

Ten years later, these papal letters were part of the Vatican exhibit at the Louisiana Purchase Exposition held in St. Louis in 1903. J.W. Buel, a Norse scholar, viewed these manuscripts and immediately sensed their historic importance. Three years later he wrote Cardinal Raphael Merry del Val, the papal secretary of state, asking permision to photograph these manuscripts. On July 14, 1906, the cardinal replied affirmatively to Buel's request, stating "the Holy Father instructs me to grant you permission to reproduce by photography any of the manuscripts referring to the Constitution of the Church in Greenland." Thanks to the initiative of Buel and the scholarship of Rasmus Anderson, these papal documents were published for the first time in English in *The Flatey Book* in 1908. Those who claimed that the accomplishments of the Norse people in the western hemisphere were no more than romances were compelled by this evidence to change their minds; photographs of these papal letters appeared in Anderson's book and were also deposited in the library of St. Louis University.

In introducing these letters to the reading public in 1908 Anderson noted that the letters he published were chiefly concerned with the tithes and liturgical prescriptions. At the same time, however, they offer many insights into the condition of the Church in Greenland. Pertinent passages from these letters in the translations made in 1908 follow.[26] The reader will note that the *stylus curiae* was already refined in the thirteenth century.

Pope Innocent III

Addressing his letter to Archbishop Ivarson of Trondheim on February 13, 1206, Pope Innocent III, recalled the work of Cardinal Breakspeare as papal delegate to Norway. In citing the creation of the ecclesiastical province of Trondheim, he mentioned Greenland in the following passage:

"...he conferred the pallium upon your predecessor, John; and in order that the rest of the Norwegian province might not lack the attention of a metropolitan, he decreed that the city of Nidaros (Trondheim), committed to your direction, be the permanent metropolis of the province and that Oslo, Hamar, Bergen, Stavanger, the Orkney Islands, the Faeroe Islands, the bishopric of Skaslthold, Iceland, and Greenland, be subject to it forever as their metropolis, and that their bishops obey both him (your predecessor) and his successors as their metropolitans."

Pope John XXI

This pontiff addressed three brief letters to Archbishop Jon Raude of Trondheim, each dated December 4, 1276, and given at Viterbo. Each letter contained an aspect of the universal collection taken up to support the work of the Crusades. In the following letter Pope John XXI makes specific reference to Gardar:

"... whereas in the Kingdom of Norway, the collection of the tithe for the Holy Land has been entrusted to you by Apostolic Letters, in which it is expressly declared that you shall personally visit all part of the Kingdom for that purpose, this seems in a measure impossible, since the diocese of Gardar, subject to your province and said Kingdom, is so far distant from the metropolitan church that, because of the difficulties of navigation, one can scarcely make the voyage, thither and return, in less than five years; so that you doubt that the apostolic command, on your own, can reach those parts within the time appointed for the payment of the tithe...."

Recognizing this fact, Pope John XXI granted the archbishop "permission to delegate certain prudent and able Nuncios of yours to gather the tithe in those dioceses."

Pope Nicholas III

This pontiff addressed two letters to Archbishop Jon Raude, one on January 31, 1279, and the second on June 9, the same year. In the first Pope Nicholas III grants permission to absolve those who have incurred ecclesiastical censure. He writes:

"...we gather that the island, on which stands the City of Gardar, is seldom visited by ships, because of the dangers of the Ocean surrounding it; wherefore when of late certain seamen set sail for this same island, you, embracing the opportunity, sent a certain prudent man with them to the same city, having commissioned him to collect the tithe, and, in the hope of securing Our ratification, you have empowered him to absolve the clerics from the sentence of excommunication which they have incurred for not paying the the tithe within the appointed time, and to dispense them from any irregularity which perchance they contracted therefrom."

The pope granted the archbishop the power to delegate, stating, "We invest you with authority to grant free|y to those whom you have sent to said island in the matter of the collection, or perhaps will send in the future, the function of absolving the clerics, as well in said island as in others of the same Ocean."

In the second letter Pope Nicholas replied to a query concerning the use of money in what later came to be called founded Masses. He wrote:

"...there exist certain endowments established by the devotion of the faithful, out of which, year after year, wine and hosts are provided for the priests of the churches in those Kingdoms (Denmark and Sweden) by a person specially appointed for this office. We... entrust to your discretion, by Apostolic Letters, that, if the income is so great that you know there will be much left over after the wine and hosts have been supplied, the tithe be taken from those revenues; but if little or nothing of the aforesaid income would remain, let nothing be paid therefrom...."

Pope Martin IV

The same Archbishop of Trondheim addressed another letter to Nicholas' successor, Pope Martin IV, inquiring about the tithe submitted by the Church of Gardar. The pope's reply offers an insight into the economy of Greenland:

"...You have added, moreover, that the tithe of Greenland is received entirely in cattle-skins, the skins and tusks of seals, and whale-bone, which you assert, can hardly be sold at a fair price.... We, therefore,...reply to your inquiry that you endeavor to convert into silver or gold the tithes both of Greenland and of the said islands...and that you send this, together with the rest of the tithe collected in that Kingdom for the good of the Holy Land."

Pope Nicholas V

The concern of the papacy for the welfare of the distant members of the Church in far-away Greenland is revealed in this letter that Pope Nicholas V addressed to the bishops in Iceland. The letter, incidentally, bears witness to the fact that Europeans were aware of the existence of that diocese "at the world's end" fifty years before the voyage of Columbus. The letter reveals the difficulties the Christian people in Greenland were experiencing and also indicates how well informed the papacy was of these sad conditions in that distant diocese. The pope wrote:

"...as regards Our beloved sons, the natives and all the inhabitants of the Island of Greenland, which is said to lie in the province of Trondheim, in the extremity of the Ocean, in the northern region of the Kingdom of Norway. We have heard with sad and anxious heart the doleful story of that same island, whose inhabitants and natives, for almost six hundred years (*sic*), have kept the Faith of Christ, received under the preaching of their glorious evangelist, the blessed King Olav, firm and unspotted under the guidance of the Holy Roman Church and the Apostolic See, and where for all succeeding time the people, inflamed with eager devotion, erected many temples of the Saints and a famous Cathedral, in which divine worship was sedulously carried on; but at length, thirty years ago...the barbarians, gathering together in a fleet on the neighboring shores of the Pagans, attacked this entire people in a cruel invasion, devastating their fatherland and sacred temples by fire and sword, leaving in the island only nine parochial churches, these, it is said, extend into the farthest districts, which they could not approach conveniently because of the defiles of the mountains, and carrying away captive to their possessions the natives of both sexes, especially such as they deemed brave and fit to undergo the burden of perpetual slavery, just as it adjusted to their tyranny. As the same report subjoins, however, very many, after a time, returned to their own from said captivity, and having thenceforth repaired the ruins of those places, desired to renew and extend the divine worship as much as possible after the pristine fashion but because, overwhelmed by the past calamities, and laboring under famine and want, they were unable to support priests and a bishop, they were deprived, for that entire period of thirty years, of the consolation of a bishop and the ministry of priests, except when anyone, in the desire of serving God, after traveling far and long, had succeeded in reaching those churches which the barbarian hand had passed unhurt....

"We, therefore, favorably disposed towards the just and worthy prayers and desires of said natives and inhabitants of the aforesaid island of Greenland, but having no certain knowledge of the foregoing events and their circumstances, commit to and command your Fraternity, whom We understand to be one of the nearer bishops of the aforesaid island, that you, or one of you (nearer bishops), ordain fit and exemplary priests, provide parishes, and establish rectors, who will govern the restored parishes and churches, and administer the Sacraments; and, furthermore, that, if it will finally appear to you or one of you as opportune and expedient, you will, with the advice of the metropolitan, provide the distance of the place permit, ordain and establish as their bishop some practical and able person, in communion with Us and the Apostolic See, and impart to him the grace of consecration in Our name, according to the usual ecclesiastical forms...."

Pope Alexander VI

With more than a touch of historic irony, at the time Christopher Columbus was unfurling the sails for his voyage to the fabulous Cathay, the Bishop of Rome was writing in 1492 a letter to Archbishop Gaute Ivarsson of Trondheim about the "new world" which was known to the Norsemen for almost five hundred years. The Borgia pope succeeded

Pope Innocent VIII who appointed Mathias, a Benedictine monk living in Denmark as the Bishop of Gardar. Mathias had professed poverty as one of his religious vows and thus the pope waived all the fees of all the officials in the chain of command from Rome to Denmark, forbidding these officials "under pain of excommunication" to accept any honoraria or fees. Pope Alexander's letter, addressed to Mathias, shows, again, how well aware officials in the Church were of circumstances in Greenland. His touching reference to the Corporal is the only knowledge we have so far of this unusual devotion.

"Since, as We have heard, the Church of Gardar is situated at the extremity of the earth in the country of Greenland, whose inhabitants are accustomed to use dried fish and milk because of the want of bread, wine and oil, wherefore and also on account of the rare shipping to said country due to the intense freezing of the sea no vessel is believed to have put to land there for eighty years back, or if it happened that such voyages were made, surely, it is thought, they could not have been accomplished save in the month of August, when the ice was dissolved; and since it is likewise said that for eighty years, or thereabout, absolutely no bishop or priests governed that Church in personal residence, which fact, together with the absence of Catholic priests, brought it to pass that very many of the diocese unhappily repudiated their sacred baptismal vows; and since the inhabitants of the land have no relic of the Christian religion save a certain Corporal, annually set forth, upon which, a hundred years ago, the Body of Christ was consecrated by the last priest then living there; – for these, then, and for other considerations, Pope Innocent VIII, of blessed memory, Our predecessor, wishing to provide a suitable pastor for that Church, at that time deprived of the useful solace of the same, at the advice of his brethren, of whom We were then one, appointed bishop and pastor to that place Our venerable brother Matthias; the latter was Bishop-elect of Gardar, a professed member of the Order of St. Benedict, and intending to sail personally for said Church, inspired with great fervor of devotion to lead back the souls the strayed and apostate to the way of eternal salvation, and to expose his life to the greatest danger, freely and spontaneously, to obliterate such errors...."

These papal letters authenticate the existence of the Diocese of Gardar and Christian life in Greenland during the Middle Ages. Although minor incidents may be inaccurate or confused – given the nature of communications at that time – the basic facts in the papal letters confirm what is said about Greenland in the Icelandic sagas. The archeological expeditions which have uncovered many of the Christian churches in medieval Greenland as well as Helge Ingstad's remarkable discovery of the Norse settlement near L'Anse aux Meadows, Newfoundland, also confirms the Icelandic sagas.[27]

In conclusion, this writer makes his own the words Rasmus Anderson wrote in *The Flatey Book* in 1908: "The matter will doubtless never cease to be a subject for interesting study and investigation by both European and American scholars.... Our sons and daughters will be taught that Leif Erikson was the first white man who turned the prow of his ship to the west and landed upon the shores of this vast continent; nor shall Thorvald Erikson, the first European, and the first Christian buried beneath American sod, be forgotten. We shall not forget Thorfinn and Gudrid, who established the first European colony in the western hemisphere, nor their infant son Snorre, the first child of European blood to open his eyes in the New World."[28] ∿

REFERENCES

1. Cindy Wooden, "Vatican yearbook paints church by numbers," *The Catholic Review,* July 31 (Vol. 56, no. 15) 1991, p. 1. The yearbook also notes that the world average is one priest for every 2,258 Catholics; in the United States, with a Catholic population of 50.4 million, one for every 1,010; Brazil, the country with the largest Catholic population of 129.6 million, one priest for every 9,306.

2. For example, in its issue of April, 1990, *The Catholic Historical Review,* in reviewing *Columbian Consequences,* stated, "This is the first of a series of three volumes planned to be published by the Smithsonian Institution among its activities commemorating the quincentennial of the discovery of America." Again, in Foster Provosts's *Columbus – An Annotated Guide to the Scholarship of His*

Life and Writings, 1750-1988, Norman Fiering in his foreword writes: "This unification and integration began at a precise moment in 1492 when permanent contact was first made between inhabitants of the two halves of the globe who hitherto had been totally unknown to each other and, in fact, totally unimagined."

3. E. J. Marcus, "Gardar, the Diocese at the World's End," *Irish Ecclesiastical Record,* 79 (1953), p. 94.

4. This is a summary of the account of Olav's life in Snorre Sturlason's *Heimskringla – The Olaf Sagas,* E. P. Dutton & Co., New York, 1915. The "King Olaf Trygvesson's Saga" is found on pp. 5-99.

5. Thomas B. Willson, *History of the Church and State in Norway,* Archibald Constable & Co. Ltd., Westminster, England, 1903, p. 2.

6. This account is a summary of "The Saga of Eric the Red," in Rasmus B. Anderson, *The Norse Discovery of America,* Norroena Society, New York, 1907, pp. 29-63. The author of the article "Iceland" in the *Encyclopedia Britannica* (vol. 12, p. 52, 1960 ed.) offers this explanation of the word "saga": "In Icelandic the word 'saga' is used for any kind of story or history, whether written or oral.... In English, on the other hand, this word has a narrower sense and is generally applied to biographies of one hero or a group of heroes written in Iceland between the 12th and 15th centuries. Sagas are generally based upon native tradition, whether preserved orally or in writing."

7. Willson, pp. 41-2.

8. Sturlason, *Heimskringla,* p. 881.

9. Anderson, *The Saga of Eric the Red,* pp. 16-62.

10. Magnus Magnusson and Hermann Palsson, ed. *The Vinland Sagas,* Penguin Books, London, England, 1965, p. 71.

11. Anderson, pp. 102-105.

12. Sturlason, p. 101.

13. Carl H. Meinberg "The Norse Church in Medieval America, " *The Catholic Historical Review*, vol. 5 (July, 1925), pp. 179-216. This was the first article I read on this subject in 1984 and it set me on an extensive journey of research over the past seven years.

14. Meinberg, p. 198.

15. Laurence M. Larson, ed., *The King's Mirror,* Twayne Publishers,

Inc., New York, NY, 1917, p. 144.

16. P. DeRoo, *History of America before Columbus,* J. P. Lippincott Co., Philadelphia, 1906, pp. 351-367.

17. DeRoo, p. 433.

18. Meinberg, p. 193.

19. Thomas B. Willson, *History of the Church and State in Norway,* Archibald Constable & Co. Ltd., Westminster, England, 1903, pp. 137-38.

20. Quoted in DeRoo, p. 590.

21. Thomas O'Gorman, *History of the Roman Catholic Church,* Christian Literature, New York, NY, 1895, p. 11.

22. Marcus, pp. 110-14.

23. *Greenland,* published by The Royal Danish Ministry for Foreign Affairs, A. Rasmussens Bogtrykkeri, Ringkjobing, Denmark, 1952, p.32.

24. Letter from Chaplain, Major General, USAF John P. McDonough to the author. Oct. 3, 1991.

25. Cf. "The Medieval American Church", *The Catholic Historical Review,* vol. 3 (July-October, 1919), no. 2, pp. 210-227. This article contains the complete text of the papal letters in Latin and English.

26. Anderson, p. 133. The account and quotations of the papal letters are taken from this work which includes photographs of the original documents, the Latin text and English translation of these papal letters. The subtitle of Anderson's book is, "Documents now published for the first time, which establish beyond controversy the claim that North America was settled by Norsemen five hundred years before the time of Columbus." The author is grateful to Mr. Raymond Gadke, librarian of the University of Chicago, for making this work available.

27. Helge Ingstad, *Westward to Vinland,* St. Martin's Press, New York, NY, 1969.

28. Anderson, p. 8.

SELECTED BIBLIOGRAPHY

Anderson, Rasmus B., ed. *The Anglo-Saxon Classics,* Norroena Society, New York, NY, 1911.

____, ed. *The Flatey Book,* Norroena Society, New York, NY, 1908.

Bure, Kristjan, ed., *Greenland,* Royal Danish Ministry for Foreign Aff✝airs, A. Rasmussens Bogtrykkeri, Ringkjobing, Denmark, 1952.

DeRoo, P., *History of America before Columbus,* vol. 2, J. P. Lippincott Co., Philadelphia, 1900.

Haugen, Einar. *Voyages to Vinland,* Alfred A. Knopf, New York, NY, 1942.

Heyerdahl, Thor, *Early Man and the Ocean,* Doubleday & Company, Garden City, NY, 1979.

Ingstad, Helge, "Vinland Ruins Prove Vikings Found the New World," *National Geographic,* vol. 126, no. 5 (November, 1964), pp. 708-34.

____, *Westward to Vinland,* St. Martin's Press, New York, NY, 1969.

Jones, Gwyn, *A History of the Vikings,* Oxford University Press, New York, 1984.

Larson, Laurence M., "The Church in North America (Greenland) in the Middle Ages," *The Catholic Historical Review,* vol. III (July, 1917), no. 2.

____ ed. *The King's Mirror,* Twayne Publishers, Inc., New York, NY, 1917.

Marcus, E.J. "Gardar, the Diocese at the World's End," *Irish Ecclesiastical Record,* 79 (1953), pp. 94-114.

"The Medieval American Church," *The Catholic Historical Review,* 3 (July-October, 1919), nos. 2-3, pp. 210-217. No author given. This article contains the complete texts of the papal letters.

Meinberg, C.H., "The Norse Church in Medieval America," *The Catholic Historical Review,* 5 (July, 1925), pp 179-216.

Morison, Samuel Eliot, *The European Discovery of America,* Oxford University Press, New York, NY, 1971.

O'Gorman, Thomas, *History of the Roman Catholic Church,* Christian Literature, New York, NY, 1895.

Rosedahl, Else, *The Vikings*, The Penguin Press, New York, NY, 1987.

Smiley, Jane, *The Greenlanders*, Ivy Books, New York, NY, 1988. This historical novel describes life in Greenland during this period. It is an epic narrative, written in the style of, and comparable to, Sigrid Undset's Kristin Lavransdatter. No other popular work captures so well the spirit of the Norse Church in medieval America.

Sturlason, Snorre, *Heimskringla or The Lives of the Norse Kings*, Dover Publications, Inc., New York, NY, 1990.

___, *Heimskringla – the Olaf Sagas*, E.P. Dutton & Co., New York, NY, 1915. (Translated by Samuel Laing)

Wilson, Thomas B., *History of the Church and State in Norway*. Archibald Constable & Co., Ltd., Westminster, England, 1903.

1992

 HILD ABUSE

Archbishop Robert F. Sanchez of Santa Fe, New Mexico, urged me in 1984 to undertake the research and writing of an essay on child abuse. At that time the subject was becoming a widely discussed issue in the mass media. I spent several years in research and submitted the manuscript to some leading psychologists, sociologists, welfare workers and theologians. After many revisions, it finally appeared in the pages of The Living Light, *a publication of the National Confraternity of Christian Doctrine, in the Spring, 1992, issue.*

The alarming increase of child abuse in all its forms in our society in the past generation is the saddest measure of how disoriented and disorganized our society has become. It is a problem that touches, in some way, every family in our nation and causes increasing distress among religious, education, and governmental leaders.

It is hoped that this essay both will add a religious dimension to every consideration of the problem and will form the basis for serious reflection and discussion among all religious people striving to give a Christian response to this problem.

This "working paper" has been studied and discussed by more than a score of theologians, sociologists, educators, pastors, and social workers throughout the United States. After several major revisions, incorporating the corrections and suggestions of these competent readers, it has been their unanimous opinion that it should be presented to a broadly based audience of religious men and women. In this process I have served chiefly as reporter and editor.

This study is divided into four parts: 1) the nature of child abuse; 2) the causes of child abuse; 3) a theology of the child; and 4) healing and reconciliation. Although all four aspects of the problem demand the reader's attention, the third section, dealing with religious attitudes toward child, forms the heart of the matter.

The Nature of Child Abuse

One of the most baffling aspects of child abuse is the shroud of secrecy that surrounds it. Few people are willing to give much thought to the subject, and even fewer want to speak about it. Many people seem to feel that the less that is thought and said about child abuse, the sooner it will go away. Unfortunately, the exact opposite is happening.

Specialists in child abuse report that never before in our national history have so many cases of child abuse been reported as in the past two decades. A national conference on the subject was held in April 1985, and two committees of the U.S. House of Representatives are studying the problem. Hardly a day passes that the media does not call public attention to a problem that specialists say is rapidly reaching epidemic proportions.

Four Crimes and Sins

Child abuse involves four different manifestations of crimes (for so they are considered by federal and state laws) and sins (for so they are considered in ordinary religious teaching). These are physical abuse, sexual abuse, physical neglect, and emotional neglect. Physical abuse is any act of violence that inflicts injury on the child, such as slapping, spanking, beating, and whipping to an excessive degree. Sexual abuse has been defined as "exposure to sexual stimulation inappropriate to age and development."[1] Physical neglect arises when the parent, guardian, or responsible person fails to meet a minimum of needs for the child, such as adequate food, clothing, and shelter. Emotional neglect is inflicted upon a child who is constantly criticized, ignored, ridiculed, or shouted at, causing emotional scars that are often carried into adult life. The last is often the most difficult to detect and in most cases is not reported until long after the psychological damage has been done, if even then. According to laws concerning child abuse, anyone from birth to eighteen years of age is considered a child when subjected to any of these four kinds of abuse.

Child abuse was first recognized as a clinically observable problem by C. Henry Kempe in 1962. The following year the federal government passed laws mandating the reporting of cases of child abuse. Similar laws were also passed by all fifty states within the decade. Although child abuse has always been a problem in society, the passage of such legislation has helped to break the conspiracy of silence and has made everyone more aware of its existence.

Authorities in this field point to several reasons that child abuse is more prevalent in our society today than in past generations. I will examine these shortly. The laws regarding child abuse are, however, both humane and Christian in their purpose, for they aim at helping rather than punishing the child abused, the child abuser, and the family. Recent figures reveal that one million cases of child abuse (including two million children) were reported in 1985.[2]

SEXUAL ABUSE

The form of child abuse that receives most of the headlines in the national media has been child sexual abuse. Such cases centering around a child day-care center, a baby-sitting service, and a small community in places as divergent as California, Florida, and Minnesota made alarming headlines in 1986. The American Humane Association of Denver has reported that since 1977 – the first year records were kept – child sexual abuse has increased 400 percent. One authority has recently stated that in 1980 there were 336,000 cases of child sexual abuse reported, and that 90 percent of these were perpetrated by a parent or other person in trust.

Two popular myths about child abuse must be put aside before one can begin to approach reasonable solutions. One myth is that the child abuser is the traditional "dirty old man" who sits on the park bench waiting to molest children. The other myth is that the abused child is a precocious, unruly, flirtatious little scamp who deserves everything he or she receives. The truth of the matter is far removed.

Both the abused child and the child abuser are victims. Both need and deserve a great deal of compassion, understanding, and affection. In over 70 percent of cases the abuser is either a member of the family or a close friend. In over 90 percent of cases the abused child is confused and frequently distressed about his or her role in the case. Only rarely do total strangers enter into the case. For this reason it has been frequently stated that child abuse involves the whole family, and it is the whole family that needs the support of the community, the state, and the Church. We shall return to the role of the family later.

Another misunderstanding needs clarification. Cases of child abuse are often quickly seized upon by the media and surrounded with the sensationalism of a media event. This type of publicity runs counter to the very purpose of the law, whose aim is to reconcile and provide assistance to the abused, the abuser, and the family. In reporting cases of child sexual abuse, one would like to think that the communications industry would be more conscious of its responsibility and would strive to aid, rather than exploit, the parties concerned.

Physical Abuse and Physical and Emotional Neglect

By fixing the public's attention on cases of child sexual abuse, the real danger is that the public will be less concerned with, or even be ignorant of, other causes of child abuse involving physical abuse and physical and emotional neglect. This type of sensationalism can easily lead the public to think that other causes of child abuse are not too serious. Thus, both the child abused and the child abuser continue to suffer and do not receive the assistance they both so badly need.

For example, a professional journal recently carried an exceptionally fine article on the definition of child abuse. Then immediately beneath this article the editor inserted the following filler, which completely destroyed the purpose of the article: "Too many woodsheds have been converted into garages. In fact, they didn't call it juvenile delinquency in the old days, because father had a woodshed and a razor strap to combat it." A "woodshed" and a "razor strap" are hardly suitable means to employ in the prevention of juvenile delinquency!

This example is but a reflection of an all too common popular misunderstanding of discipline expressed in the old adage, "Spare the rod and spoil the child." Many people who employ this as a rule of thumb in the formation of the child mistakenly believe they are quoting Sacred

Scripture. Nothing could be further from the truth. The adage, which most child specialists would disagree with today and which has been used for many decades as a cloak for child abuse, emanated from the stern, strict, and self-righteous puritanical soil of American colonial days.

Both this terrible saying, which served as justification for the suffering and harmful effects that many have endured, and the sensationalism that screams from the headlines of newspapers or the news desks of television and radio, are nothing but subtle forms of a malaise that afflicts American society. That sickness is the cult of violence that permeates almost every aspect of our national life. As ugly and painful as it is to examine this, we must do so, for no remedial hope can be given to lessen the incidence of child abuse until we examine the violent nature of our society and related causes.

THE CAUSES OF CHILD ABUSE

From serious studies of child abuse, many causes have been discovered. Violence and the inability to cope with the stress of modern life are two. Another cause is a lack of appreciation and understanding of the rights and dignity of the child.

Any act of child abuse is an act of violence. Sociologists have noted that child abuse in our society increases in direct proportion to the increase in violence in our way of life. In a violent society, an innocent child will always be the most vulnerable, for he or she is incapable either physically or emotionally, or both, to resist.

Recently Dr. Vincent J. Fontana, a national authority on the problem of child abuse, stated that within one year 50,000 children were expected to die and 300,000 were expected to be permanently injured by child abuse in the United States. Dr. Fontana said, "It is a disease of violence that breeds more violence, for the abused children of today, if they survive, will grow up to be the abusing parents of tomorrow."[3]

One of the keen observers of the American scene, Max Frankel, summarized our national addiction to violence in these words:

"We are known for our violence, we Americans. The creative violence with which we haul down the good for what we fancy the better. The cruel violence with which we have treated the red men, and black.

The intoxicating violence of our music and art. The absurd violence of our comics and cartoons. The organized violence of our athletic and corporate games. The coarse violence of our speech, even our jokes.... Our young deplore the violence of the old and are tempted to use violence against them. The old deplore the ferocity of the young and are tempted to use violence to suppress them."[4]

So deeply imbedded in our national consciousness is violence that we have become insensitive to the forces within us that are destroying us. Robert J. Keeshan, television's "Captain Kangaroo," has these words: "This diet of violence has created an immunity to the horror of violence. The young child may even come to believe that the use of violence is justified."[5]

Child abuse, as well as other crimes, will continue to increase as long as we as a nation continue to accept and even glamorize it as acceptable. The world of entertainment carries a great responsibility for many of these crimes against children. One authority stated the solution succinctly: "The successful answer to violence in the family is to end the violence, not the family."[6]

Dr. Thomas Radecke, chairman of the National Coalition on Television Violence, recently made a similar observation: "Prime-time TV violence has increased sixty-five percent since 1980 to an all-time high." In the same article he added. "This intense violence is now brought into the American home by pay-cable television. Violence in movie videos, rock music lyrics, pornography, and children's toys has increased to record levels following television's example."[7] He then drew this conclusion: "Based on the available scientific information, I estimate that twenty-five to fifty percent of the violence in our country is coming from the culture of violence that has been established and is reinforced daily by violent entertainment."

Teenage Suicide and Abortion

Two other forms of child abuse must be noted as particularly tragic acts of violence. The first is teenage suicide and the second is abortion. Most people do not generally consider these tragedies as acts of child abuse.

In the case of teenage suicide, columnist Cal Thomas has sadly noted the cause: "Teenagers alone are not responsible," he wrote. "It's a failure of adult commitment to…marriage and of commitment to children as something more than a tax deduction."[8] Dr. James Dobson, a well-known clinical psychologist, has stated that the increase in the suicide rate among teenagers is a proof that as a nation we have become prisoners of our own materialistic society. This type of materialism, he said, manifests itself not only in the pursuit of an accumulation of things, but, even more sadly, in the loss of appreciation of the worth of the individual person.

We do not like to think about teenage suicide for the thought itself is so terrible. Suicide, especially in the case of the very young, is total defeat and completely devastates the family and friends, and even the broader community. It is, however, a shattering reality, being the second most common cause of death among adolescents. In 1986, an estimated 6,000 teenagers committed suicide in our country. This represents a 41 percent increase within the period of one decade.

Tottle Ellis, vice-president of Eagle Forum, cited this as one reason: "In the quest for affluence, parents are often more involved with careers and keeping up with the Joneses than with their children." It is a striking statistic that the incidence of teenage suicides is higher in affluent communities than in those that are called centers of poverty.

The child abuse inflicted upon a victim of teenage suicide is largely the emotional neglect of the young person. In most cases it is not one person responsible – least of all the victim – but many complex factors created by society itself. One might even say that the suicide of one young person in a community is the responsibility of the entire community. "Never in human history," Ellis noted, "have we been so close and yet so far apart. We are living in a world where we have proximity without community."

Abortion is also child abuse in one of it most pitiful forms. In this case the child has no defense – not even the ability to whimper – and absolutely no hope for recovery. Our concern about the abused child and the child abuser must also include the aborted child and those who are involved in the performance of an abortion. As Christian people, we believe that abortion is a sin, an act of an unjust aggressor upon the very life of an innocent victim.

At one time in U.S. history, Americans believed that abortion was a crime. It is hoped that those who are rightly concerned about child abuse will come to see that abortion is the ultimate crime of child abuse. As U.S. citizens strive to improve the country's legal system and its adjuncts to give aid to the abused child and the child abuser, one hopes that the legal system will also be improved to include abortion within the ambit of the law's concern.

In no way can a Christian accept or condone any form of violence as a lifestyle. The Christian is called by baptism to be a person who promotes peace. Thus Jesus declared on one occasion, "Take my yoke upon you and learn from me, for I am meek and humble of heart…" (Mt. 11:29). On another occasion, in the Sermon on the Mount, Jesus gave us another directive to follow: "Blessed are the peacemakers, for they will be called children of God" (Mt 5:9).

Although written in another context, the words of the Second Vatican Council apply with equal force here: "That earthly peace which arises from love of neighbor symbolizes and results from the peace of Christ who comes forth from God the Father…. For this reason, all Christians are urgently summoned 'to practice the truth in love' (Eph 4:15) and to join with all true peacemakers in pleading for peace and bringing it about" (*Gaudium et Spes*, n. 78).

STRESS OF MODERN LIFE

Another cause of child abuse is the stress and strain imposed upon the family today by many external factors. The abuse of alcohol and drugs has multiplied tensions in the home and has wrought untold havoc. Inadequate housing is also an obvious factor in increasing tensions because of lack of space, fuel, light, and even air. Every person has a right to decent housing: when that right is denied, a heavy burden is placed upon all the members of the household.

The economic situation also plays its role. Families with economic difficulties are victims of unhealthy stress, causing nerves to be on edge, tempers to flare, words uttered, and deeds performed that would not happen as easily in normal situations. Statistics have shown that families in which the father is unemployed have a 62 percent higher probability of child abuse than in other families. Mothers who are forced to enter the workplace because of economic oppression also have a higher proportion of child abusers in their ranks. Such mothers labor under great strain, as do those in the one-parent home, and need all the support that the community, the state, and the Church can give them.

Obviously, there are distinctions to make in the case of working mothers. At the present time there are millions of women with children in our country working outside the home. If this should be the case because a woman has succumbed to the notion that only being a mother is no great challenge for an intelligent woman, nothing could be further from the truth. If, however, the mother must leave her children at home or in a day-care center and enter the workplace for economic reasons, this is a blight on our society. "To trade a baby's tender years for a TV or a trip to Europe," wrote one woman, "is a bad bargain for the child, the mother, and society."

Those women with children who enter the work force because they seek a "career" or "creative expression" would be well advised to listen to further advice from this same woman: "For parents to take a new-born child, who is only a bundle of needs and potentialities and love, and guide and develop the child until a fully functional human emerges is a great art. It is totally necessary if society is to continue."

Stress and strain within the family circle will always be a part of the human condition. But undue, unwarranted, unnecessary, and unwanted stress is the result of a society that has lost a sense of both human and Christian values. In these cases it seems, according to most reports, that child abuse is not so much a physical act as the neglect – and most unconscious – to meet the emotional needs of the child.

Other causes have been and could be given for child abuse. I have outlined these because they seem to be the most adduced by the specialists in this area. Underlying all causes of child abuse, however, is a factor that is most fundamental, touching the very heart of the problem. This factor has not been given the attention it deserves. If it received more consideration, many cases of child abuse would be eliminated. This is a greater understanding of a theology of the child.

A Theology of the Child

When one turns to the Church to examine a theology of the child, one is struck by the fact that theologians have paid scant attention to the child. They have, indeed, given extensive attention to the obligations and responsibilities of parents toward the child. This may be because for many centuries the child had been considered an "extension of the parent" and had no legal identity in his or her own name. This may also be due to the fact that only in comparatively recent times have so many problems arisen concerning the child.

One theologian stated the problem most clearly: "Out of the vast flood of recent theological literature one can find scarcely anything that deals with the Christian significance of childhood. Children, apparently, are an unresolved problem – not only for parents, but for educators and theologians as well."[9]

If theologians have not directed their attention to the role of the child, the Church does, indeed, offer us more than enough to consider and meditate upon in the pages of her Sacred Scriptures and in her liturgy. First will be considered the Word of God and then the acts of worship of God's people.

Sacred Scripture affords numerous examples of the special favor of God for children. The great desire of Abraham and his wife, Sara, was a prototype of the desire of all God-fearing married couples for a child. Upon the birth of their child they too are able to exclaim, as Sara did, "God has given me cause to laugh, and all who hear of it will laugh with me" (Gn 12:6).

The story of Joseph and his brothers' treatment of him is surely a biblical prototype of child abuse. His brothers were jealous of him and said one to the other, "Come on, let us kill him and throw him into one of the cisterns here; we could say that a wild beast devoured him…" (Gn 37:20). On the other hand, the forgiveness and reconciliation of Joseph with his brothers in the later chapters of Genesis is an example of what should happen among God's people in every case of child abuse.

The tyranny of the pharaoh against the children of the Hebrews in the land of Egypt is a terrible example of mass racial child abuse. The action of the sister and the daughter of pharaoh in rescuing Moses from the waters and sparing his life are also examples of what everyone can do in the cases of child abuse.

On the other hand, the confidence and support that the aged Eli offered the young Samuel as the latter was growing up in the shadow of the temple are examples of love for the child that all can imitate. In the biblical account the ancient Eli gives the child Samuel advice that parents might well give their children: "Go to sleep, and if you are called, reply, 'Speak, Lord, for your servant is listening'" (1 Sm 3:9).

Few works in all the world's literature excel the Book of Tobit in the marvelous bond between the old and the young, the father Tobit and the son Tobiah. They offer inspiration for both the abused child and the child abuser. All can benefit when dealing with the problem of child abuse, in taking to heart the words of the elder to the younger: "Do not be discouraged, my child, because of our poverty. You will be a rich man if you fear God, avoid all sin, and do what is right before the Lord your God." (Tob 4:21).

In the pages of the Old Testament, too, the Child above all other children is announced by the prophet Isaiah. He proclaimed, "...the virgin shall be with child, and bear a son, and shall name him Immanuel.... The calf and the young lion shall browse together, with a little child to guide them" (Is 7:14; 9:5; 11:6). This Child, we know, is the Eternal Son of God, the Divine Word Incarnate, Who first appeared among us – marvel of marvels! – as a Child.

One of the mysteries of God's providence is recorded in sacred Scripture on almost the same page as the birth of Christ the Child. Matthew gives us the account of the mass murder of all the infant boys of Bethlehem following the birth of that Child called the Prince of Peace. No other page in the New Testament records a more violent crime of child abuse. For over fifteen hundred years the Church has held these Holy Innocents in loving memory, marking their feast three days after the birth of the Child called the King of Martyrs.

Victims Include Martyrs and Saints

In her liturgical rites and prayers, the Church holds the child in the greatest reverence. Its list of martyrs and saints includes victims of child abuse. There are children and teenagers who surrendered their very lives rather than deny God. These include such ancients saints as the boy Thuribius, who was murdered by his older playmates for bringing Holy Communion to the Christians in prison, and the virgin martyrs Agnes and Lucy, who chose death rather than surrender their virginity to their cruel oppressors. The Church continues to show her love and reverence in the calendar of saints for these young saints who suffered child abuse.

The Church also shows her love and respect for children in the prayers and in the actions of her worship. For many centuries she has employed a blessing for mothers before childbirth, praying that the child in the womb "may happily see the light of day." After childbirth the Church invokes a special blessing upon the mother and her child, praying that "she together with her offspring may merit the joys of everlasting happiness." As the child grows throughout his or her tender years, the Church has a special blessing, asking God "to show upon this Your child blessings and assistance, considering the faith and devotion of the Church and the parents." When the child becomes ill the Church has a special blessing, imploring God to "extend Your right hand upon this child who is afflicted at this tender age; and being restored to health, may he reach maturity, and ceaselessly render you a service of gratitude and faithfulness all the days of his life."

Then, on the feast day of the Holy Childhood – often celebrated on the feast of the Holy Innocents – the Church again invokes a special blessing upon children, praying: "Strengthen their hearts by the power of the Holy Spirit, sanctify their lives, foster their innocence, keep their minds intent on good, grant them to prosper, give them peace, health, and charity, and by Your strength and protection deliver them from temptation of men or demons."

In the waters of baptism the Church recognizes the sublime dignity of the child. In that sacred rite the Church prays: "Set him free from original sin, make him a temple of your glory, and send your Holy Spirit to dwell with him." In those clear and concise words the Church proclaims the dignity of every child, both in this life on earth and in the life of the world to come. The child's innocence is declared by his freedom from original sin; his dignity is proclaimed as being a living temple of the glory of God; his destiny is sealed as the dwelling place of the Holy Spirit.

In more recent years the Church has restored special rites for children's and young people's Masses. Many older people can recall when there was each Sunday a special "children's Mass." Children's Masses should be encouraged as a regular part of the liturgies in the parish.

THEOLOGICAL REFLECTION

As we have said, the child has generally been neglected in the Church's speculative theology. Our inability to recognize the child in our theology and in our daily consciousness indicates our preoccupation with other, perhaps lesser, values. A contemporary theologian who urges more attention be given to the child has expressed his thought thusly: "…from earliest times, the Christian community has taken children seriously. Children are significant for the Christian life of faith and grace not primarily because they are symbols of innocence or nostalgic reminders of what we once were or potential soldiers of the church, but because every Christian believer must be a once and future child. In children the Christian recognizes both the origins of life and the future of life; he affrms both what he has been and what he is destined to become; he discerns the power of human past and the pull toward a human future in the presence of God."[10]

Another theologian stated the problem recently in different terms. He noted that in more recent years we have been so preoccupied theologically with the paschal mystery of death and resurrection that we have overlooked the incarnational aspect of our redemption. In other words, Jesus has redeemed us as our Savior, not only by his passion, death, and resurrection, but also by his incarnation. The incarnation and birth are also part of the paschal mystery.

In other times, perhaps, the Church understood this better than we do today, and for that reason the feasts of Christmas and Epiphany rank as great feasts on the calendar of the Church's year. The early fathers of the Church, especially Athanasius, did not fail to see the unity within the work of our salvation between the incarnation and birth and the death and resurrection of Jesus. For this reason they had a better grasp of the holy childhood of Jesus and of the sacredness of all children. St. John Chrysostom exclaimed in one of his Christmas sermons:

"This day the ancient slavery is ended; the devil confounded, the demons take to flight, the power of death is broken, paradise is unlocked, the curse is taken away, sin is removed from us, error driven out, truth has been brought back, the speech of kindliness diffused and spread on every side, a heavenly way of life has been implanted on the earth, angels communicate with men without fear, and men now hold speech with angels."

Another reason for our seeming theological neglect of the child might be found in our reluctance to dwell very long upon the future or recall very often our past. We are all too much a part of the "now" generation. Our culture makes us desire instant remedies, instant answers, instant successes. We are an impatient society, and that very impatience induces us to be abrupt with children who need, most of all, time – time to grow, time to mature, time to be just children, time to develop their potentialities to the fullest. In our own eager desire to become perfect, we have in many cases become more imperfect. Our impatience with ourselves is reflected in the demands we place upon our children. Too many of us have forgotten what it is to be a child.

Jesus, however, did not forget. It is more than just a coincidence that on the two occasions when Jesus spoke of children He did so in terms of eternity.

It is also remarkable that Jesus referred to his own disciples as children. After their return from what appeared as a successful missionary journey, Jesus offered a hymn of praise to his heavenly Father, saying: "I give praise to you, Father, Lord of heaven and earth, for although you have hidden these things from the wise and the learned you have revealed them to the childlike" (Mt 11:25). On two other occasions he referred to his disciples as children. On the eve of his own death, Jesus spoke to them, saying, "My children, I will be with you only a little while longer" (Jn 13:33). After his resurrection he spoke to them again: "Children, have you caught anything to eat?" (Jn 21:5). So great was his respect for children that he did not hesitate to call even his closest friends, who were grown men, children!

The most familiar scene of Jesus blessing little children appears in the gospels of Matthew, Mark, and Luke. Each of them recount the same incident in order to underscore the great love Jesus had for children. Each, however, added a dimension to the story to impress upon the hearer the importance of becoming and remaining like a child in our relationship with God our Father.

In Matthew's account, the disciples were disputing among themselves as to whom would be the greatest in the kingdom of God. Jesus rebuked them for their pride, took a child from the surrounding crowd, and said, "Amen, I say to you, unless you turn and become like children, you will not enter the kingdom of heaven. Whoever humbles himself like this child is the greatest in the kingdom of heaven" (Mt 18:3-4).

Mark places the incident in another context, and in so doing he reveals Jesus not only as a teacher, as Matthew does, but also as a very warm, loving person. In Mark's account, the disciples were rebuking the crowd for bringing their little children to be blessed by Jesus, as was the custom among the Jews to show respect for a great teacher. The disciples busied themselves by scolding the people for doing this, Jesus, however, rebuked his own disciples and said, "Let the children come to me; do not prevent them, for the kingdom of God belongs to such as these" (Mk 10:14). Jesus is telling us to become like children for, as one scholar remarked, only children can fully "call God 'Abba' with childlike confidence, safe under his own protection, and conscious of his boundless love."

In Luke's account, the same incident is recorded; Jesus blessing the children and scolding the apostles for trying to keep them away. Luke, however, uses the incident to introduce the encounter of the rich young man with Jesus. A fine man he was, indeed, for he had kept all the commandments. Then Jesus invited him to seek higher goals by saying to him, "There is still one thing left for you: sell what you have and distribute it to the poor, and you will have treasure in heaven. Then come, follow me" (Lk 18:22). The young man turned away, for he could not or would not become like a child.

Luke is too sensitive to say it, but Mark does: "Jesus looking at him, loved him," and the young man "went away sad, for he had many possessions" (Mk 10:21-22). It is not easy to be like a child with trust and confidence in God our Father when we think our security lies in an accumulation of wealth and power and possessions.

Jesus has shown us that the child is precious precisely because he is a child, and, as such, a complete person in his own right, not simply, as they say, "the father of the man." The child has value, too, because it is by the practice of the virtues of a child that he and we, following his example, gain entrance into heaven. Finally, the child is priceless simply as a child because he is a sign and symbol of what we all must remain or become if we wish to enter the kingdom of heaven.

The child in each of us is past, present, and future. The child in our past directs our present and points to our future. The child in us is, indeed, part of each one's history, but also a part of each one's present, and by becoming or remaining childlike, a promise of each one's future immortality. In this sense the child in each of us always remains. For this, if for no other, we must respect all children, lest we fail to respect ourselves in the present or future. Karl Rahner summarizes this idea: "We only *become* the children who we *were* because we gather up time – and in this our childhood too – into our eternity."[12]

This leads us to the keystone of Christian theology concerning childhood, namely, the acceptance of the fact that the child is a real and complete human person. No other religion or philosophy of life insists so strongly upon this fact. Christianity insists, in Rahner's words, "that the child is already the man, that right from the beginning he is already in possession of that value and those depths which are implied in the name of man. It is not simply that he gradually grows into a man, he *is* a man. As his personal history unfolds he merely realizes what he already is."[13]

This principle underlies every legal and moral consideration concerning the child. The child, as child, already possesses the rights of the human person. The child's rights are inherent and inalienable; they are not derived from the parent and they justly enjoy the protection of the state.

In Christian theology these natural rights that endow the child with a human dignity are enhanced and ennobled through the waters of baptism. In that sacrament the human child becomes a child of God and thus his dignity becomes an eternal one. Rahner points out:

"It is the totality of this experience as summed up in the word 'child' that holy scripture draws upon when it tells us that we must become as children, that we are 'children' of God by grace, that even the children can come to the messiah, and that they both need and are capable of attaining the kingdom of heaven, that they can believe in Jesus, that to give scandal to them is a crime to be punished by a terrible death."

With such consideration in mind it is easier to see why Jesus identified himself with children. He pronounced woes upon those who scandalize children, reminded his audience that God has given them a guardian angel to watch over and protect them, that they are among those whom Jesus himself can receive most easily and lovingly into his own heart. The fullness of childhood – and adulthood as well – is rooted in being the children of God. For that reason Jesus taught us to call God "our Father."[14]

To be a child of God, then, is our noblest dignity as creatures, both in the biological and spiritual order. In fact, biological childhood is the prelude, the foundation, of spiritual childhood. Even in adulthood, the more we preserve and cultivate the virtues of innocence, wonderment, trust, confidence, and willingness to accept authority without questioning, the more perfect we will be as children of God.

The most noble task of a person's maturity lies in preserving and developing the virtues of childhood. To refer to Rahner once more:

"Man remains religious when he experiences the childhood which is an elemental factor in his nature, when he adopts this and maintains it as his basic attitude and outlook, and allows it to develop to the full and without limitation. Childhood is only truly understood, only realizes the ultimate depths of its own nature, when it is seen as based upon the foundation of childhood of God."[15]

HEALING AND RECONCILIATION

It is hoped that these thoughts will enable all of us to grow in reverence and respect for the child. As a Christian people we, especially, must look upon every act of child abuse with deep compassion both for the child abused and the child abuser. This is the Christian imperative that Paul placed upon us when he wrote, "Bear one another's burdens, and so you will fulfill the law of Christ" (Gal 6:2). By the very fact that we are Christians, we are expected to exercise a ministry of healing and reconciliation. Paul also reminds us that God has reconciled us to himself through Christ and thus has "given us the ministry of reconciliation" (2 Cor 5:18).

It should be noted that the civil law that requires us to report cases of child abuse guarantees anonymity to the one who reports the case. However, those same laws specifically do not protect the one who makes the report if he or she is acting out of a base motive, such as malice, hatred, envy, or revenge. In this case, as in all cases, our motives must be pure, prompted by our concern for the welfare of the child and the abuser, for all too easily sentiments of anger, hatred, disgust, and revenge can render an objectively good action a bad one by our own reprehensible motives. Such sentiments are but forms of violence and only tend to make the work of reconciliation and rehabilitation more difficult for all parties concerned.

In the ministry of reconciliation, the Church has a most important role to play. Experts tell us that the increasing number of cases of child abuse have taxed social service offices beyond the limits of their personnel and resources. Government cuts in spending have also drastically curtailed the assistance such offices have rendered in the past.

More and more these officials are turning to churches for assistance. More and more, too, the abused child, the child abuser, and the family are turning to churches for guidance and support. It is no more than right that they do so, for the Church might well be considered as one great sacrament of reconciliation. All members of the Church must become more actively engaged in this ministry of reconciliation.

The fact that 75 percent of the reported cases of child abuse involve an adult who is related to the child gives us the clue as to where to begin this ministry of reconciliation. The healing must begin with the family and in the family – the entire family. The writer of a recent article was the mother of an abused child and the spouse of the abuser. She literally cried out in print, "We are unseen victims who are ignored." A few observations may make it easier to aid in the reconciliation of a broken family.

We must not think of the child abuser as an evil or malicious person. Dr. Richard Klugman, director of Denver's Child Abuse Center, says that child abusers "are like the rest of us except that they know less about how to handle children effectively." The distinguished anthropologist Margaret Mead once made the observation that child abusers are no more evil than other people but are perhaps more broken and hurt than most others. Simple punishment of the child abuser is not enough; too often it does no more than perpetuate the cycle of abuse. All too often the offended child is punished by the very act of punishing the parent.

Nor would it be correct to assume that love is lacking in an abusive family. In most cases there is an abundance of love but it is smothered under heavy layers of worry and anxiety, stress and strain. Experts tell us that the abusive family needs most of all to develop the skills necessary to cope with problems. In this area especially all families in a community need to be able to lean on one another, to support and sustain one another, in the manner of that almost forgotten virtue of *neighborliness.*

In some cases the local parish church has taken the lead in this direction; more parishes can become conveners of families who can learn from each other the skills of parenting. In these centers, too, children can be taught what they need to know about child abuse and how to cope with it in their own lives. "Church-sponsored support groups," wrote one authority in this field, "are the least threatening and the most productive."

The Second Vatican Council's *Pastoral Constitution on the Church in the Modern World* holds up for our admiration and imitation a model of the Christian family in action:

"Among the multiple activities of the family apostolate may be enumerated the following: the adoption of abandoned infants, hospitality to strangers, assistance in the operation of schools, helpful advice and material assistance for adolescents, help to engaged couples in preparing themselves better for marriage, catechetical work, support of married couples and families involved in material and moral crises, help for the aged, not only by providing them with the necessities of life but also by obtaining for them a fair share of the benefits of economic progress (*Gaudium et Spes*, n. 78).

Child abuse will continue as long as there are hurting and broken families. Restoration of Christian values, such as those mentioned above, might be the longest route in reducing child abuse, but it is the surest route. There is not a member of the Church who cannot in some way, both large and small, be involved in this important and imperative ministry of reconciliation. ∾

REFERENCES

1. National Catholic News Service, "NCEA Workshop Tells Teachers How to Help Children Avoid Sexual Abuse," May 2, 1985, p. 5.
2. *Ibid.*
3. Arthur Daigon, *Violence: USA* (New York: Bantam Books, 1975), 42.
4. *Ibid.*, 27.
5. *USA Today*, November 20, 1984, p. 10A.
6. *Ibid.*
7. *Ibid.*
8. USA Today, October 30, 1984, p. 10A.
9. Nathan Mitchell, "The Once and Future Child: Towards a Theology of Childhood," *The Living Light* 12:3 (Fall 1975): 423.
10. *Ibid.* 427.
11. M.F. Toal, ed., *The Sunday Sermons of the Great Fathers*, vol. 1 (Chicago: Henry Regnery Co., 1957), 115.
12. Karl Rahner, "Ideas for a Theology of Childhood," *Theological Investigations*, Vol. VIII (New York: Herder & Herder, 1971), 36.
13. *Ibid.*, 37.
14. *Ibid.*, 40.
15. *Ibid.*, 49.

1993

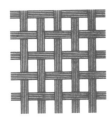

HEOLOGY OF COMMUNICATIONS

The Church, someone remarked, is a vast communications network. As such, the Church depends for its life and vitality upon the mass media. Events within and outside of the Church in recent years prompted me to write this essay concerning the relations of the Catholic Church vis-à-vis the mass media. In early 1993 I wrote this essay.

A recent survey reveals that leaders and members of the Catholic Church place communications very low on their list of priorities. We live in a century of unparalleled transformation of the world, chiefly due to the revolution brought about by the communications industry. I have tried for more than 35 years to bring about a greater awareness and appreciation of a theology of communications among all the members of the Church. In this effort I have relied heavily upon papal documents and the writings of the German theologian, Karl Rahner.

Papal Documentation

During my years in Washington Jerry Renner and I tried to take every available opportunity to sketch, at least, the general directions such a theology of communications might take. We wrote numerous articles and delivered only God knows how many speeches and addresses before scores of audiences on what we considered this vital subject of the continual growth and development of the Church as the People of God in the area of communications. Here I will make a few observations and cite only a handful of documents.

First, the documents. The one book that influenced my thinking most of all was Karl Rahner's small but significant work, *Free Speech in the Church*, published by Greenwood Press. The one papal address that also profoundly influenced my own thinking was the talk of Pope Pius XII of Feb. 18, 1950, entitled "Public Opinion in the Church." In my opinion it is more significant than his encyclical letter of Sept. 8, 1957. A few other theologically significant and important statements are Pope John XXIII's enunciation of the "right to information" in his encyclical letter, *Pacem in Terris*; the Second Vatican Council's Decree on the Instruments of Social Communications, *Inter mirifica* of Dec. 4, 1963; Pope Paul VI's of Apr. 17, 1965, on the right to information; and the Jan. 29, 1971, pastoral instruction on the means of social communication from the Pontifical Council for the Instruments of Social Communication. There are, of course, other pertinent documents.

Before making a few comments concerning these documents I feel I should preface them by a brief remark concerning what I believe to be the dominant characteristic of our times.

Change Is Change

The philosopher, Leslie Dewart, wrote: "The price that the Church would one day have to pay for resisting gradual change would be the need to undergo sudden, painful and traumatic change. The accumulated pressures in the Church were bound to find a sudden avenue of escape as soon as a crack in the monolith would develop." I personally do not think we have yet arrived at that "crack in the monolith" but if resistance continues at its present pace, I believe the crack might soon become a collapse of the monolith. And I am not prepared to say that would be a bad thing; it depends, I suppose, on what you mean by the monolith.

Many church leaders of two generations ago, unlike some church leaders today, tried to prepare us for change, as did the Second Vatican Council. In *Growth or Decline? – The Church Today* Cardinal Emmanuel Suhard of Paris wrote shortly after World War II:

"Something is dead on the earth which will not rise again. The war therefore assumes its true meaning. It is not an intermission but an epilogue. It marks the end of a world. The confusion, the feeling of maladjustment which results in all fields justifies the feeling so often expressed in the ambiguous phrase: 'The world is in revolution.'"

Pope Pius XII expressed the same message on Feb. 10, 1952. Speaking to a throng of people in St. Peter's Piazza on that day he said: "The whole world must be rebuilt from its foundations, transformed from savage to human, from human to divine, that is to say, to make it as God would have it. Millions of men plead for a new way." The significant phrase there, in my view, is "as God would have it." Not as this or that churchman would have it. Humankind is called to serve and worship God, not His Church.

Pope John XXIII also challenged us with the vision of change in his magnificent address at the opening of the Second Vatican Council. He said: "In the present day Divine Providence is leading us to a new order of human relations. By man's own efforts, and beyond the greatest expectations, we are being directed towards the fulfillment of God's higher and inscrutable designs."

Communications, as everyone knows, is all about change. The mass media have much to teach the Church about change, but only if church leaders are *honest* and *open*. The devil of secrecy was a terrible mark of the nineteenth and early twentieth centuries. Those who attempt to return to that kind of secrecy are leading the Church into the dark chasm of terrible trouble. As one of my friends says, "Another ten million Catholics will shrug their shoulders and quietly take a walk."

FREEDOM OF INFORMATION

Following the Second Vatican Council, I had thought that few people within the Catholic Church would oppose the fundamental principle of humankind's inherent right to information. That was my belief until in very recent years when it seems some church leaders are attempting to turn back the clock. They are like the fearful ostriches who bury their heads in the sand. They are *not* bad or evil men and women, they are simply afraid – afraid of the press, afraid of their flocks, afraid of Rome.

They deceive themselves, and unfortunately others, into thinking that in this era of instantaneous communications medieval expressions still have validity. You know, phrases like "no comment," or "strictly confidential," or "I don't know." Of course, there is a place for such expressions, such as in some cases where sensitive situations or individuals are concerned. In such cases the good name of an individual must be preserved or, perhaps, in a given situation, not all the facts have been ascertained. This is then appropriate and reporters generally respect such a reply. However, generally speaking, such remarks are not appropriate in a Church which claims to be the People of God.

Such church leaders would be among the first to disavow the comment made by James P. Shannon which he made in 1967 upon receiving the St. Francis de Sales award from the Catholic Press Association. At that time, as the Auxiliary Bishop of the Archdiocese of St. Paul and Minneapolis and member of the American Bishops' Committee on Communications, he said:

"I have tried to be as open with the press as possible and I have never found the press betraying that confidence. I have found that when you level with the press, the press will level with you.... We must not make the mistake of continuing to use double-talk with the press. The press recognizes double-talk and if it catches you using double-talk it will not regard you as a reliable source of information."

Four brief quotations might be the best rebuttal to these fearful people who seem to prefer to be ostriches.

1. In an address delivered on Apr. 17, 1964, Pope Paul VI said: "Information by this time is unanimously recognized as a universal, inviolable and inalienable right of modern man.... Information must be true, honest, and faithful to facts to fulfill its social role, and it will never be so unless he who gives information is always anxious for objectivity. That is to say that information must before all else correspond to truth."

2. *The Decree on the Instruments of Social Communication* of the Second Vatican Council states this right most emphatically: "The prompt publication of affairs and events provides every individual with a fuller, continuing acquaintance with them, and thus all can contribute more effectively to the common good and more readily promote and advance the welfare of the entire civil society. Therefore, in society men have a right to information... about matters concerning individuals or the community." If this be true for civil society, much more, indeed, does it apply to the Church.

3. Pope Pius XII in his address on Feb. 18, 1950, concerning public opinion in the Church described it "as a natural echo, a more or less spontaneous common resounding of acts and circumstances in the mind and judgment of people who feel they are responsible beings, closely bound to the fate of their community." He then sounded this warning if public opinion is thwarted by church leaders: "When so-called public opinion is dictated or imposed... (it) makes a mockery of the just rights of men to their own judgments and their own convictions. Then it creates a heavy, unhealthy, artificial atmosphere which in the course of events... compels (men) to give their wealth and their blood for the defense and triumph of a false and unjust cause. In truth, where public opinion ceases to function freely, there peace is in danger."

4. Pope Paul VI, son of a newspaper publisher, delivered an address to participants in a United Nations seminar on freedom of information on Apr. 17, 1965. He said clearly and forcefully:

"Information by this time is unanimously recognized as a 'universal, inviolable and inalienable' right of modern man; in him it answers to a deep need of his social nature.... Since this is a question of a right founded in the very nature of man, it evidently does not suffice to proclaim it in theory; one must also recognize it in practice, defend it, serve it, and so direct its exercise that it remains faithful to its natural purpose. It is a right at once active and passive; the seeking of information and the possibility for all of obtaining it."

Finally, the pastoral instruction of the Pontifical Council for the Instruments of Social Communication dealt this blow to those who would hide behind the cloak of secrecy:

"On those occasions when the affairs of the Church require secrecy the rules normal in civil affairs equally apply. On the other hand, the spiritual riches which are an essential attribute of the Church demand that the news she gives out of her intentions as well as of her works be distinguished by integrity, truth and openness. When ecclesiastical authorities are unwilling to give information or are unable to do so, then rumor is unloosed, and rumor is not a bearer of the truth but carries dangerous half-truths. Secrecy should therefore be restricted to matters that involve the good name of individuals, or that touch upon the rights of people whether singly or collectively."

These statements prompt me to draw five corollaries. I do so by citing the words Karl Rahner wrote in his book, *Free Speech in the Church*.

1. "We can only speak of a 'public opinion' when we can observe the public's reaction to the views and attitudes of an individual. But if the situation can only be satisfactorily known in this way, then it will be necessary, or at least useful, to give public opinion a chance to develop, by allowing the individual to address the general public. The fact that this holds true in Church matters also means that, to a certain extent, the individual within the Church must be allowed to address the Church community in general as a publicist – not only to make direct representations to the Hierarchy."

2. "If there is any real desire to know the current situation – spiritual, psychological, social, etc. – then Catholics must be allowed... to talk their heads off."

3. "In matters apart from "the Church's unchanging deposit of faith and her divinely ordained constitution... public opinion has a still more vital function to perform within the Church, and hence a still greater right to freedom. At this level any form of 'top secret' government would be a really great danger."

4. "Apart from anything else, the Church today should be more careful than ever before not to give even the slightest impression that she is of the same order as those totalitarian states for whom outward power and sterile, silent obedience are everything and love and freedom nothing, and that her methods of government are not those of the totalitarian systems in which public opinion has become a Ministry of Propaganda."

5. "If the clergy and hierarchy do not allow the people to speak their minds, do not, in more dignified language, encourage or even tolerate, with courage and forbearance and even a certain optimism free from anxiety, the growth of a public opinion within the Church, they run the risk of directing her from a soundproof ivory tower, instead of straining their ears to catch the voice of God, which can also be audible within the clamor of the times.... Freedom is an essential part of any public opinion...."

WE ARE IN TROUBLE

Item. When a certain bishop cancels Father Richard McBrien's column from his diocesan newspaper arbitrarily and without reason and in opposition to the newspaper's editor — *the Church is in trouble.*

Item. When 22 editors of diocesan newspapers quit in one year, 1992, because of conflicts with their publisher-bishops — *the Church is in trouble.*

Item. When an archbishop of an eastern see and his chancery officials refuse to answer any questions or be interviewed by the religion writer of the metropolitan newspaper — *the Church is in trouble.*

Item. When a bishop announces that he will not allow any dissent in his local church from the new catechism — *the Church is in trouble.*

Unfortunately, the list goes on and on. I have noted many such items reflecting a sad return to the "cult of secrecy" on the part of too many bishops in the United States who are in direct violation of these papal and Vatican statements. "Secrecy," wrote James Gaffney, an ethicist, in *A Catholic Bill of Rights,* "becomes an instrument of vice when information is withheld in order to maintain power over those who are denied it, or so put them at some practical disadvantage."

"Creeping secrecy" is a close first cousin, if not a brother, to "creeping infallibility." Even that great son of St. Benedict, St. Bernard of Clairvaux, did not hesitate to admonish and correct one of his disciples, Pope Eugene III. The Dominican theologian at the Council of Trent, Melchoir Cano wrote:

"Peter has no need of our lies or flattery. Those who blindly and indiscriminately defend every decision of the Supreme Pontiff are the very ones who do most to undermine the authority of the Holy See – they destroy instead of strengthening its foundations."

The danger of this kind of "creeping secrecy" was pointed out in an article in the Nov. 14, 1992, issue of *America* by William E. McManus, retired Bishop of the local Church of Fort Wayne-South Bend. He wrote:

"The U.S. conference of bishops has a right to hold a secret session for a preliminary discussion of a controversial matter of faith and morals, but its decisions, with rare exceptions, always should be in the open. But they are not. Of late, the bishops' conference has been going into executive session to shield its deliberations from scrutiny by the media. That abuse of its executive session prerogative denigrates the status of the conference's official observers and demeans the media."

Archbishop Francis T. Hurley of Anchorage, Alaska, writing in his weekly column in the *Catholic Commentary* on June 4, 1993, sounded a similar warning:

"The bishops (we bishops) might be setting ourselves up too. That is one of the by-products when bishops hold confidential meetings and executive sessions on high profile, public policy issues that involve the entire Catholic population. The National Health Plan, whatever it will be, is not just the bishops' concern and responsibility; it is the concern and the responsibility of the entire Catholic family."

I hope the observations I have made on the past few pages, as well as the passages cited, someday will be picked up by a theologian and he or she might be able to bring to life a full-blown Christian theology of communications. Perhaps these words, written by the British theologian, A.E.C.W. Spenser in the pages of *The Clergy Review* in the mid-1960's are a point of departure:

"Communications has a place of special importance in Christian theology. You don't have to be a theologian to recognize the repeated stress on communication in both the Old and New Testaments. Christ is the 'Word of God.' The Church exists to 'teach all nations.' Prophecy, promises, preaching, parables, prayer, epistles, message, communion all refer to communication. For this reason it is natural to think of the Church as a communications system." ᴄᴠ

ATRONS

GOVERNOR AND MRS. ELMER ANDERSON	ARDEN HILLS, MN
DOROTHY AND JAMES BLOMMER	WAITE PARK, MN
JIM AND BARBARA BRUM AND FAMILY	DALLAS, TX
NATALIE AND THOMAS CAREY	ANCHORAGE, AK
CATHOLIC AID ASSOCIATION	ST. PAUL, MN
CHRIST THE KING CHURCH	CAMBRIDGE, MN
KENNA AND BILL CONLIN	ST. CLOUD, MN
REV. JAMES MICHAEL DOYLE	BROOKINGS, SD
REV. FRANK EBNER	ELK RIVER, MN
JOAN AND FRANK FEHRMAN	RUSH CITY, MN
RAYMOND GADKE	CHICAGO, IL
DR. AND MRS. GREGORY GIBBONS	CAMBRIDGE, MN
MARILYN AND WERNER GRUBER	SPRING HILL, MN

Dawn and Matt Herkenhoff	Eden Prairie, MN
Joseph Holig	Swanville, MN
Rev. Arthur Hoppe	St. Rosa, MN
Bishop Mark J. Hurley	San Francisco, CA
Rev. Wilfred A. Illies	St. Cloud, MN
Mary Helen Kavanaugh	South Bend, IN
Mr. and Mrs. Donald Kolb	Holdingford, MN
Ted and Rosemary Kruger	St. Cloud, MN
Charles Main	Seattle, WA
Rev. Thomas Meyer	Swanville, MN
Monks of Blue Cloud Abbey	Marvin, SD
Monsignor Terrence J. Murphy	St. Paul, MN
Monsignor Hugh Nolan	Norristown, PA
Stuart and Jeanne Olson	Escondido, CA
Bishop Francis Quinn	Sacramento, CA

MONSIGNOR JOHN S. QUINN	CHICAGO, IL
ARCHBISHOP JOHN R. ROACH	ST. PAUL, MN
ST. SEBASTIAN'S CHURCH	AKRON, OH
REV. RAYMOND SCHULZETENBERG	GILMAN, MN
ROBERT SPAETH	SAUK RAPIDS, MN
ADMIRAL AND MRS. EMORY STANLEY	SEATTLE, WA
URBAN AND AUGUST TOENIES	FREEPORT, MN
MONSIGNOR C. W. TRAUTNER	EDEN, SD
REV. ROBERT VOIGT	ST. CLOUD, MN
JOHN AND MARY WEITZEL	ST. CLOUD, MN
REV. RICHARD WEY	BIG LAKE, MN
REV. NICHOLAS ZIMMER	BRAHAM, MN

PONSORS

Maggi and Bill Adams	Roseau, MN
Anonymous	Freeport, MN
Anonymous	Woodbury, MN
John and Lillian Arnzen	Freeport, MN
Jerry and LeMay Bechtold	Rockville, MN
Alphonse and Esther Beuning	Melrose, MN
Mr. and Mrs. Jerry Billig	St. Cloud, MN
Mr. and Mrs. Stephen Blattner	Avon, MN
Christian Heritage	Cold Spring, MN
Church of St. Henry	Perham, MN
Church of St. John Cantius	St. Cloud, MN
Church of St. Matthew	St. Paul, MN
Church of St. Mary	Holdingford, MN
Church of St. Rose of Lima	St. Rosa, MN

Mr. James A. Clark	Fall River, MA
Rev. T. William Coyle, C.SS.R.	Fargo, ND
Bishop John Cummings	Oakland, CA
Rev. Raymond Donnay	Sobieski, MN
Bishop Paul V. Dudley	Sioux Falls, SD
Rev. Harvey Egan	Minneapolis, MN
Ron and Mary K. Engelmeyer and Family	Melrose, MN
Rev. John Whitney Evans	Duluth, MN
Rev. Charles Froehle	St. Paul, MN
F. C. Gessell	Swanville, MN
Sylvester and Mary Giese	Freeport, MN
Andrew and Donna Glatzmaier	Albany, MN
Martha Goettertz	Freeman, SD
Rev. Eugene Hackert	Morgan, MN
Myron and Fridge Hall	St. Cloud, MN
Rev. Roger J. Hessian	Canon Falls, MN
Jim and Rita Higgins	Lakeville, MN
Monsignor John V. Horgan	Stamford, CT

David and Mary Ann Klasen	Albany, MN
Jerry and Pat Klasen	New Richmond, WI
Rev. William Kloeckner	Alma, TX
Rev. Thomas E. Kramer	Bismarck, ND
Mrs. Vera Kutzera	St. Cloud, MN
Vincent and Diane Kvidera	Ortonville, MN
Rev. Nicholas Landsderger	St. Cloud, MN
Rev. Donald Liepold	Sioux Falls, SD
Mrs. Rose Laugerin	Cottage Grove, MN
Alma Lucas	Browerville, MN
Rev. Arnold Luger	St. Paul, MN
Mrs. Donna Monette	Albuquerque, NM
Ann Mack	Ortonville, MN
Rev. Paul McDonald	San Antonio, TX
Rev. Richard McGuire	Elizabeth, MN
Rev. Charles Hubert McTague	Newark, NJ
Rev. Lloyd Murrak	Virginia, MN
Rev. Lawrence J. Murtagh	Stockholm, SD

Mrs. Roman Niedzielski	Gilman, MN
Monsignor Allan Nilles	Park River, ND
Rev. Jerry Nordick	Chokio, MN
In Memory of Rev. Otto Neudecker	R.I.P.
The Edward O'Malley Family	Lawrenceburg, IN
James W. and Audrey O'Malley	Portland, OR
Kevin O'Malley	Carmel, IN
The Michael Edward O'Malley Family	Jacksonville, FL
Rev. John O'Toole	Crookston, MN
Our Lady of Sorrows Church	Bernalillo, NM
Rev. Jerry Paulson	Montevideo, MN
Mr. Julian Plante	St. Cloud, MN
Mrs. Lorayne Primus and Family	Swanville, MN
Harriet Rausch	Big Stone City, SD
Jerry and Jacqueline Renner	Norwalk, CT
Lawrence and Margaret Roettger	Holdingford, MN
Rev. Gerald Ruelle, O.S.B.	Killdeer, ND
Rev. Donald Rieder	St. Cloud, MN

George and LaDonna Riesdorf — Avon, MN

Mr. and Mrs. Sylvester Salzl — Melrose, MN

Santuario de San Martin — Albuquerque, NM

Bishop George H. Speltz — St. Cloud, MN

Rev. Raymond Steffes, O.S.C. — Onamia, MN

Rev. John Sankovitz — St. Paul, MN

Deacon John and Mrs. Mildred Scott — New Hope, MN

Rev. Bernard Schreiner — Ivanhoe, MN

David and Clarice Schroeder — St. Cloud, MN

James and Ruth Shannon — Wayzata, MN

Frank and Leona Silbernick — Little Falls, MN

Ralph and Mary Stich — Albany, MN

John Stoermann — Freeport, MN

Mrs. Eleanor Sullivan and Family — Lakeville, MN

Nell Sullivan — Chokio, MN

Rev. Al Svobedny, O.M.I. — Buffalo, MN

Rev. Donald Tomlinson — Sartell, MN

Fran and Mil Voelker — Sartell, MN

Rev. Arthur Vogel	St. Stephen, MN
Claude and Janice Vogel	Albany, MN
Gerald and Karen Voller	Albany, MN
Mr. and Mrs. Ralph Vos	Holdingford, MN
Rev. Roger Vossberg	Melrose, MN
Gregor Wessel	Swanville, MN
Wilbert and Alice Wedel	Albany, MN
Dr. Robert and Mrs. Alice Wick	St. Cloud, MN
Patricia and Robert Witte	Clearwater, MN
Jim and Teresa Zakrzewski	Woodbury, MN